Lesbian & Queer Plays
from the
Jane Chambers Prize

*Featuring Plays by Mary F. Casey,
Claire Chafee, Meryl Cohn,
MJ Kaufman, and Gina Young*

Edited by Maya E. Roth and
Jennifer-Scott Mobley

NoPassport Press

Lesbian & Queer Plays from the Jane Chambers Prize
Edited by Maya E. Roth and Jennifer-Scott Mobley
Volume copyright 2018.

This publication is a collaboration between WTP and the Jane Chambers Prize and NoPassport Press.

Cover design by Bill Talcott.
Image from the premiere of *Femmes* by Gina Young.

NoPassport theatre alliance and press
PO Box 1786
South Gate, CA 90280 USA. www.nopassport.org

ISBN: 978-0-359-05806-8

Acknowledgements

This project was inspired by the creative talents and generous support of many others, most visibly the talented honorees of the Jane Chambers Prize over the past decade. Your plays and creative contributions have moved, motivated, challenged and connected us in ways that shape how we see the world, ourselves, America, theater and feminism: we are better teachers, researchers, people and artists as a consequence. We also thank everyone from the WTP community who believed in this project's necessity, with special thanks to Jill Dolan and Sara Warner, as well as Kimberly Dark, Carolyn Goelzer, Kristen Rogers and Christine Young, among others. We thank all of the more than 2000 playwrights who have shared submissions since 2006, when Maya began to steward the Contest, as well as the over fifty feminist adjudicators who have helped us to identify feminist artistic excellence during that time. Thank you to the ATHE colleagues and professional artists who have joined us for staged readings of these plays and yearned for more... Thank you always to Jane Chambers for the inspiration of her plays and her unfolding legacy. We are profoundly grateful, too, to the Arch and Bruce Brown Foundation, and its Board led by James Waller, whose grant generously supported our publication preparation and targeted public events leading up to it, convinced of the importance of this anthology to LGBTQ cultural history and literature, as well as to feminist studies and theater, more broadly. Thank you to Bill Talcott for his design and technical expertise, as well as to our families who understood when our focus stayed here. All respect and gratitude, finally, to Caridad Svich and NoPassport Press for welcoming us into this series geared toward creative, university, and activist communities alike, and for valuing artists' work and diverse American cultures over market. Theater, like research praxis and teaching, indeed like life, is a collaborative endeavor. Thank You to All who helped these plays, and this publication of winners, to live —and reach others.

Dedicated to Jane Chambers

"I feel an extreme gratitude to (this Prize) ... and to Jane Chambers for writing *Last Summer at Bluefish Cove* and taking it on faith that you could put a lesbian at the center of a world and call it wild, or kingdown, or Acapulco, and get on with writing what the world feels like for you."

— Claire Chafee, ATHE Awards, 2013

In Memory of Jane Chambers (1937-1983)

Preface

I distinctly remember the first time I bought a book of plays by women. The 1981 collection was Judith Barlow's first in her several edited volumes of plays by American women. This one focused on work from the 1900s to the 1930s and included Rachel Crothers, Susan Glaspell, Zona Gale, Georgia Douglas Johnson, and Sophie Treadwell. The collection taught me a history I hadn't learned as a theater major in college about the existence of women playwrights. I also recall the thrill I felt around the same time, when I found the first collection of plays from the Women's Project that producer Julia Miles edited in 1980, when she was still at American Place Theater. That collection introduced me to the remarkable plays of Joan Schenkar, which rocked my world with their radical form and incisive content.

These crucial volumes represented to me, a young feminist theater scholar and critic, a pathway into the theater I knew would speak to the lives of women and, with any luck, change the world. Before the feminist movement began to agitate broadly for the representation of women in theater and performance and before feminist theory and criticism offered critical perspectives on the work and its profound potential, these prescient volumes seemed nuggets of female gold in a mainstream of otherwise straight white male theater.

I want to be hopeful, 40-odd years later, that this new collection of Jane Chambers Award-winning plays won't startle readers or spectators with its idiosyncrasy. But sadly, I'm not so sure. When feminist activists first used theater to make their political claims, and when feminist theater-makers refashioned their craft to embody new visions of gender, race, and social relationships, they were certain of the profound cultural shifts the work would inspire. But in 2018, so much work remains to be done: for women, for women in theater, for us all. In other words, this volume isn't the icing and sugary flowers on the rich cake of women's theater achievements; it's another contribution to the recipe book of how to make sure women playwrights remain seen and heard, performed and produced.

Alongside those ground-breaking published play collections, the Women and Theater Program (WTP) of the Association for Theater in Higher Education (ATHE) pioneered specific awards for women playwrights when it established the Jane Chambers Award in the early '80s. Long a forward-thinking advocacy organization for feminist theater-makers and feminist theater critics, the WTP realized early on that visibility for women who were otherwise disregarded in the theater industry would promote the circulation of women's plays and productions of their work.

Over the awards' many years of bestowing such notice on deserving, sometimes ignored artists, the Jane Chambers award has recognized women who went on to successful careers in theaters around the world. Naomi Wallace, for only one of many examples, one of the earliest winners, has achieved renown in the U.S. and in the U.K. as a playwright who continually innovates with form and content. In addition to her sharp deconstructions of gender inequity, Wallace homes in on all systems of social and cultural power, creating theater that chisels out an image of what inequality looks and feels like across identities, cultures, and histories.

Such diversity of form, content, and identities has always marked the Jane Chambers Playwrighting Award. Vetted by practitioners and scholars committed to widening the scope of plays available to see and consume, to teach and to rehearse, the texts honored with this award continually challenge readers and spectators to see, feel, and experience their lives differently. The award's interventions extend beyond the recognition of a play and its author each year. Bestowed annually at ATHE, the preeminent conference for college and university theater educators, the Jane Chambers Award demonstrated the primacy of the text even when feminist theoretical work subscribed to post-structuralist notions that decried authorship as a patriarchal constraint.

That is, even as theory took the field in one direction, the practice of giving out an award to an author for an excellent play grounded us in creative written work by women that required us to see, hear, and engage their stories. When ATHE added the Jane Chambers Award presentation to its starry roster of honors, we were all proud that a woman playwright stood on the dais to thank a feminist theater organization and was seen by thousands of conference-goers eager to present new work on the stages of their schools.

In other words, the Jane Chambers award-winning plays have always represented a gesture of advocacy and a practice of activism. Named for one of the very first openly lesbian American playwrights, the Jane Chambers Award early on specified in its nomination invitation that the plays submitted should address the lives of women and/or lesbians in its content, themes, and form.

Now, the WTP rhetoric says the award honors "plays and performance texts created by women that present a feminist perspective and contain significant opportunities for female performers." The award is given to plays with themes that address women's lives from an avowedly political perspective and, as such, is singular and distinctive. The award doesn't just recognize the gender of the writer; it emphasizes the importance of writing feminist plays about women that consider structures of power in society and in the theater industry. Too often, still, even plays written by women boast male protagonists or embed female characters in generic worlds, rather than those more distinctively women-oriented. Artists rarely want to be called a "woman playwright"; they want their work to extend into a much broader cultural sphere.

But to be a woman writing about women certainly doesn't imply a narrow perspective. As the Jane Chambers

Award-winning plays have shown over the years — and as those collected here demonstrate — the notion of "woman" isn't singular by any means. The concept has always signaled an enormous diversity of genders, sexualities, races, ethnicities, classes, ages, abilities, and religions. It's always pointed to all the intersections of these and many more identity vectors and the various ways in which they're experienced and performed.

And after all, even in 2018, the "arrival" of women as fully human, fully enfranchised human beings seems to recede farther into the future. The right to control our own bodies retreats daily in the U.S., as the Supreme Court veers sharply to the right and the political climate becomes more virulently anti-abortion. The #MeToo movement might currently call attention to sexual harassment and assault, but when the trend ebbs, what will happen to women who continue to be subjected to the violence of men who hold the power to make or break their careers or their daily lives? What of women in industries who find themselves hitting "pregnancy walls" when they take time off to have children? What of the multiple injustices poor women, women of color, incarcerated women, and differently abled women regularly incur, sometimes across those identities all at once? What of women married to one another in the U.S. and elsewhere who can't rest assured that their rights to legal relationships and their attendant benefits are secure? What of women fleeing from national violence, who find themselves and their families uprooted and migrant, or who suffer their children being wrenched from their arms at the U.S. border? Who will tell all these stories, if not women playwrights committed to writing about women's lives?

Until she died of cancer in 1983, Jane Chambers wrote plays about women who otherwise remained invisible, unknown, and uncelebrated. *Last Summer at Bluefish Cove* tells the story of a chosen family of lesbians who gather annually at the beach to create their own enclave of relationships and histories, who lose one of their own to cancer shortly after she meets the love of her life (the straight woman vacationing next door). Chambers' plays *A Late Snow, My Blue Heaven,* and *Kudzu* explore similar communities of women. And her play *Quintessential Image* tells the poignant, wry story of an internationally known photographer who is celebrated for capturing significant historical images when all she really meant to do was photograph the woman she loved.

The plays honored by the Jane Chambers Award continue her legacy. They urge us to witness stories necessary to move humanity forward. They admit to injustice while they offer a glimpse of better worlds. They champion love, they taxonomize loss, and they restructure our imaginations. Collected, they represent their own community of a few selected to be honored and who lift up so many more.

The great work continues.

— Jill Dolan
Princeton, New Jersey
June 2018

Contributor Bios

Mary F. Casey is a Los Angeles based playwright and scholar. Mary's plays often explore the lives of non-traditional women who challenge the status quo, occasionally on horseback. Her rodeo play, *Women and Horses and a Shot Straight from the Bottle* received its world premiere at Echo Theatre in Dallas, where it was nominated for three Leon Rabin Awards through the Dallas Theatre League. Her play *Wide Open Spaces* was given a reading at the Autry National Center of the American West, where Mary received the Butcher Scholar Award. She is a three-time finalist for Actors Theatre of Louisville's Heideman Award for ten-minute plays, and her short plays have been performed in assorted interesting places, from Secret Rose Theatre in Los Angeles to the Six Women Theatre Festival in Manitou Springs. Her proudest theatrical achievement is the full-length play *Unspeakable Acts*, which won the 2008 Jane Chambers Award. She is pursuing graduate studies in Borderlands History and continues to explore the meeting place of history and theatre.

Claire Chafee's play *Why We Have a Body* opened at The Magic Theatre in San Francisco (1993) where it ran for seven months, and was later produced Off-Broadway by The Women's Project. It won Claire the Dramalogue Award, the Bay Area Critic's Circle Award and New York Newsday's Oppenheimer Award. *Why We Have a Body* was published in *Best Women Plays 1993* (Smith and Krauss), *The Actors Book of Gay and Lesbian Plays* (Penguin) and *HERE TO STAY: 5 Plays by The Women's Project* (Applause). Her play *Even Among These Rocks* premiered at The Magic Theatre (SF) and was published in *NuMuse* (Brown University). She was commissioned by Berkeley Rep to collaborate with composer Beth Custer to create the original musical *A Practical Guide to the Night Sky*. Other plays include *5 Women on a Hill in Spain*, produced in the Lesbian Playwright's Conference in San Francisco and the Minneapolis Fringe Festival, and *Darwin's Finches*, which premiered at The Thick House, produced by Encore, and nominated for the Bay Area Critics Circle for Best Original Script in 2004. Her recent script, *Whisper from The Book of Etiquette*, was the recipient of a Special Projects Princess Grace Award and was presented as a reading in New York City at New Georges, and at New York Stage and Film at Vassar College and the Bay Area Playwrights Festival in 2008. Claire's play *FULL/SELF* won the Jane Chambers Award in 2013. She also writes fiction.

Meryl Cohn is a two-time semifinalist for the O'Neill National Playwrights Conference (*Reasons To Live* and *And Sophie Comes Too*), a finalist for the Massachusetts Cultural Council Playwriting Grant (*Naked With Fruit*), a Lark Play Development Center semifinalist, a *Cape Cod Times* Favorite Play of the Year, and the recipient of the Eventide Arts Playwriting Award. Seven of her full-length plays have been commissioned for productions at Provincetown Theatre. Her recent work has been presented at The Skylight Theater, The Open Fist

Theater, Counter Productions, TOSOS, Smith College, The Road Theatre, The NY International Fringe Festival, The Cherry Pit, and Soho Playhouse, among others. Cohn studied playwriting at Smith and received an M.F.A. in Dramatic Writing from NYU's Tisch School of the Arts. Her articles have appeared in *The Village Voice, The Boston Phoenix,* and *The Washington Post.* She is the author of the best-selling humor book *Do What I Say: Ms. Behavior's Guide to Gay and Lesbian Etiquette* (Houghton Mifflin), and for many years offered irreverent advice in her nationally syndicated humorous advice column (for which she appeared on Oprah et al.). She is the founder of the Northampton Playwrights Labs and a member of the Dramatists Guild. She is trained as a mediator but realized she doesn't like conflict. She just finished her first novel, *Actually Zelda,* which she hopes her agent will sell soon. Meryl lives with her wife, novelist MB Caschetta, in Massachusetts. Her play *The Siegels of Montauk* won the 2009 Jane Chambers Contest for feminist playwriting.

Jill Dolan (Preface) is the Dean of the College and the Annan Professor in English and Professor of Theater at Princeton University, where she also directed the Program in Gender and Sexuality Studies. She is the author of *The Feminist Spectator as Critic* (1989, reissued in a 2012 anniversary edition); *The Feminist Spectator in Action: Feminist Criticism for Stage and Screen* (2013); *Utopia in Performance: Finding Hope at the Theatre* (2005); *Theatre & Sexuality* (2010); and many other books and essays, including a critical study of the plays of Wendy Wasserstein (2017). Dolan received the 2013 Distinguished Scholar Award for Outstanding Career Achievement in Scholarship in the Field of Theatre Studies from the American Society for Theatre Research. In 2011, she won the Outstanding Teacher Award from the Association for Theatre in Higher Education and a lifetime achievement award from the Women and Theatre Program. She won the 2010-2011 George Jean Nathan Award for dramatic criticism for her blog, The Feminist Spectator. Dolan is the editor of *Menopausal Gentleman: The Solo Performances of Peggy Shaw* (2012) and co-editor (with Holly Hughes and Alina Troyano) of *Memories of the Revolution: The First 10 Years of the WOW Café Theatre* (2016). Dolan was inducted into the American Academy of Arts and Sciences in 2016.

MJ Kaufman is a playwright and devised theater artist working in New York and Philadelphia. Their work has been seen at the Huntington Theatre, New York Theater Workshop, the New Museum, Clubbed Thumb, New Georges, Page73, Colt Coeur, Yale School of Drama, National Asian American Theater Company, Lark Play Development Center, Bay Area Playwrights Festival, Aurora Theatre, Crowded Fire, Fresh Ink Theatre, New Harmony Project and performed in Russian in Moscow. MJ has received awards and commissions from the Playwrights Foundation, the National Foundation for Advancement in the Arts, Young Playwrights, Inc., and the Huntington Theatre. MJ received the 2013 ASCAP Cole Porter Prize in Playwriting, the 2013 Global Age Project Prize, and the 2010 Jane Chambers Prize in Feminist

Playwriting. MJ co-curated the 2016 and 2017 Trans Theater Festivals at The Brick. MJ is currently a member of the Public Theater's Emerging Writers' Group, WP Theater Lab, and a resident playwright at New Dramatists. Originally from Portland, Oregon, MJ attended Wesleyan University and Yale School of Drama. They have taught playwriting at Fordham University, Wesleyan U, SUNY Purchase, and University of the Arts. *A Live Dress* was begun in a Playwriting course and then developed at the Huntington Theatre, where Kaufman was a resident playwright prior to graduate school. Find out about their upcoming shows by joining MJ's mailing list at: <https://tinyletter.com/mjkaufmanster>.

Jennifer-Scott Mobley is an Assistant Professor in the Department of Theatre and Dance at East Carolina University. Her book *Female Bodies on the American Stage: Enter Fat Actress* (Palgrave) explores cultural constructions of the fat female in representation. As a dramaturg and feminist scholar, her work focuses on female playwrights and the female body in performance. In 2017, she was co-program chair for the American Society of Theatre Research Conference: "Extra/Ordinary Bodies: Interrogating the Aesthetics of Difference." Her critical reviews and essays have appeared in *Theatre Journal, Ecumenica,* and *The Critical Companion to Lynn Nottage* (Routledge). Prior to co-coordinating the Jane Chambers Award, Mobley was a finalist reader from 2011-2014 and coordinated the student Jane Chambers contest from 2006-2009. She served as Vice President and President of the Women and Theatre Program of ATHE from 2010-2014. Since 2016, she has led adjudication for the Jane Chambers Prize together with Roth.

Maya E. Roth is the Della Rosa Associate Professor at Georgetown University, where she was founding Artistic Director of the Davis Performing Arts Center (2005-07) and founder of the Theater & Performance Studies major. Since 2007, Maya has stewarded WTP and ATHE's national award for feminist playwriting, the Jane Chambers Prize, which inspired this anthology. She directed the Student Jane Chambers Prize from 1999-2001. She has directed over three-dozen plays, including world and area premieres, classics, and collaboratively-devised works. Her critical essays and performance reviews have appeared in volumes such as *Feminist Theatrical Revisions of Classic Works, Theatre of War and Exile,* and *Dramatic Revisions of Myths, Fairytales and Legends,* as well as scholarly journals. She is best known for her expertise on the plays of Timberlake Wertenbaker, including her co-edited book (with Sara Freeman) *International Dramaturgy: Translations and Transformations in The Theatre of Timberlake Wertenbaker* (2008). As dramaturge, she has collaborated closely with Iraqi-American Playwright-Performer Heather Raffo, including for the new play *Noura* from its incubation in 2015 through its 2018 world premiere at The Shakespeare Theatre (DC) as well as for Raffo's libretto *Fallujah* (City Opera of Vancouver 2012). Recent honors include the Georgetown College Dean's Excellence in Teaching Award (2014) and the Women and Theatre Program's Service to the Field Award (2016).

Sara Warner (Afterword) is Associate Professor in the Department of Performing and Media Arts at Cornell University, where she is a Stephen H. Weiss Junior Fellow, the highest teaching honor for a recently tenured professor. Sara has published widely on dramatic literature and performance studies; feminist and queer art; lesbian, gay, and trans studies; the prison industrial complex; and academic labor. Sara's book, *Acts of Gaiety: LGBT Performance and the Politics of Pleasure*, received the Outstanding Book Award from the Association of Theater in Higher Education (ATHE), an Honorable Mention for the Barnard Hewitt Award from the American Society for Theatre Research (ASTR), and was named a Lambda Literary Award finalist. She has served as President of the Women and Theatre Program, Drama Division Delegate for the Modern Language Association, Secretary of ATHE, and as a member of several Boards of Directors, including the Center for Lesbian and Gay Studies (CLAGS), the Arch and Bruce Brown Foundation, and The Cherry Street Art Space.

Gina Young is a playwright, director and experimental theatre artist whose work often merges movement, music and contemporary queer theory. She got her start at the legendary WOW Cafe Theatre in New York City, toured the U.S. and Europe with lesbian pop duo Team Gina, and then settled in Los Angeles, where her work has been presented by The Hammer Museum, REDCAT, Highways, Los Angeles Performance Practice/LAX Festival, USC's Visions & Voices Series and the Women's Center for Creative Work. She was a Finalist for Center Theatre Group's 2018 Richard E. Sherwood Award, was selected for Directors Lab West 2018, and is a winner of the Jane Chambers Award for Playwriting for her play *Femmes: A Tragedy*. Gina is the creator of SORORITY, a hub for new queer and feminist performance in Los Angeles, and Feminist Acting Class, a revolutionary experiment in actor training. She studied Drama at NYU/Tisch and is a member of the Dramatists Guild. For more information and bookings, please visit www.ginayoung.com

Table of Contents

***

FEMINIST CULTURES AND CREATIVITY
Maya E. Roth

Rites of passage and ravishing girl-love, feminist quests and wry wit, uncertain futures and creativity: That's what you will find in this volume. Also: An offstage voice, lesbian history, and the hula; a farce in a beach-house with dark undercurrents; restless spirits and a queer love quest; a desert road trip from Manhattan, with wry insights from the afterlife; and girl on girl love, parody and betrayal, with a femmes' burlesque shaped by your (diverse) cast.

This anthology introduces our twin-set collection of ten recent prize-winning plays from the Jane Chambers Contest. Chosen for their excellence in feminist playwriting, all feature a majority of roles for women — still a rarity in mainstage theater seasons. Bold and distinctive, the winners rose from more than 2000 submissions over a decade. Honored between 2007-16 by the Women and Theatre Program (WTP) and the Association for Theater in Higher Education, the ten plays featured across two volumes are written by nine women and a genderqueer writer for the stage. By centering on women's experiences through a feminist lens, all of these playwrights also re-center something else: America, storytelling, theatrical genealogies, feminism, lesbian and queer identities, LGBTQ history, family, the future.

With this collection of winning plays, original interviews with the playwrights, and framing essays, Jen-Scott and I aim to stir focus on contemporary feminist perspectives and playwriting in the early 21st century. We also strive to intervene in the widely-documented systemic under-representation of women in theater, onstage and off, which undermines these writers — and the field. We trust that by placing these winning plays together, particularly in themed sets, their artistic and social stakes, as well as their feminist cross-currents, will call to you, like a possibility, a live conversation, or even, to invoke Claire Chafee's phrase, a "secret handshake" (Interview 2014).

The plays are at the heart of each volume. This first play anthology focuses on *Lesbian and Queer Plays from the Jane Chambers Prize*. The second volume, forthcoming, foregrounds *Cross-Cultural Feminisms: Plays from the Jane Chambers Prize*. We cluster winning plays from a single recent decade thematically, instead of organizing them into two five-year sequences, in order to deepen creative, cultural and critical focus. While each play won on *its own feminist terms*, our editorial frames allow two dominant strands of feminist playwriting from this decade of winners to gain focus; cross-over plays in each volume signal some flow, and intersectionality.

This first volume — *Lesbian and Queer Plays from the Jane Chambers Prize* — is all the more significant for the field because still today, in 2018, painfully few published or produced plays center on lesbian lives, in spite of a bounty of gems. Thus, we address a marked gap in the field more pointedly, a gap predicated in no small part on sexism and its corollary, economics, as Holly Hughes, among others, has noted (*Preface to Five Lesbian Brothers*).[1] In a similar vein, Paula Vogel attributes the marked gender and racial disparities in production and theater reviews to "market manipulation […] [that] dismisses women and POC (people of color)," more broadly (Qtd. in "A Collective Call," *HowlRound Commons*, June 15, 2017).

Volume One features lesbian and queer feminist playwrights writing "out." Mary Casey's *Unspeakable Acts* (2008), for instance, inspired by oral histories at UCLA, dramatizes the psychic and social contours for pioneering educators exiled from their livelihoods during the 1950's "lesbian scare." Written during national debates on Don't Ask, Don't Tell (Don't Pursue, Don't Harass), or compulsory closeting for LGBT individuals in the military

---

[1] In counterpoint, the production and publication of gay male plays are numerous, importantly documented as central to American and contemporary drama, as recent Broadway revivals have furthered. See the *New York Times* retrospective "A Brief History of Gay Theater, in Three Acts," for instance, by Jesse Green (February 26, 2018).

3

(and many work places), Casey exposes blacklisting and homophobia as the "unspeakable acts," not lesbian lives. (In so doing, she poses a subtle rejoinder to *The Children's Hour*). A past performer, Playwright-Director Gina Young seeks "work that […] *feels* queer, *sounds* queer." In *Femmes* (2014) she slyly queers Claire Boothe Luce's *The Women*, re-imagined in a multiracial lesbian burlesque community, full of sass, difference and experimentation. Each of the five plays in this volume re-center iconic aspects of American life and culture through lesbian and queer feminist lenses: the McCarthy era, the Yiddish theater world, the American West. Some traffic in the lesbian detective genre, like *A Live Dress'* (2010) queer coming of age tale (that reframes Broadway's first lesbian stage kiss in the 1920s as a moment of recognition, not 'indecency,' before discovering secret dybbuks) — or Meryl Cohn's *The Siegels of Montauk* (2009), where feminist ethics bubble up out of fabulous farce for a PFLAG family and two interlopers. Claire Chafee, meanwhile, follows existential questions (cum quests) in *Full/Self* (2013), by telegraphing in with exquisite detail on three generations of "spirited" women in liminal "elsewheres"— the Afterlife, out West, a Manhattan park bench. With depth and whimsy, she offers a complex meditation on growing up female, parenting, class and family roots/reinvention, as well as living lesbian in America in the early 21st century.

Volume Two features more cross-cultural plays in theme, poetics and politics. From Christine Evans' *Trojan Barbie: a Car-Crash Encounter with Euripides' 'Trojan Women'* (2007) — a post-modern feminist critique of the Iraq and Afghanistan wars via radical interaction with a classic — to Austin-based Teatrista Natalie Mayorga Goodnow's queer solo play *Mud Offerings* (2011), which stages a Chicanita having it out with the *Vergen de Guadalupe* at the borders of identity and the Americas. Featuring a radical eclecticism of characters, styles and scenes in each play, these winners creatively engage marginalized experiences, as modeled by Emma Stanton's *No Candy*, which focuses on a multigenerational mix of Muslim women who re-create their memories and lives in Srebenica, after ethnic violence (2016). These plays experiment with form, often pursuing more pointed social critiques than the ones in Volume One.

I call this a "twin-set" to suggest a shared cultural genealogy. The volumes are not birth twins, but rather, play collections that share similar cultural roots, while traveling unique routes.[2] As lesbian feminists have played such key roles in gender rights movements in the US and in feminist arts and scholarship, perhaps it is unsurprising that more than half of our winning feminist plays between 2007-16 engaged lesbian and lesbian queer lives, particularly given Jane Chambers' legacy. Similarly, in an era of globalization, international gender rights issues have garnered focus in activism, arts and the academy; it's fitting that more feminist playwrights in America chose to excavate compelling, often urgent intersections of local and global concerns (and identities), not only intersections of personal and political stakes, in this decade.

By hailing 'Lesbian' and 'Queer' in this first volume's title we respect the language the playwrights themselves use to describe their primary cultures of belonging — and, moreover, their plays' central figures and frames. In this, we gesture towards overlapping, and sometimes divergent, poetics and politics deployed by feminist and LGBTQ writers in this decade. As Mary Casey and Claire Chafee engage, explicit focus on lesbian lives and culture remains critical because lesbians are so often silenced and occluded in American history, arts and culture, including at times within feminist and LGBTQ circles. Indeed 21st century America has stewarded what Bonnie Morris calls *The Disappearing L: The Erasure of Lesbian Spaces and Culture* (2018). Meanwhile, the interrogation of gender binaries which animated much feminist living and theory in decades past has come to ally with the genderqueer movement, especially for many younger artists; thus, we

---

[2] Chafee pointed out this phrase repurposes language for a popular version of women's apparel in an earlier era: short-sleeved sweater underneath, and cardigan atop. A pleasurable redress, from clothes to books, normative to feminist, imbued with traces of disidentification.

use the phrase "queer" as an inclusive marker of sex/gender difference across a continuum that includes trans writers, such as Kaufman, now a leading voice in the trans playwriting movement, as well as Gina Young, who identifies as both femme lesbian and queer.[3] Provincetown-based Meryl Cohn (a.k.a. Ms. Behavior), writes the continuum as mainstream.

We highlight plays between 2007 and 2016 for several reasons: first, we aim primary focus on contemporary plays and women playwrights; second, I was the steward for the Contest across those years, leading to my sustained curation — and relationships with —these plays and playwrights; and third, WTP celebrated the first twenty years of the Contest in 2006 by honoring Chambers' legacy, instead of a winner, which separated "waves" of the contest—leading to active renewal of the Prize's feminist roles in changing contexts, about which I have written in *Theatre Topics*, made more pressing by the dissipation (and defunding) of feminist organizations and ethics in American society, theater, and the academy. This collection was hatched in a decade when feminist scholars, artists and activists reflected back on "the movement," and recorded its legacies to re-imagine forward, as marked by publications in theater such as *Feminist Futures? Theatre, Theory, Performance* (2006), edited by Elaine Aston and Geraldine Harris or *Contemporary Women Playwrights: Into the 21st Century* (2014), edited by Penny Farfan and Lesly Ferris. In a similar vein, we in WTP hosted a series of round-tables, which likewise inspired Sara Warner's archival research on Jane Chambers for this Afterword and mine for our Winners Archives in the Appendix.[4] The

---

[3] Queer theater accents "multiplicity," and anti-hegemonic perspectives, as Jill Dolan notes, with, as Robin Bernstein adds, "an intention to signify diversity, difference and disagreement" (*Cast Out* 7). As a verb, 'queer' means to skew normative perspectives and structures (e.g. of dramatic form or social organization) with an LGBTQ difference.
[4] The Prize's wider arc of feminist playwriting registers in our Appendix, beginning with the first Award in 1984, and 1991 for the student prize, pieced together from my research. Given our key focus for the twin-set, we record all honorees (six to eight annually) since 2007, and refer readers to the curation, annually posted on WTP's website

presidency of Donald Trump, beginning in 2017, better frames current feminist and other activism in the U.S., including our latest Prizewinners — Cary Crim for *Never, Not Once*, and Martyna Majok for *Queens*.

To be clear, from 2007-16, the publication and production challenges all playwrights face were compounded for women writers, especially for feminist and lesbian plays. The field knows this, yet systemic bias remains. Female playwrights have roughly the same chance of seeing their plays produced in mainstage seasons in the United States as a century ago, hovering below 25%. Intensified activism and annual mainstreaming of these disparities (e.g. in *American Theater* and *The Kilroy's List*) have not yielded marked culture, nor systemic, change. If some key factors persist — marked gender and race disparities in rates of production, funding levels, leadership roles in theaters and critical reception, even casting trends — some dynamics *have* shifted. The marked acceleration of technology, for instance, has enabled under-recognized writers to make their work available themselves via activist digital platforms, including via databases for women and trans artists or on the National New Play Network's database, since their works are disproportionately under-reported on "industry-leader" platforms. Theaters and teachers who want to present great plays by women can find a deluge. The Jane Chambers Prize is one of many initiatives seeking to create alternate pipelines —ours, with feminist adjudication, staged reading, and curation—to help offset systemic under-representation of women's work. We foreground feminism: complex roles for women, feminist perspectives and experimentations in form.

What is feminist in these plays? Here, you will find no tragic lesbians from the American stage archives, nor sentimental *ingenues*, no long-suffering wives nor suffocating mothers, no enchanted fairies nor evil

---

(prepared by me 2007-16, and by Jen-Scott 2017-18). In theater, works cannot become part of the future repertory, if they are not preserved. Archiving feminist history — and indeed women's creativity, achievements and labor in any era — is critical, often overlooked.

7

stepmothers. Rather you will find a diverse array of women with tenacity and creativity, questions and wit, on quests (and detours), seeking what *Full/Self* calls "some workable new way." Our Winners imagine alternatives to circumscribed (hetero) normative arcs for "women's stories" in rom-com films, and the classical set of virgin-whore-mother-muse (and eroticized victims) that dominate our stages; complex in their complicities and capacities, the plays' women interact with other women— *and* the world— feeding feminist ethics and storytelling. Feminist frameworks emerge early in these plays, often buoyed by stage interventions, stylistic and / or narrative, along the way.

Intriguingly, all five of these plays *veer* in their last scenes. Neither utopic, nor dystopic, they present an open-ended future — to evoke the possibility of change and worlds in motion.[5] In all five last scenes, central figures hail the Unknown Future: sometimes with a glimpse of joy and rare alliance across generations (as in *Full/Self*), with music to make the "hard work" ahead possible (and worth it); sometimes stepping apart to resist replaying past patterns (as in *Femmes*); sometimes, hand in hand, to quest into the Unknown (as in *Live/Dress*). Most also evoke awareness of other (unseen) women, beyond the multigenerational array they each stage: "What about the other women?" is the question that lingers beyond *Siegels of Montauk* as the three adult sisters (lesbian therapist, straight writer, sometimes pregnant surrogate for gay men) prepare to leave the family beach home forever. In *Unspeakable Acts*, the protagonist begins anew, jauntily ready to invent a next chapter as "notorious lesbians" with her lover, refusing the tragic lesbian arc society thrusts upon her, buoyed by her feminist chosen family. Tonally distinct (melancholic, unsure, resilient), their last moments remind us that the future relies (too) on us.

---

5 "Essential to any sort of feminist politics has always been the idea that 'the future' is a question, is *in* question: is not necessarily determined by the past or the present," as Elaine Aston and Geraldine Harris write in *Feminist Futures?* (3).

Each play invites inventive staging and provocative, rich discussion with audiences, artists and classrooms. Most tackle unexpected —even taboo — subjects in creative, powerful ways: All take risks. Many experiment with form in playful, bold ways. Highly original and diverse, the plays in Volumes One and Two range from magical realism to fast-moving histories, ensemble comedies to solo performance, farce to feminist burlesque, and they suit an array of aesthetic communities, ethics, and theatre venues. They also surface the vitality of feminist playwriting by lesbian, queer and straight theater folk today, with quite different generations writing and living feminist, placed side by side in our volumes.

One rare gift of this collection is that all of the playwrights came of age with feminism as a reference point in their lives, politically and/or creatively. Chafee, whose *Why We Have a Body* (1993) was an iconic (nationally-touring) feminist and lesbian play of the late twentieth century, credits the formative impact of Chambers on her life and art, as our dedication shares. In a 2014 interview, she elaborated that "getting an award in her honor is like … a secret handshake saying to keep going." In this volume's published conversation, Kaufman recalls that "something […] cracked open for me" on encountering feminist writers such as Suzan-Lori Parks, Cherrie Moraga, and Naomi Wallace as a young adult, followed by Paula Vogel's mentoring at Yale. In our edited 'Conversations' following each play, writers share insights on their work and arcs over time (influences and signature features). All also present feminist perspectives on writing—including strategies and insights for women writers, for feminists, for the field. We place artists and scholars, as well as different generations of writers, in conversation via this Prize —and in the twin-set. This praxis enacts feminist and theatrical community to make visible that we are "part of a larger movement, connected to other worlds of aesthetics and values."[6] We hope this curated collection will help to activate your imaginations, to connect generations of feminism, and to diversify season programming, teaching, funding, residencies, and readers' joyful, deeper grasp of lesbian and queer playwriting today.

Works Cited

Aston, Elaine and Geraldine Harris. *Feminist Futures?: Theatre, Performance, Theory.* Palgrave MacMillan, 2006.

Bernstein, Robin. *Cast Out: Queer Lives in Theater.* University of Michigan Press, 2006.

Chafee, Claire. Interview with Maya E. Roth, qtd. in *Women and Theatre Program Newsletter.* February 2014.

Critical Mass (24 Feminist Artists and Academics). "A Collective Call to End Critical Bias." *HowlRound Commons.* 15 June 15, 2017 http://howlround.com/a-collective-call-against-critical-bias

Farfan, Penny and Lesly Ferris, *Women Playwrights: Into the 21st Century.* Palgrave MacMillan, 2013.

Green, Jesse. "A Brief History of Gay Theater, in Three Acts," *The New York Times.* 26 February 2018. https://www.nytimes.com/2018/02/26/t-magazine/gay-theater-history-boys-in-the-band

Hughes, Holly. Preface to *The Five Lesbian Brothers (Four Plays)* by The Five Lesbian Brothers. TCG Press, 2000.

Morris, Bonnie. *The Disappearing L: The Erasure of Lesbian Spaces and Culture.* SUNY Press, 2018.

Roth, Maya E. "Renewing and Renewing Feminist Theatrical Engagement," *Theatre Topics.* J. Hopkins UP, 20: 2 (2010) 157-168.

Roth, Maya and Jen-Scott Mobley. "Previous Winners and Honorees," Jane Chambers Prize, Women and Theatre Program. http://www.womenandtheatreprogram.com/contact.html.

---

[6] Kaufman's language, from our fuller interview. Casey describes the impact of our Prize and process as feeling like "a collective action;" Cohn calls it "life-sustaining to feminist playwrights."

UNSPEAKABLE ACTS

by
Mary F. Casey

**Winner of the
2008 Jane Chambers Prize**

CAST OF CHARACTERS

MARTHA DEANE	A Professor of Physical Education, in her mid-50s. Charismatic and dynamic.
ROSALIND CASSIDY	A Professor of Physical Education, also in her mid-50s. Scholarly and sardonic.
RUTH FULTON	Assistant Professor of Physical Education, in her mid-30s. A fish out of water in academia.
DAVID DOWD	Ambitious University Dean, in his mid-40s.
PHYLLIS DOWD	Housewife, helpmate to David Dowd, in her early 40s.
ROBERT G. SPROUL	Powerful, self-assured President of the University of California, in his 50s.

NOTE ON DRAMATURGY
Original dramaturgy by Jan Lewis.

NOTE ON PHYSICAL MOVEMENT
Three of the characters are professional physical education teachers and are thus acutely aware of human movement. Their movements should reflect a grace and comfort with their physical selves. This ease is in contrast to David Dowd's physical awkwardness; he's a man out of touch with his body.

12

NOTE ON HISTORICAL SOURCES
Unspeakable Acts uses both history and fiction to tell the story of UCLA Professor Martha Deane's real-life fight to save her position and her good name.

Archives utilized in the play's creation include the UCLA Library's University Archives and the UCLA Library Center for Oral History Research. Particularly informative were the oral histories of professors Martha Deane and Rosalind Cassidy, as well as of Dean Paul Dodd.

While the events surrounding Martha Deane's suspension from UCLA and her fight for reinstatement are accurately represented, the dialogue, some characters and situations have necessarily been invented. However, the historical record does suggest Martha and Ruth ultimately enjoyed a long life together up on the Tiger Tail.

SETTING

Stage right is the outdoor patio of Martha's small but cozy 1940s modern home in Los Angeles, California. There are patio chairs, plants and a well-stocked bar. Stage left is David's office on the UCLA campus, with an appropriately large desk, chairs and appropriately impressive framed photos on the walls. In between, or above, Martha's and David's respective spaces is a third space, flexible and liminal. With different lighting, this can be a gym floor, a small insurance office, David's study or a plot of land.

TIME

The action of the play occurs between 1952 and 1955.

ACT ONE

SCENE ONE

(The stage is dark.)

MARTHA DEANE (*offstage*): Ladies!

(*Spot up on Martha Deane, a charismatic UCLA Physical Education Professor in her mid-fifties. It is the autumn of 1952.*)

MARTHA (*continuing):* Ladies, welcome to your bodies. Yes, your bodies, ladies. That amazing conglomeration of muscle, skin, bones and sensations that has got you this far. Rule number one in preparing for a career in Physical Education: Never forget you have a body. Rule number two: Consider carefully what it tells you. Chances are, it's right.

And allow me also to welcome you to your first day of training in your career as an instructor of Physical Education in the California school system. This will be the twenty-sixth year I have facilitated the Introduction to Teaching Methodology class. I assure you, you have made a choice you will never regret.

Your job will be to teach young ladies in junior and senior high schools across the state, many of them unaware they even have a body. You will teach them by offering each girl a series of experiences through which she will discover her own relationship to human movement. In so doing, in a larger sense, you will be helping her experience her own essential humanity.

While some people today question the place of physical education in the university, our philosophy is that physical education is a science as profound and complex as physics or medicine. What could be more important to the world today than teaching what it means to live and move in the world as a human being?

(*Spot out on Martha.*)

(The patio of Martha's house in Los Angeles. Small but cozy, it's ideal for modest indoor/outdoor modern California living. It's nearing sunset and a party is in progress offstage. Martha offers a martini to her best friend, Rosalind Cassidy. Also a Professor, Rosy is in her mid-fifties, a respected scholar.)

ROSALIND: I'm sure it's delicious, Martha. But one was more than enough.

MARTHA: Don't tell me I am in the presence of an academic with common sense.

ROSALIND: The world is ever full of possibilities, dear.

MARTHA: I've always feared women who could hold their liquor.

ROSALIND: Rather subversive these days, isn't it?

MARTHA: Oh, everything's subversive, to hear the Republicans talk.

ROSALIND: I wouldn't let the Democrats off the hook so quickly.

MARTHA: Well, I don't recall Roosevelt looking for spies and microfilm in a pumpkin patch.

ROSALIND: He's been dead since 1945. Surely, you've noticed.

MARTHA: Only because you keep reminding me.

ROSALIND: Oh, I suppose I'll vote for Stevenson like every other egghead. But he won't win. Not while McCarthy rules.

MARTHA: I'd like to think we're safely out of that madness, but the Un-American Committee is practically next door.

ROSALIND: Home on the range. Where the deer and the antelope name names.

MARTHA: You're altogether too clever and too sober for your own good.

> (Ruth Fulton enters, a strikingly attractive Assistant Professor in her mid-thirties. She's carrying a drink tray.)

RUTH (to Martha): Martha, what on earth did you say to Jim Barton?

> (Martha moves to help her refill glasses.)

MARTHA: Not a thing that wasn't warranted.

RUTH: He practically bit my head off in the driveway. (To Rosalind) He's put in this swimming pool next door—

MARTHA: I don't know which is worse — the noise from the motor or having to admit we now live next door to someone who owns a swimming pool.

ROSALIND: You mean that sound like a freight train outside the living room window?

MARTHA: I told him the noise was unacceptable.

RUTH: Martha!

MARTHA: Well, it is.

RUTH: All right. Yes, it is. You win. But did you have to bring out all the artillery? Now you've really made him angry.

MARTHA: Let him be angry!

RUTH: He lives fifteen feet from us!

MARTHA: All the more reason he should respect the eardrums of his neighbors.

RUTH: Oh, why do I even bother to argue with you?

ROSALIND: You may have noticed, Ruth, everything's a matter of justice to Martha.

MARTHA: There's another way in the world?

ROSALIND: Complacency, I suppose.

MARTHA: Appeasement.

ROSALIND: If only you'd been at Munich instead of Chamberlain.

RUTH: The swimming pool motor is not a Nazi tank, Martha. Sometimes it's okay to compromise. In Nebraska, we called it getting along.

MARTHA: Your preference is to live in Nebraska?

(Ruth touches Martha affectionately.)

RUTH: My preference is to live with Martha Deane and take my lumps.

MARTHA: It can be a bit lumpy sometimes, can't it?

ROSALIND: Ruth's Midwestern politeness doesn't allow her to tell you you're a bull in a china shop, Martha, dear. It's a wonder the swimming pool isn't littered with broken crockery.

MARTHA (*to Ruth*): How's the party going?

RUTH: David Dowd is telling us all about his last trip to some country in Africa to recruit an anthropologist.

MARTHA: And Phyllis?

RUTH: Riveted.

ROSALIND: A brave soul, Phyllis.

MARTHA: Courageous.

ROSALIND: Ever sacrificing.

MARTHA: Ever sacrificed.

ROSALIND and MARTHA (*toasting*): To Phyllis!

RUTH: Shhhhhh. He'll hear you.

ROSALIND: Ears ever alert for the slightest inchoate mutiny. You're very tolerant to invite the Dowds, Martha.

MARTHA: I'm trying to kill him with kindness. And my canapé recipe.

RUTH: So, maybe he won't cut the PE Department's program —

ROSALIND: — if he tastes your hors d'oeuvres?

MARTHA: You both know me too well. I am nothing if not strategic. (*Takes drink tray from Ruth.*) As an apology, let me take these in.

RUTH: Dowd's probably still talking. (*Takes back drink tray from Martha.*) Consider it a gift.

(*Ruth kisses Martha. Rosalind turns away politely.*)

MARTHA: Excuse us, Rosy.

RUTH: Sorry —

ROSALIND: Quite all right. It's your home.

MARTHA: You're very broad-minded.

ROSALIND: You forget I've worked in women's Physical Education departments all my adult life. I must say I prefer displays of tenderness to screaming fights over boyfriends.

(Ruth exits with drink tray.)

MARTHA: She's a trouper.

ROSALIND: She makes you happy. And she's lovely.

MARTHA: Do I say thank you? When you say that to a man about his wife, he's supposed to be complimented.

ROSALIND: So be complimented.

MARTHA: I am happy.

ROSALIND: But —?

MARTHA: Does it sound like there's a "but"?

ROSALIND: Something is making you uncomfortable and you won't talk about it unless I browbeat you sufficiently.

MARTHA: I'm not saying there's a "but", Rosy —

ROSALIND: But if there were?

MARTHA: If there were, it would be that I live in terror of having to admit I'm too old for her.

ROSALIND: Oh, stop it, Martha.

MARTHA: It's twenty years —

ROSALIND: She doesn't seem to care. That's what matters.

MARTHA: I don't know if it's the actual years so much as the experience of them. Not that I'm wiser — by any means. But I'm not afraid. Ruth and her generation are cautious in a way ours isn't. Oh, when we were her age did we have a time, Rosy. Eleanor Roosevelt was in the White House —

ROSALIND: And there was mass poverty and millions of people went hungry. You have a selective memory.

MARTHA: We got through the Depression somehow, Rosy, thank God. The War was horrible, of course, but it did open up all kinds of possibilities for women —

ROSALIND: Which have all but disappeared now. No more Rosie the Riveter, the last I looked. They want us back in the kitchen where we belong. And those of us lucky enough to have careers make less than our male colleagues. Is it any wonder Ruth is cautious?

MARTHA: The pendulum will swing back. She just hasn't seen it swing as many times as I have. I must seem like a relic to her, a throwback.

ROSALIND: You've got past the first year with flying colors. Surely by now all your secrets have been revealed. She's seen you unwashed and unkempt. She's heard all of your stories at least once, many twice. She's tolerated innumerable faculty parties, including the likes of David and Phyllis Dowd, for God's sake. Martha, I think it's safe to say the girl isn't going anywhere.

MARTHA: Knock on all the wood you can find.

ROSALIND: It must be nice to have someone to come home to every night.

MARTHA: At my age, it would be nice to think that part of my life is settled.

ROSALIND: Well, my life is certainly settled, I suppose. But in a different way.

MARTHA: What about the new fellow in architecture?

ROSALIND: Married. Well, separated. Very touch-and-go. The wife doesn't understand him, etc. etc. etc.

MARTHA: I knew I shouldn't have wasted the good silver on him.

ROSALIND: You need to accept my obvious spinsterhood, Martha, dear. God knows I have. I love teaching and having a career, and that truly is enough for me. And that's a good thing because it's damn hard to find a man willing to marry an intelligent woman over thirty.

MARTHA: For all intents and purposes, I suppose we're both spinsters. As far as the world knows.

ROSALIND: Your spinsterhood, however, appears to be significantly more satisfying than mine.

(Police siren wails off stage.)

MARTHA: Oh, for heaven's sake!

ROSALIND: Barton again?

MARTHA: Who else would complain about the noise made by a group of addle-pated academics?

ROSALIND: I'm almost flattered he finds us a nuisance.

MARTHA: Don't tell that to Ruth or she'll have your head.

ROSALIND: You'll be polite to the nice officer?

MARTHA: When have you known me to be anything but the soul of discretion? *(They laugh.)*

SCENE THREE

(David Dowd's office on the campus of UCLA. Phyllis Dowd, a woman of gentle strength in her forties, looks at the framed photo on the desk while her husband, Dean David Dowd, rummages through some papers. Once a man on a career fast track, he finds himself now in his mid-forties, engine idling.)

PHYLLIS: Gad, David. Where did you find this?

DAVID: What's wrong with it?

PHYLLIS: The angle. I look like I'm a hundred and ten.

DAVID: Hardly.

PHYLLIS: We've got all those Hawaii pictures. Put one of them in.

DAVID: I like that one, Phyllis. I like looking at you at the Boardwalk.

PHYLLIS: With the wind howling and the water spraying. Please, David. All your colleagues must think I've let myself go.

DAVID: I'm the only one who looks at it.

PHYLLIS: All the more reason.

DAVID: What brought you by today, Phyllis?

PHYLLIS: I can't just drop by spur of the moment to have lunch with my handsome husband?

DAVID: You haven't been here in months.

PHYLLIS: All the more —

DAVID: Why?

PHYLLIS: You know why, sweetheart.

DAVID: You can stop worrying about me.

PHYLLIS: You're tired all the time. Distracted —

DAVID: I work hard —

PHYLLIS: Too hard.

DAVID: Now is my chance to —

PHYLLIS: — move up. Yes, I've heard all this before, David.

DAVID: I'm fine, Phyllis.

PHYLLIS: You need a vacation.

DAVID: We just got back from Hawaii.

PHYLLIS: That was a year and a half ago.

DAVID: Okay, okay. Let me pencil you in.

PHYLLIS: Dorothy says they're looking for a Chancellor at one of the teachers' colleges —

DAVID: No.

PHYLLIS: David, maybe you should consider it.

DAVID: UCLA is my home.

PHYLLIS: I know it wouldn't be as prestigious —

DAVID: I _am_ moving up, Phyllis. You know that. It just takes —

PHYLLIS: A fresh start might be just the thing.

DAVID: — time.

PHYLLIS: It couldn't hurt to think about it.

DAVID: It just takes time.

PHYLLIS: You seem tense. You're fighting with Martha again, aren't you?

DAVID: She's got forty teachers all doing Group Process, whatever that is. If I had my way —

PHYLLIS: Yes, I know. You'd cut her program.

DAVID: It's an educational —

PHYLLIS: — frill. So I've heard.

DAVID: Do I really talk about it that much?

PHYLLIS: Yes, constantly. But I don't think that's what's really bothering you.

DAVID: Nothing's bothering me.

PHYLLIS: David, listen to me. It's just a rumor, what that Regent supposedly said.

DAVID: What?

PHYLLIS: It doesn't mean anything. To me or to anyone else. He's just an ignorant fool.

DAVID: Will you stop bringing that up, Phyllis!

(She stares at him in surprise, silent.)

DAVID *(continuing)*: Oh, I'm sorry, dear. You're right, I am tense these days. *(He kisses her.)*

PHYLLIS: What about France this year, David?
    (The telephone rings.)

DAVID: France? *(Picks up telephone.)*

PHYLLIS: We've never been.

DAVID *(on telephone)*: Oh, hello, Mr. President.

PHYLLIS: You've always wanted to.

DAVID *(on telephone)*: Yes, of course. *(He hangs up.)*
Another time.

PHYLLIS: You don't want to go? Why not?

DAVID: Talk about it, I mean. Another time.

PHYLLIS: It's just, you've been so —

DAVID: I'm fine.

PHYLLIS: So. How is President Sproul?

DAVID: He's in town from Berkeley.

PHYLLIS: And he needs to speak with you. Right now.

DAVID: It's highly confidential.

PHYLLIS: It's always highly confidential with him. You drop whatever you're doing, he swears you to secrecy on some important thing he wants you to take care of and you can't sleep for a month.

DAVID: That's not true, Phyllis.

PHYLLIS: He may be the President of the University of California, David, but you don't owe him your heart and soul.

DAVID: It will be quick, dear. Do you mind?

PHYLLIS: Does it matter?

DAVID: Of course, it matters.

PHYLLIS: But Robert Gordon Sproul matters more.

DAVID: He pays the bills. And for the trip to France.

PHYLLIS: So he does. I'll wait outside.

DAVID: Thanks, honey.

> (*Phyllis exits. Only a moment later, longtime President of the University of California, Robert Gordon Sproul, enters. A middle-aged man, he has retained the dynamism of youth. His presence is imposing.*)

DAVID (*continuing*): Mr. President.

SPROUL: Phyllis is looking well.

DAVID: Oh, you bumped into her —?

> (*They shake hands. Sproul walks around the room restlessly. He looks at the photo on David's desk.*)

SPROUL: Windy that day, wasn't it?

DAVID: Very.

SPROUL: How do you like Adlai's chances?

DAVID: It would be nice to have an intellectual in, for a change.

SPROUL: He's as good as Stalin to the Regents. I'd have my hands full. Look, Dave, there's a situation down here. I've been talking to the Regent's counsel about taking care of it. Your name came up.

DAVID: A situation —?

SPROUL: An unfortunate one.

DAVID: I'd be happy to handle it —

SPROUL: It could get messy.

DAVID: Fair warning.

SPROUL: Odd times we live in these days. They say Communists are infiltrating your school paper now. Just how I want to spend my time — investigating the *Daily Bruin*.

DAVID: The situation —?

SPROUL: It's regarding Martha.

DAVID: Martha Deane?

SPROUL: I don't like putting you in this position. Investigating a colleague is never easy. We've both known her for years.

DAVID: She was the campus representative to —

SPROUL: — my twentieth anniversary dinner. Yes, and she gave a marvelous speech. Some would say she's still the most powerful woman on campus — certainly when Clarence Dykstra was still alive.

DAVID: She's quite an advocate for the women's PE program.

SPROUL: Bulldog, I think you mean to say.

DAVID: Has there been a complaint of some kind?

SPROUL: Complaints.

DAVID: From students?

SPROUL: No.

DAVID: Parents?

SPROUL: Neighbors.

DAVID: Neighbors? Martha's neighbors?

SPROUL: Look, I know you've seen a lot of the world, Dave. That war service in Washington, all the traveling you've done. As a dean, you deal with people a lot. You've read the Kinsey findings? Well, skimmed it — no one reads the whole thing.

DAVID *(uncomfortably)*: I've glanced at it.

SPROUL: I'll stop beating around the bush. You know as well as I do it's not just Communists they're letting go at the State Department. I've heard they're firing a homosexual a day right now. I suppose it was bound to hit the academy sooner or later.

DAVID: I'm not sure that I'm following —

SPROUL: There have been complaints from neighbors about Martha's activities.

DAVID: Activities?

SPROUL: At her house. A young woman. A roommate.

DAVID: Inappropriate activities?

SPROUL: Seen through an uncurtained window. I don't want to go into it further. The implication for the university — well, it's most unfortunate. The neighbor's an alum. He contacted the head of the alumni committee — he's got a daughter in Martha's department — and he says he'll go to the papers if we don't get this taken care of right away.

DAVID: I'll look into it, Mr. President.

SPROUL: You have the authority to take whatever action is necessary to facilitate the investigation and to protect the University.

DAVID: She's tenured, of course.

SPROUL: I'm well aware of that. We all know there are very few reasons tenure can be revoked. Look, Dave, I have known Martha Deane for over twenty years. I consider her a friend as well as a colleague. She is a particular favorite of Mrs. Sproul.

DAVID: I understand the difficulty for you.

SPROUL: Sometimes our jobs have unpleasant but unavoidable aspects. If I could, I would let this one die on the vine. But we don't have that option. I just ask that you allow her to retain her dignity as much as possible.

DAVID: I'll talk to her today.

SPROUL: About the roommate —

DAVID: Oh, yes.

SPROUL: A young graduate student or assistant professor or something. Quite striking girl, as I recall. I remember her creating a certain stir when she arrived.

DAVID: I believe I know who you mean.

SPROUL: Talk to her first.

DAVID: All right.

SPROUL: Have you done this kind of investigation before? I assume in your labor work or at the War Board … Now, I'm not suggesting Tailgunner Joe tactics. The girl's new here. From Iowa, I believe. She'll probably just quietly resign. You'll have more trouble with Martha.

DAVID: Could I get more details —?

(Sproul opens a briefcase and hands David a file. Lights down on David's office.)

SCENE FOUR

(A basketball dribbles furiously off stage. Lights up on Martha's patio, later that day. Ruth stands tensely dribbling a basketball. She tosses it away, then begins to pace the room, adrenaline pumping. She stops at the bar and tries to pour herself a drink, but her hands are shaking too much. She paces more.)

ROSALIND *(offstage)*: Martha? *(Ruth does not answer.)* Did I get the time wrong? *(Ruth tries to light a cigarette, but can't. Back to pacing. Rosalind enters the patio.)*

ROSALIND: Oh, Ruth. I'm sorry. Martha said to come by after four o'clock. *(Ruth tries to pour herself a drink again.)* What on earth? *(She moves to the bar.)* Here. Let me. *(She pours a drink for Ruth.)* What on earth is wrong, Ruth? *(Ruth takes a sip of the drink, puts it down, starts pacing again.)* Ruth! *(She stands in front of Ruth and puts her arms on her shoulders, stopping Ruth in her tracks.)* Tell me what is going on!

RUTH: Martha …

ROSALIND: What about Martha? What's happened to her? Is something wrong with Martha?

RUTH: She's with Dowd.

(Ruth sits down, tries to sip her drink again.)

ROSALIND: Martha's with Dowd? Well, I suppose that is enough of a horror on its own —

RUTH: He knows.

ROSALIND: He knows what, Ruth? What are you saying?

(Ruth cries out, gets up again. Rosalind stops her.)

RUTH: Let me up, Rosy.

ROSALIND: Tell me what's going on.

RUTH: I can't.

ROSALIND: I've known Martha forever, dear. She's my closest friend in all the world. If something's wrong with her, you have to tell me.

(Ruth forces Rosalind's arms away from her as she rises.)

RUTH: Dowd knows about us. About Martha and me. He brought me into his office —

ROSALIND: Damn!

RUTH: He asked me … he asked me … I just wanted it over.

ROSALIND: What did you say?

RUTH: I could hear ringing in my ears.

ROSALIND: Ruth —

RUTH: I couldn't hear what he was saying and his mouth kept moving and all I heard in my head was talking and then he was waiting, he was waiting for me to talk, and all I could say was —

ROSALIND: Stop!

RUTH: Martha! All I could say was "Martha."

ROSALIND: It's all right now, Ruth. It's over.

RUTH: It's not over. You don't understand.

ROSALIND: Ruth, I certainly understand how you must have —

RUTH: No, you don't! How could you? You're not like us.

(Beat.)

ROSALIND: I suppose you're right.

RUTH: I'm sorry, Rosy —

ROSALIND: No, you're right. As much as I may think I understand, it isn't the same for me. I don't suppose I've ever really thought about it. It's rather like discovering there's always been an open chasm between you and someone, but you just never saw it.

RUTH: Forgive me, Rosy. I'm not angry with you —

ROSALIND: You'll find another job.

RUTH: No, I won't. Not in teaching. I'm not like you two. I don't love the university life. I don't love teaching and I certainly don't love the politics. But it's losing Martha I'm worried about. Oh, Rosy, I can't lose Martha! Do you understand?

ROSALIND: You didn't tell Dowd anything? *(Ruth shakes her head.)* Nothing?

RUTH: No.

ROSALIND: Good girl.

RUTH: I just resigned.

SCENE FIVE

(David's office. Martha enters holding a large paperbag.)

DAVID: Martha, hello.

(She hands him the bag.)

MARTHA: Phyllis's dessert dish. It was nice seeing you both the other night.

DAVID: Look, Martha —

(She notices a framed photo on desk.)

MARTHA: I had forgotten you went to Hawaii last year. Phyllis looks so happy on that boat. Perhaps you should buy her one, David. You know I've often thought I'd like to go to Hawaii myself —

DAVID: There's a matter of some urgency —

MARTHA: Oh, for heaven's sake, David. Is this about department staffing again? Really, let's just call a truce and have done with it, shall we? You agree not to cut my budget and I agree not to go behind your back and get it reinstated. Deal?

DAVID: This isn't a budgetary matter, Martha.

MARTHA: Well, I'm relieved to hear that. Sorry, David. I didn't mean to jump down your throat —

DAVID: I've just been talking to Ruth.

MARTHA: Ruth. Fulton?

DAVID: Yes.

(Beat. Martha knows something's up.)

MARTHA: She didn't mention it.

DAVID: I just saw her now.

MARTHA: Oh, you did.

DAVID: I asked her to come in to answer some questions.

MARTHA: Questions.

DAVID: Look, Martha. This is very difficult for me. You and I have been colleagues for many years.

MARTHA: Yes, we have, David.

DAVID: Phyllis and I have spent a number of lovely evenings in your home.

MARTHA: I'm glad you've enjoyed yourselves.

DAVID: I don't relish having to do this —

MARTHA: Don't relish doing what?

DAVID: I want you to understand that.

MARTHA: Get to the point, David. Is there a problem with Ruth?

DAVID: Actually, the problem is with you.

(A beat. Not what Martha was expecting.)

MARTHA: What do you mean?

DAVID: The University will be initiating an investigation regarding you, Martha.

MARTHA: What on earth are you talking about?

DAVID: Your activities.

MARTHA: My "activities"? I am a tenured professor. I have been at this institution longer than you have. What exactly am I being investigated for?

DAVID: The details are confidential, Martha. I'm sorry.

MARTHA: I'm being investigated but I'm not allowed to know what about?

DAVID: In a general sense, your fitness to teach.

MARTHA: My fitness? I'm healthy as a horse, David, so you can't possibly mean my physical health.

DAVID: Your overall fitness. Mental, psychological. Moral.

MARTHA: This is an outrage! If you don't back off immediately, David, I will make an official complaint about you to Bob Sproul —

DAVID: The Privilege and Tenure Committee will be making a recommendation on your overall fitness to teach here.

MARTHA: Privilege and Tenure … I am on that committee.

DAVID: Oh, yes, of course.

MARTHA: I was one of its original members.

DAVID: We'll need to have you step down until this is settled.

MARTHA: Step down!

DAVID: This is very difficult for me to say, Martha, but it's necessary for the university to have you step down from your teaching as well.

MARTHA: I will not "step down," as you keep saying, just because you have the temerity to question my ability as a teacher.

DAVID: You will do as I say, Martha. Effective immediately, you are suspended from the university.

MARTHA: Have you lost your mind?

DAVID: I will be preparing a report on the investigation for Privilege and Tenure. Once they've reviewed it, a decision will be made at that time whether to reinstate you and continue your salary —

MARTHA: Reinstate?

DAVID: — or proceed with the termination process.

MARTHA: You're telling me I am suspended without pay indefinitely?

DAVID: Yes. *(Martha picks up the phone on his desk.)* Who are you calling?

MARTHA: Bob.

DAVID: Put the phone down, Martha.

MARTHA *(on telephone):* Yes, hello, Roberta? Fine, thanks. Yes, nice to hear your voice, too. Is President Sproul in?

DAVID: I advise you not to speak with President Sproul right now.

MARTHA *(on telephone):* When will he be in, then?

DAVID: He authorized the investigation, Martha.

MARTHA *(on telephone):* Yes, I would. Just ask him to call Martha at his earliest convenience. Thank you. *(She hangs up.)* What's going on, David?

DAVID: Ruth admitted … well, certain things about your relationship —

MARTHA: What things, David?

DAVID: She said very little, actually.

MARTHA: We're roommates. Neither of our salaries allows us to live alone. I wasn't aware that would be of concern to you.

DAVID: Aren't you a bit more than roommates, Martha?

MARTHA: No. We're not.

DAVID: You are entitled to seek legal counsel —

MARTHA: For what reason? What charge am I defending myself against?

DAVID: I believe you know there are very few actions that can break tenure. Unprofessional conduct is one of them —

MARTHA: You can't be serious, David! I'm no more guilty of unprofessional conduct than you are.

DAVID: I am truly sorry.

(A beat. A hundred angry retorts run through Martha's mind. She controls herself with effort.)

MARTHA: So am I, David. So am I.

(Martha exits. David moves agitatedly around his office, stopping to stare at the photo of Phyllis.)

SCENE SIX

(Martha's patio. It's twilight now. Ruth sits in the half-light smoking and slowly sipping a drink. The front door slams loudly. Martha enters and stops. She and Ruth stare at each other for a moment, gauging the other's response. Martha holds out her arms.)

MARTHA: Oh, darling.

(Ruth runs to her and they embrace.)

RUTH: I'm so glad you're home, baby. I was worried.

MARTHA: Are you all right?

RUTH: I don't know. It's all so … strange. Like a nightmare. I keep thinking it's not happening. Hold me closer. … How are you?

MARTHA: Oh, I'm fine. I can't believe it, Ruthie. I can't believe that pompous little ass had the nerve to suspend me. Suspend me! I have been at this university longer than he has. He has no right to do this to me! *(She disentangles from Ruth and exits to the living room.)*

RUTH: Where are you —?

MARTHA *(offstage)*: He's lucky I didn't get hold of Sproul on the spot. I've always thought he was incompetent. *(Martha enters with a telephone and long cord, which keeps getting tangled; she jerks it after her.)* But I tried to give him the benefit of the doubt. Idiot! Privilege and Tenure will never agree to this. They will never back David Dowd.

RUTH: Let me help you, baby.

(Ruth easily untangles cord.)

MARTHA: I've got to get Mac. Employment law is his specialty.

RUTH: What did you say to Dowd?

MARTHA: I never imagined in a million years I would need legal advice.

RUTH: Martha, what did you say to him?

MARTHA: Not a damn thing. I will fight that man to the grave, Ruthie.

RUTH: We need to talk a minute.

MARTHA: Hopefully his and not mine.

RUTH: Before you call Mac.

MARTHA: If he thinks he can destroy my program by destroying my reputation, then he's got another —

RUTH: Damn it, Martha! *(She takes the telephone out of Martha's hands.)* Will you just listen to me!

MARTHA: We have to speak to Mac!

RUTH: I have to speak to you!

MARTHA: We have to do something. Right now. I can't just stand here and —

RUTH: I resigned.

MARTHA: You what?

RUTH: I resigned, Martha. Mac needs to know that.

MARTHA: Oh, no, Ruthie.

RUTH: I tried to call you but they said you were already in his —

MARTHA: And I've been going on and on… I just assumed —

RUTH: That I'd put up a fight? I'm not you, Martha.

(Martha hugs her.)

MARTHA: Why didn't you just tell me to shut up?

RUTH: Well, you were right. We do need to call Mac.

MARTHA: Dowd had no right to ask either of us about our private life. We don't owe him an answer, Ruthie. Our private life is none of his business.

RUTH: You know that and I know that. But we're not the ones making the rules.

MARTHA: If I went by the rules I'd be a housewife in Wilkes-Barre. What did Dowd say to you?

RUTH: I don't know if I remember. I know I don't want to remember. Something about living with you, what you mean to me — the room started to spin and my stomach … I knew what was coming suddenly and I could feel my body tense, all the muscles in my back and along my shoulders. And then he was asking questions and I couldn't say anything, Martha. I was so … so embarrassed … and humiliated. David Dowd asking me that kind of question — David Dowd!

MARTHA: Bastard.

RUTH: And I thought of my mother and my father and my poor grandfather and the way his face always lit up when I came in the room —

MARTHA: He won't get away with this. Don't worry.

RUTH: I felt like a bad child, like I'd been caught stealing candy and now the whole world would know and I would be punished and my grandfather would never smile at me again.

MARTHA: I'm so sorry.

RUTH: I just wanted it over, Martha. I thought if I resigned, they would leave you alone. I can't imagine what you would do if you didn't teach, sweetheart. And I can't imagine what I would do if I didn't have you.

MARTHA: I can't imagine that either.

(They kiss. Ruth breaks it off.)

RUTH: Is it okay for us to —? I mean …

MARTHA: It's our home. If it isn't safe here —

RUTH: It must have been Barton. Who went to Dowd, I mean.

MARTHA: Yes, I suppose it was. God knows what he saw or thought he saw.

RUTH: I think it was that time last month, when it was so hot and the window was open, and now I feel like he's watching.

MARTHA: He can't see us on the patio. Come here. *(They embrace again, trying hard to make it feel natural.)* We'll get through this, Ruthie. Don't worry. You'll get another job. Privilege and Tenure will reinstate me.

RUTH: How can you be so sure?

MARTHA: Because … Because the sun keeps coming up every morning. Because it's how I see the world. Because I have you.

RUTH: I'm glad you're not a housewife in Wilkes-Barre.

MARTHA: Are you sure?

(They kiss, neither relaxed. Martha leans over and turns off the light.)

SCENE SEVEN

(David's office, later that evening. David stands staring out the window.)

PHYLLIS *(offstage)*: David? *(He doesn't notice her.)* Honey, I saw you through the window as I was walking up. Open the door, David. *(He still doesn't notice.)* David!

(He rouses himself to open the door. Phyllis enters. She goes to hug him but he moves away from her.)

PHYLLIS *(continuing)*: What's happened, David?

DAVID: Oh, sorry, Phyllis. Hard day at the salt mines. Did you come for a visit?

PHYLLIS: We were going to meet for dinner, remember?

DAVID: Oh, yes. That's right.

PHYLLIS: You stood me up for lunch.

DAVID: Yes, yes. It's all coming back.

PHYLLIS: And then you had another meeting.

DAVID: Yes. With Martha.

PHYLLIS: And we agreed we'd meet in the Village at eight o'clock for dinner.

DAVID: Yes, well, and here you are.

PHYLLIS: Yes, well, and it's nearly midnight and I never heard from you.

DAVID: Oh, forgive me, dear. It's been a very complicated day.

PHYLLIS: What's going on, David?

DAVID: Nothing's going on.

PHYLLIS: Am I a fool not to think you're having an affair?

DAVID: An affair? What are you talking about?

PHYLLIS: It just doesn't seem like you, but you're so distracted, missing appointments, hardly remembering your own name —

DAVID: I'm not having an —

PHYLLIS: Then what is it, David? You're not being honest with me about something.

DAVID: It's just this position. You see, Phyllis, some-times —

PHYLLIS: — you forget I've heard all this before, David. "It's just this position. You see, Phyllis, sometimes there are things I can't tell you. Confidential things."

DAVID: Is that what I say?

PHYLLIS: Over and over. This is about Martha, isn't it?

DAVID: How did you know it was about Martha?

PHYLLIS: Most things about Martha upset you.

DAVID: I'm not upset —

PHYLLIS: You're pretty upset for someone who's not upset.

DAVID: I'm tired.

PHYLLIS: Is there a new problem with Martha?

DAVID: Some complaints.

PHYLLIS: It must be more than that.

DAVID: He wants me to investigate.

PHYLLIS: Investigate Martha? We just had dinner at their house.

DAVID: He has no choice, Phyllis. He has to maintain the university's reputation.

PHYLLIS: And Martha somehow threatens it? Martha Deane?

DAVID: You probably think I'm jumping for joy, but I'm not.

PHYLLIS: Wasn't she the campus's representative at his twentieth —?

DAVID: Yes, yes. That was before any of this came to light.

PHYLLIS: Gad, she's been here forever. You would think all the skeletons would be out of the closet by now. What could be so horrible you have to drop what you're doing and investigate her right now?

DAVID: She and Ruth Fulton have apparently had an illicit relationship for some time.

PHYLLIS: And President Sproul wasn't aware of this? There have been rumors about Martha for years. He's not deaf. Why all of a sudden are you —?

DAVID: The complaints allege unspeakable acts observed through uncurtained windows.

PHYLLIS: Oh, you can't be serious! What on earth is an "unspeakable act"? Oh, I'm sorry, honey, I'm embarrassing you. It's just hard to imagine, even in this day and age, that the University has you investigating two women through a window.

DAVID: You don't understand how important —

PHYLLIS: It just seems so beneath him, David, and you. She's always been a complete lady when she's been around me.

DAVID: Why are you defending her?

PHYLLIS: I'm not. I just hate to see you brought in as a hatchet man to do someone else's bidding.

DAVID: I'm not a hatchet man!

> (Lights up on Martha's patio, simultaneous. Rosalind and Martha are in a heated discussion. Intercut scenes.)

ROSALIND: You should listen to Mac. He's an attorney, for goodness's sake.

MARTHA: I listened to him.

ROSALIND: In one ear and out the other.

MARTHA: It's his job to advise. It doesn't mean I have to take his advice.

ROSALIND: You're digging your heels in.

MARTHA: I'm considering his counsel.

ROSALIND: He's right. Consider mine, too.

MARTHA: I need time to think. You can't expect me to decide something like this without at least talking to her —

ROSALIND: Then talk to her. Now.

MARTHA: No.

ROSALIND: Mac says you can't wait. Do it now. Tonight. Before something happens.

MARTHA: It's easy to give advice from the sidelines, isn't it? When it doesn't affect you one way or the other.

ROSALIND: Your life affects mine every day, Martha. I'm sorry, I know it could be a few months until Privilege and Tenure —

MARTHA: A few months! You say that as though it's nothing.

ROSALIND: Listen to me, Martha. You two can't risk being seen together. You don't know what kind of cameras or surveillance —

MARTHA: Surveillance! My God, am I Alger Hiss suddenly? Ethel Rosenberg? Have I committed some horrible crime?

ROSALIND: Apparently to some, you have.

MARTHA: I need Ruth with me, Rosy. Now more than I ever have. This whole investigation, this insanity, is about us, our relationship, who we are to each other. You can't expect me to give her up — that's doing exactly what they want. That's letting them win.

(Ruth enters wearing a robe and with a towel over her head from a shower.)

ROSALIND: It's temporary.

MARTHA: It's too much to ask. I'll take the risk.

ROSALIND: Don't be a fool.

MARTHA: Too late.

ROSALIND: Oh, you are so aggravating sometimes.

(Rosalind stalks past Ruth to the door and exits.)

RUTH *(lightly)*: I'm sure I don't know what she means. *(She kisses Martha on the cheek.)* It feels good to be clean finally. What were you and Rosy fighting about?

MARTHA: Nothing.

RUTH: You and Rosy were fighting about nothing?

MARTHA: We weren't fighting.

RUTH: I've never seen you two even raise your voices at each other before —

MARTHA: Forget it, Ruth.

RUTH: Stop protecting me, Martha.

MARTHA: I'm not —

RUTH: You are. I know that tone in your voice. What did Mac say to you?

MARTHA: He thinks Privilege and Tenure will vote to reinstate.

RUTH: That's wonderful news, baby —

MARTHA: We just have to get through the next five or six months.

RUTH: It could take that long?

MARTHA: David Dowd is nothing if not thorough.

RUTH: What else did Mac say?

MARTHA: Don't let's talk about it right now, all right?

RUTH: Fine … When, then?

MARTHA: Later.

RUTH: When you've decided it's the right time?

MARTHA: Oh, darling. Don't let's fight.

RUTH: I'm not fighting with you. Just like Rosy wasn't.

MARTHA: Will you let us have just a moment's peace. We haven't had a chance to really hold each other since this whole thing blew open.

(Martha opens her arms to Ruth, who doesn't move.)

RUTH: Tell me what Mac said, Martha.

MARTHA: Leave it alone, Ruthie. I'm asking you.

RUTH: We're in this together.

MARTHA: He thinks I have a chance.

RUTH: But —?

MARTHA: But it's a hard road to hoe.

RUTH: Because of me.

MARTHA: No. Not exactly.

RUTH: Because of our … relationship.

MARTHA: Please, Ruth —

RUTH: Because of how it looks with us living together —

MARTHA: All right — yes, damn it! Mac thinks it would look better during Dowd's investigation if we didn't see each other.

RUTH: Not see each other!

MARTHA: I didn't say I agreed with him —

RUTH: Not see each other for six months!

　　　(Back to David Dowd's office.)

PHYLLIS: What is President Sproul's hold over you, David? I'm not understanding this.

DAVID: Well, he didn't come right out and say it …

　　　(Beat.)

PHYLLIS: Oh, my God. Forgive me. (She hugs him.) I'm sorry, David. I've been thoughtless.

DAVID: But I'm sure it's on his mind.

PHYLLIS: No, no, sweetheart. You're wrong. The President asked you because he trusts you and he knows you'll do a good job. Not because he's trying to test you —

DAVID: Don't let's talk about it any further.

PHYLLIS: But we have to, don't you see? Not talking about it is what's eating you up — eating us up.

DAVID: It's been a long day, Phyl. Did you park the car near?

PHYLLIS: It's just outside. Please don't shut me out, David.

(Back to Martha's patio.)

MARTHA: I'm not arguing with you! I told him six months was impossible. That's why Rosy's angry.

RUTH: I can't imagine a day without you, Martha, let alone six months.

MARTHA: You know I feel the same way.

RUTH: I'm in love with you. Your life is so much a part of mine I don't even know where one ends and the other begins.

MARTHA: I haven't a clue either. I need you right here beside me during this. We need each other.

RUTH: What did he say, then?

MARTHA: You mean after I told him I was going to ignore him and take my lumps with you?

RUTH: Yes. What did he advise?

MARTHA: Oh, you know lawyers and their advice.

RUTH: You're doing it again. You're protecting me from something you think I shouldn't hear. What did he say after that? I'm asking you —

MARTHA: And I'm asking you not to ask me.

RUTH: Why?

MARTHA: Because I need you to stay. More than anything.

RUTH: Why wouldn't I stay, baby? That's what I want, too. More than anything.

MARTHA: Then please, please, leave it at that, Ruthie.

(*Back to David Dowd's office.*)

DAVID: I'm tired.

PHYLLIS: Speak to me!

DAVID: You take the car. I'll make my own way home.

(*He moves toward the door.*)

PHYLLIS: David! Are you crazy? You're letting a piece of gossip tear you apart.

DAVID: I don't want to talk about this!

PHYLLIS: Well, I do. (*David opens the door.*) I don't care if that Regent thinks you're a homosexual. He's wrong. I should know, for heaven's sake.

DAVID: The word he used was *pansy*.

PHYLLIS: Forget it, David. You don't know he said it. Even if he did, who cares? It doesn't matter.

DAVID: You're wrong, Phyllis. It matters. That one word matters more than anything else about me. More than all the professors I've recruited from all over the world, all the budgets I've balanced, the classes I've taught, the students whose hands I've held through one crisis or another over the last twenty years. I thought I knew what mattered, Phyllis. Hard work. Effort. Experience. But now my whole career, my chance for advancement, the respect of my peers — it all boils down to that one word. Don't tell me it doesn't matter.

> *(He exits. She starts to follow him, then stops. Lights down on David's office.)*

> *(Back to Martha's patio.)*

RUTH: Oh, my God, Martha. I just realized why you won't tell me.

MARTHA: Slow down, sweetheart. You're getting upset—

RUTH: He told you to get another lawyer, didn't he?

MARTHA: I'll fix you a drink.

> *(She moves toward the bar. Ruth stops her.)*

RUTH: Didn't he?

MARTHA: I'll fix us both drinks.

RUTH: But he said you wouldn't be able to find one, right? *(Martha does not respond.)* Because as long as I stay in this house, you have no defense. Isn't that what he said, Martha?

MARTHA: All right. Yes, damn it! That's what he said. *(Ruth exits to living room)*. Where are you going? Ruth, please. We need to talk this through.

> *(Ruth enters with a suitcase and some clothes. She begins to pack hurriedly.)*

RUTH: Six months! Martha, I can't imagine being away from you for six months.

MARTHA: Then stop. We'll figure something out. Don't go, Ruth.

RUTH: But I can't just stand here and watch you lose.

MARTHA: I won't lose.

RUTH: Don't be so damned stubborn!

MARTHA: This is outrageous! They can't do this to us, to me —

RUTH: They can and they have. Let's just not make it any worse, Martha.

MARTHA: Stop it, sweetheart. Stop packing. I wish I'd never told you —

RUTH: You should have told me the minute you got off the phone with Mac. I'm not that twenty-one-year-old wide-eyed Midwestern girl you met in 1938. I'm not one of your students anymore. I stand toe-to-toe with you, baby, whether you like it or not. I'm your friend, your companion, your confidante. But most of all, Martha, I'm your lover.

> *(She kisses Martha with passion, then pulls away. Ruth exits. Martha moves to follow, then stops...)*

ACT TWO

SCENE ONE

> *(The stage is black.)*

ROSALIND (*offstage*): Ladies!

> *(Spot up on Rosalind as she addresses a class of PE students. It is spring 1953.)*

ROSALIND *(continuing):* Ladies! May I have your attention? I've asked you to assemble today so that I could meet you each personally and as a group. Miss Deane, who has handled these duties so well for so many years, continues to be on a leave of absence to handle some compelling family matters. We've all missed her presence over the last six months and I know we all hope things will be quickly resolved. Were she here, she would tell you at this juncture that you are on the noblest of paths and one which you will never regret, as she has not. She would tell you to listen to your body — and you would laugh, wouldn't you? Because it's funny and odd and very Martha Deane. But in time I think you will come to see her point — the importance of listening to and observing the body and understanding it.

The scientific study of the body's muscles and their movement has been a practice since the time of Aristotle and Archimedes. However, it was only recently, with our society's eagerness to name every last concept, creature, malady and human act, that we have a scientific word for it. *Kinesiology.* As we begin to explore kinesiology this semester, you will start to notice how people live — or don't live — in their bodies. Who is comfortable … and who is not. You will study body language: people who talk with their hands … people who slouch in dejection … people who invite our interest. You will study how people's bodies mirror what they feel … and who they are.

Many people outside our field — some even in academia — see the study of physical education as a lesser field, something vaguely about calisthenics, unworthy of actual academic significance. But through physical education, we study so much more than sports — we are actually exploring the individual and his relationship to himself, his body and his world. What better occupation for any of us in these difficult times than the study of humanity and its betterment.

SCENE TWO

54

(Martha's patio, night. It is the spring of 1953. Rosy watches as Martha brings the telephone from another room and plugs it into the wall. Martha places the phone right next to her, willing it to ring.)

ROSALIND: What time did Mac think the committee vote would come?

MARTHA: An hour and twenty minutes ago. Drink?

ROSALIND: Yes, thanks. *(She notes that Martha keeps glancing at the telephone.)* Perhaps there's hope for Ike after all.

MARTHA: Olive?

ROSALIND: Please.

MARTHA: What's he said? I haven't been following the papers.

ROSALIND: He called McCarthy "a pimple on the path of progress."

MARTHA: Apt enough.

ROSALIND: Oh, it won't take long now, his public demise.

MARTHA: You're awfully optimistic.

ROSALIND: They're in office now so the Republicans don't need him.

(Martha hands her a drink.)

MARTHA: You're trying to distract me by talking about politics.

ROSALIND: Well, clearly it isn't working.

MARTHA: Engage me, then.

ROSALIND: Any suggestions?

MARTHA: Something meaningful.

ROSALIND: How's Ruth enjoying insurance? (*Beat.*) Well, you're engaged now, aren't you?

MARTHA: Indeed. Well, she loves it. She's a natural. It runs in the family, apparently. I suspect she'll do quite well.

ROSALIND: It's a talent. I couldn't sell ice cream to Eskimos.

MARTHA: They probably make their own.

ROSALIND: Does she visit?

MARTHA: We were advised not to see each other.

ROSALIND: You were advised not to do many things, as I recall.

MARTHA: Occasionally even I follow the rules, Rosy. We write, we call. Daily. Sometimes hourly.

ROSALIND: I think I'm uncomfortable talking about this, for some reason.

MARTHA: You're worried you're invading my privacy.

ROSALIND: Am I?

MARTHA: If I had privacy to invade, you would be.

ROSALIND: It must be difficult for you both.

MARTHA: Difficult! It's excruciating. Pretending to the world we have no feelings, no needs. Isn't it all rather baffling — that half the world thinks we have no sexual feelings at all and the other half thinks we have nothing but?

ROSALIND: It's all Kinsey's fault, and Freud before him. Sex didn't exist before 1948 and now it's everywhere.

MARTHA: I do miss the quieter days, Rosy. When you could live happily with another woman and no one batted an eye.

ROSALIND: You mean in 1893?

MARTHA: It wasn't that long ago, was it? It seemed like after the War, everything changed somehow. There's all this bother now about masculinity and femininity and men feeling threatened if their wives work.

ROSALIND: Well, your neighbor was certainly anxious living next door to two spinsters.

MARTHA: Ah, yes. And one so young and attractive — what a waste. Must get those perverts out of the neighborhood.

ROSALIND: Times do change, Martha.

MARTHA: But love is eternal. At least that's what I'm hoping.

ROSALIND: I'll knock on all the wood I can find.

(The telephone rings. Martha quickly picks it up.)

MARTHA (on the phone): Hello, Mac? (She listens attentively. Her face breaks into a smile.) Yes! Thank God! (She hangs up the phone.) It's over, Rosy.

SCENE THREE

(The study of David and Phyllis's home. David sits next to a telephone.)

PHYLLIS *(offstage)*: It's over now, David. You did the best you could. It's not your fault you couldn't get any witnesses —

DAVID: There were witnesses.

PHYLLIS *(offstage)*: You mean, that neighbor?

DAVID: Yes, that neighbor who saw Martha and that young woman —

PHYLLIS *(offstage)*: Ruth Fulton.

DAVID: — through the window.

(Phyllis enters wearing an apron.)

PHYLLIS: That wasn't enough for the committee, apparently.

DAVID: It should have been.

PHYLLIS: It's over, David. You can have your life back — all those things you've put on the back burner. Even better, we can have our life back. We've put off France for months now —

DAVID: It's not over.

PHYLLIS: What do you mean? Privilege and Tenure —

DAVID: It's an incompetent committee.

PHYLLIS: But you've always supported its decisions.

DAVID: I've told President Sproul I think the committee's verdict should be overruled.

PHYLLIS: Overrule Privilege and Tenure?

DAVID: They're all Martha's friends.

PHYLLIS: This is Sproul's idea?

DAVID: He agrees.

PHYLLIS: So, it's your idea. Can't someone else take this on?

DAVID: She refuses to resign.

PHYLLIS: An attorney? The Regent's counsel? Surely a legal person should —

DAVID: The committee was spineless.

PHYLLIS: — take over. Martha will fight you tooth and —

DAVID: Someone has to protect the University's interests.

PHYLLIS: — claw. Tooth and claw. The University could lose. You could lose, David.

DAVID: I have to do this!

(She stares at him for a beat.)

PHYLLIS: Why, David?

DAVID: Because it's the right thing to do. I'm convinced of it, Phyl. You know, at first, I thought the neighbor had gone a bit overboard with the complaint and all. I thought, who really cares what people do in their own home? But I could see this was serious to him. He wanted to be sure his family was safe.

PHYLLIS: From Martha?

DAVID: Yes, from Martha. From things that frightened him, things he didn't understand. You know what it was like living through the Depression. The fear you wouldn't have enough to eat or you'd lose your house. We all remember. We all just want to keep what we have and not go backward. The times are different now, thank God. But the fear doesn't go away.

PHYLLIS: You don't have to do this, David. There are other ways to show you're as tough and smart as any of the rest of them. Let President Sproul or the Regent's counsel or Staff Warren handle this.

DAVID: Please understand, Phyllis. I have to see this through.

> (Beat.)

PHYLLIS: All right. How much longer will this take?

DAVID: I don't know.

PHYLLIS: Six months? A year?

DAVID: I said I don't know.

PHYLLIS: It's my time, too, David. You've forgotten my life gets put on the back burner right next to yours. We are in this together, at every point, lockstep. Husband and wife. I need to know how much time it will take until I have you back. *(He does not respond.)* It's cold now.

DAVID: What?

PHYLLIS: Your dinner.

> (She exits. He picks up the telephone.)

SCENE FOUR

MARTHA (*offstage*): To justice!

(Lights up on Martha's patio. The telephone has been moved back into the living room. Rosy and Martha are clinking champagne glasses. An open bottle of champagne sits in an ice bucket.)

ROSALIND: To reinstatement.

MARTHA: To having Ruth home!

ROSALIND and MARTHA: To Ruth!

MARTHA: How long until that giant scarlet letter on my forehead fades?

ROSALIND: No one cares, Martha.

MARTHA: Everyone cares. It's titillating. I'm a topic of conversation.

RUTH *(offstage)*: Martha!

ROSALIND: The girl drives quickly.

(The telephone rings.)

MARTHA: Tell Ruth I'll only be a minute.

ROSALIND: You think it's Sproul?

MARTHA: He's overdue.

(Martha exits. Ruth enters.)

RUTH: I don't know when I've been so happy. *(She hugs Rosalind.)* I have my Martha back.

ROSALIND: I do, too, thank God. I can't tell you how little I like teaching there without her. It's complete chaos on the best of days.

RUTH: You've been a good friend to her, Rosy.

ROSALIND: I've been a horrid pain in the ass is what I've been. The mark of a true friend.

RUTH: She thinks the world of you.

ROSALIND: When she doesn't curse my name for lecturing her unabashedly and at regular intervals.

RUTH: Rosy, there is one thing. I lost my temper with you back in the fall —

ROSALIND: Forget it. I have.

RUTH: No. It's important. I hurt your feelings.

ROSALIND: You pointed out the obvious.

RUTH: I didn't mean —

ROSALIND: — that I'm not part of the club?

RUTH: It doesn't matter.

ROSALIND: No, it matters. It makes all the difference in the world, in fact. You were right. David Dowd would never have called me into his office, sat me down and interrogated me about my relationships. It would never have happened, Ruth. Through no fault of my own, I am apparently incapable of committing unspeakable acts. Lucky me.

MARTHA (*offstage*): That bastard.

> (*Martha enters. Upset, she picks up a champagne glass and throws it across the room. She sits down and puts her head in her hands.*)

ROSALIND: Martha, what on earth has happened?

MARTHA: I haven't had a minute's peace and now it's going to just keep on —

RUTH: But Privilege and Tenure —

MARTHA: Dowd's overruled them.

ROSALIND: What?

MARTHA: He's continuing the investigation.

ROSALIND: That sanctimonious little ass.

RUTH: Does Sproul know?

MARTHA: He's blessed it. I can't believe it, Rosy. I've known Bob Sproul for twenty years. (*Ruth hugs Martha. Gently, Martha pushes her away.*) *(To Ruth)* You'll have to leave now.

ROSALIND: What kind of investigation?

RUTH: No, Martha —

MARTHA *(to Rosalind):* Witnesses, oaths, depositions. The whole nine yards.

ROSALIND: I'd love to wring his smarmy little —

MARTHA *(to Ruth):* Please, Ruth. Go now.

RUTH: We haven't even had a moment alone —

MARTHA: We can't be seen together. Mac says it's even more important now than before.

(*Rosalind sizes up the situation, hugs Martha.*)

ROSALIND *(to Martha):* Call me later, dear.

RUTH: Then you're going to keep fighting this?

(Rosalind exits.)

MARTHA: Tooth and claw. He's trying to ruin me! I have to fight back. I have no choice.

RUTH: It is always about justice for you — Rosy's right.

MARTHA: Justice! Of course, it's about justice. It's about standing up and doing what's right. If this were happening to someone else, I would be just as outraged. But it's also about me, damn it, living my life. Ruthie, if I stop now, I have nothing. No job, no income, no pension—

RUTH: You have me.

MARTHA: What a catch I am these days! Savings run through now, legal bills —

RUTH: I would support us both.

MARTHA: I know you would, darling, but this would always be hanging over my head. "The Martha Deane Scandal." I can't let him run my name into the ground. I don't care what it takes!

RUTH: Oh, Martha, don't do this! You could waste years — you could waste the rest of your life trying to get justice from David Dowd and the Board of Regents. It's not going to happen.

MARTHA: Why do you say that?

RUTH: They hold all the cards.

MARTHA: They're in the wrong!

RUTH: Sometimes that doesn't matter, Martha! Do you think McCarthy is in the right? Look how many lives and careers he's destroyed.

MARTHA: So, we turn our backs and let him triumph?

RUTH: Of course not —

MARTHA: I'm going to fight this, Ruth. You can be by my side —

RUTH: No, I can't! That's the whole point. Why won't you get it through your stubborn head — if you fight this, I have to disappear again for — what, months? Years? I have to pretend we're not lovers, that I don't have my whole world wrapped around you. I need you, Martha. Doesn't that matter to you?

MARTHA: Of course, it matters. But I can't let them do this to me —

RUTH: Well, I can't let them do this to me, either. *(Martha does not respond.)* I mean it. The last six months have been unbearable for me. And now, not to know how much longer —

MARTHA: We'll get to the end of this together, Ruth. I promise.

RUTH: Together?

MARTHA: Yes, of course, together.

RUTH: When?

MARTHA: Later. When it's over.

RUTH: It may never be over. I can't wait that long.

MARTHA: Well, damn it, maybe you should just go then. Go on and make a new life for yourself. Find someone who's less difficult for you. Someone your own age.

RUTH: That's a cheap shot.

MARTHA: You're at the beginning of your career, Ruth. Starting over is different for you. I'm at the height of mine. I have seven to ten good years left when I can really accomplish what I want. Leave my mark. I can make it all matter. To give up that chance — not to fight to clear my name — you ask too much of me.

RUTH: I never thought you would pick something — anything — over me.

MARTHA: You're the one who's forcing me to choose.

RUTH: We can start over together, Martha. Leave California — maybe it would be easier in New York or Europe —

MARTHA: This is my home. Why should I leave it? I've done nothing wrong. I am a good person, a sane person, a moral person — regardless of what David Dowd and the Regents may think of me. My darling girl, I love you more than I can say, but I have to do this. Rosy says I'm just an old fool, and maybe she's right. But I have to do this. They have no right to treat me this way!

RUTH: Damn you!

(She hugs Martha fiercely, then exits.)

SCENE FIVE

(David's office, the next day. He sits at his desk, distracted. There's a knock.)

DAVID: Yes?

(Rosalind enters.)

DAVID (continuing): Ah, Rosalind.

ROSALIND: David.

66

DAVID: Sit down. Thank you for coming by.

ROSALIND: You did call.

DAVID: Yes, yes. You're probably wondering why.

ROSALIND: I am assuming it's not because you wish to interrogate me about my private life. Which is much less sordid than I would prefer, I must say.

DAVID: No, of course not.

ROSALIND: Well, one can't take anything for granted these days, can one?

DAVID: Look, Rosalind, I've been speaking with Ben Miller and, well, it would be most helpful if you could take over the leadership of the women's PE program.

ROSALIND: Why, David?

DAVID: Why?

ROSALIND: I'm not sure I'm following you.

DAVID: Well, you know as well as I do you're the obvious choice. You're the senior professor now in the department, you're tenured, your scholarship is recognized nationally —

ROSALIND: What about Martha?

DAVID: The program lacks leadership right now, Rosalind. It's a bit adrift. We wanted to bring in a rudder.

ROSALIND: I suppose I should be flattered. I've never been called a rudder before.

DAVID: So, you will accept the chairmanship?

ROSALIND: Certainly.

DAVID: That's marvelous, Rosalind. We both thank you—

ROSALIND: On an interim basis.

DAVID: Why interim?

ROSALIND: Until Martha returns.

DAVID: That may well never occur.

ROSALIND: Well, once the whole thing is resolved, we can speak again, then. *(She rises.)*

DAVID: Wait. Professor Cassidy, the University badly needs your assistance. This is a very difficult time. We are all aware of your allegiance to Miss Deane, but what matters here is the program and the girls we are bound and obligated to teach. I urge that you strongly consider the situation.

ROSALIND: I have strongly considered it, Dean Dowd, and my answer remains the same: I would be honored and happy to take over on an interim basis, pending the long-awaited return of Miss Deane.

DAVID: You assume she will return.

ROSALIND: Oh, I assume nothing. Believe me.

DAVID: All right. Perhaps we can address some of the issues that may concern you. We are all aware that the chairmanship of a program may require significant time above and beyond a teaching and research load. Additional compensation is certainly to be considered here.

ROSALIND: David, I understand the pressure you are under. It must be formidable. I understand you and Ben want to do what's right for the program and I appreciate the offer of the chairmanship. But Martha Deane is my friend.

DAVID: That is not relevant.

ROSALIND: But it is. She recruited me down here from Mills. She helped me find a place to live. She introduced me to Clarence and to Bob Sproul and made me feel welcome. Her friends were my friends. Martha is the reason I came here and the reason I have been successful here.

DAVID: Your loyalty is commendable —

ROSALIND: — but I am paid to do a job, is that what you were going to say?

DAVID: We all work at the University's pleasure.

ROSALIND: The pleasure has gone out of my University work.

DAVID: You must separate your own feelings from your duty as a professional.

ROSALIND: Then let us both agree that I must do what is best for the young women for whom I am responsible.

DAVID: Agreed. I am glad we have reached the point of amity, Rosalind.

ROSALIND: As am I, David. So, in that case, I will be the interim chairman of the program until the matter with Martha is resolved.

DAVID: You are every bit as impossible as she is!

ROSALIND: I consider that a compliment.

DAVID: Professor! *(Beat. He slowly wilts physically, his body too exhausted to fight another battle. His voice is now oddly gentle, calm. He is for a moment the man Phyllis fell in love with.)* Rosalind. I do understand your dilemma. Like you, I value friendship more than gold. In many regards, Martha is a fine woman, an excellent teacher. A good cook, too, as we both know. A wonderful conversationalist. All of these things can remain true at the same time we acknowledge that for certain reasons she can no longer be a part of the University.

ROSALIND: Certain ridiculous, foundationless "reasons" —

DAVID: I won't argue the point with you — Rosy, isn't it? That's what Martha calls you, I know. This whole matter has quite exhausted me and I have no fight left. In good faith, I have tried to do what was asked of me. Perhaps in your eyes I have failed. Certainly, in my wife's eyes I have come up short. It is a painful time for me and one I do not think I will ever look back on without regret. If you will agree to be the interim chairman, I am sure Ben will be pleased. Thank you, Rosy.

　　(Beat.)

ROSALIND: I appreciate your candor, David. I know this is not easy for you. Regarding the interim chairmanship, I hope that perhaps an interim salary adjustment might be possible in light of the extra duties you've mentioned. I support my mother, you know, as well as myself.

　　(David pulls himself together, his old demeanor quickly returning.)

DAVID: I will discuss the matter with Ben. I should forewarn you, however, the department's budget remains tight.
　　(Rosalind exits quickly.)

SCENE SIX

(Martha's patio at dusk. She is sipping a drink listlessly and watching the sun set. Phyllis enters, startling Martha.)

PHYLLIS: Hello, Martha.

MARTHA: Phyllis.

PHYLLIS: The back door was open.

MARTHA: I was watering the flowers.

PHYLLIS: I've tried to call you.

MARTHA: I've been in and out.

PHYLLIS *(overlap):* I wanted to talk to you.

MARTHA *(overlap):* It's not a good time.

PHYLLIS: I'm sorry for how this has turned out.

MARTHA: You really must go.

PHYLLIS: He's not himself these days. It's the stress.

MARTHA: You'll excuse me.

PHYLLIS: Whatever you may think, Martha. It isn't personal.

MARTHA: That's a relief. Why are you here, Phyllis? Why did you call me?

PHYLLIS: I want this all to stop as badly as you do.

MARTHA: No one could want this to stop as badly as I do.

PHYLLIS: Then stop, Martha.

MARTHA: It's hardly that simple.

PHYLLIS: They'll give you money.

MARTHA: It isn't about money.

PHYLLIS: Listen to me, Martha! I don't condone what David is doing. I think you know that on some level.

MARTHA: If you don't condone it, then your conversation should be with your husband, not me.

PHYLLIS: I think this whole thing is a witch hunt. It's the pressure from the Regents that's making David keep on.

MARTHA: He should learn to resist pressure.

PHYLLIS: Well, he can't.

MARTHA: And you want me to stop this whole thing because he can't, because he won't.

PHYLLIS: I suppose that's what I'm saying.

MARTHA: Then talk to him, Phyllis.

PHYLLIS: I have.

MARTHA: And?

PHYLLIS: And he's a man. You know how it goes with men. Well, I mean —

MARTHA: I know what you mean.

PHYLLIS: It's like a bear fighting a bull. You're both locked in this mortal combat.

MARTHA: I prefer to think of myself as the bear, in that case.

PHYLLIS: But those kinds of fights don't stop until one or the other — or both — are dead.

MARTHA: I didn't begin this, Phyllis. Your husband did. He could have stopped with Privilege and Tenure's decision, but he didn't. No, this is his fight. As much as I might take it personally, this is not about me. I understand that now. It's about him. It's about his career. This fight will either make it or break it.

PHYLLIS: I know.

MARTHA: Why did you come to me?

PHYLLIS: Because —

MARTHA: I'm a woman? *(Phyllis nods.)* And you think women are more likely to back down.

PHYLLIS: We're more sensible.

MARTHA: Indeed, we are. Now would you please leave before I fly into a sensible but very loud rage?

PHYLLIS: Martha —

MARTHA: I am not kidding, Phyl.

PHYLLIS: Damn you.

> *(Phyllis exits.)*

SCENE SEVEN

> *(Spot up on Rosalind, addressing a small gathering of women. It is spring 1954.)*

ROSALIND: Ladies, thank you for coming tonight. Special thanks to Josie for providing the living room and the coffee. I know we all feel safer exchanging information here than in the ladies' room in Royce Hall. We just hope that Josie's neighbors are less inquisitive than Martha's.

Speaking of Martha's neighbors — we understand that some of them have now come forward with their concerns about her and are being interviewed by David Dowd and his people. Dean Dowd continues to refuse to speak with any of us in a civil manner regarding any of this. We have been told repeatedly and in no uncertain terms that the Martha Deane case is not to be discussed on campus in any way and that it is purely an administrative matter.

I know you are all wondering about how Martha is doing, how she is holding up throughout this difficult and crazy time. Most of you haven't seen her since she left campus nearly two years ago. In many ways, I think you would find her the same old Martha — fit as a fiddle, still passionate and opinionated about everything. I saw her last week and she was so very appreciative of the checks you continue to send. That is what is sustaining her now, your help and your friendship. She thanks you for your support and she knows how difficult this is for all of you, her friends. She understands very well the consequences you might face in openly showing support for her. *(A police siren's offstage wail startles her. It takes her a moment to continue.)* If anyone had ever told me I would be meeting in shrouded secrecy like nothing so much as an underground cell, I would have laughed them out the door. But times change — sadly, often — and we do what we must. Let's hope that by this time next year it's Martha who is addressing us and celebrating her return to the University.

(Spot out.)

SCENE EIGHT

(Martha's patio. It is virtually bare now. Dressed in a robe and slippers, Martha stacks a last box on a pile. Three boxes remain on the floor. The doorbell rings.)

MARTHA: Rosy?

SPROUL *(offstage)*: No, Martha. It's me, Bob.

> *(Martha stops in her tracks. With effort, she pulls herself together.)*

MARTHA: Bob. What a surprise. You're alone?

SPROUL *(offstage)*: No. Hoover and Nixon are here with me. *(Martha smiles despite herself.)* Forgive my poor attempt at humor.

MARTHA: Haven't I always?

SPROUL *(offstage)*: Touché. I'm alone. Ida's in the car reading *Sunset*.

MARTHA: How is Ida?

SPROUL *(offstage):* Hale and hearty. She sends her best.

MARTHA: The door's open, Bob. Tell Hoover and Nixon they can wait on the step in the heat.

> *(Sproul enters wearing casual clothes, as if on the way to a golf game. He carries a briefcase, which catches Martha's eye.)*

SPROUL: Martha.

MARTHA: Forgive my appearance. I've been under the weather a bit lately.

SPROUL: Was that a television set I saw in the living room? I never took you for a TV viewer.

MARTHA: Rosy suggested I might enjoy the hearings.

SPROUL: I hadn't realized the junior Senator from Wisconsin was a particular favorite of yours.

MARTHA: So, we're off the record?

SPROUL: Regent's Counsel was told only that I was considering contacting you in some fashion. Casual attire and feeble attempts at a light ambiance were not discussed and would not have been encouraged. *(He looks around the patio.)* It's a good market to sell in, I hear.

MARTHA: The scotch and gin are packed away. Sorry.

SPROUL: You know why I'm here, I suspect.

MARTHA: You were in the neighborhood?

SPROUL: That's right.

MARTHA: So, you thought you'd drop by.

SPROUL: Exactly. Go on.

MARTHA: Let me guess. You've been thinking it over now for quite some time.

SPROUL: That I have.

MARTHA: We've been colleagues and friends for many years, you and I, and you've been President of the University for many years. This has presented for you an irresolvable conflict and you have been forced to delegate to others duties you wish you had been able to retain. You have not at all times been pleased with the results.

SPROUL: That's right, Martha.

MARTHA: You want this resolved now. You have the authority to end it today — if we are in agreement. And if I sign on the dotted line whatever document you have in your briefcase.

SPROUL: There's full back pay.

MARTHA: A resignation?

SPROUL: The University would not contest your right to your pension.

MARTHA: Which I've been paying into for years.

SPROUL: No more interviews, no more depositions.

MARTHA: No more allegations that I solicit my students and set fire to orphanages.

SPROUL: You would have your life back.

MARTHA: My life teaching? No, of course not … So what do you think my response will be to your kind offer?

SPROUL: My official thoughts? I think you'll see the light of day, take the offer, allow the department to give you an appropriately moving sendoff and allow the Regents to do something other than tear their hair out at every meeting.

MARTHA: And your unofficial thoughts?

SPROUL: Off the record? I think you'll throw me out of here on my ear — but politely and without obvious undue anger. Your parting words will be to tell me to give your regards to Ida.

> *(She smiles. Gets out her handkerchief and dabs her eyes.)*

MARTHA: Excuse me. Allergies. You know I won't resign, Bob.

SPROUL: Yes, I know that.

MARTHA: So why —?

SPROUL: Look, Martha, the Regents are for the most part very successful businessmen. They didn't get that way by being patient and reasonable. Regent's Counsel told me this morning they'll take the offer off the table if you don't come around soon.

MARTHA: So, I should take what I can get before the offer goes away, is that it?

SPROUL: I will not denigrate our friendship by telling you I am here solely out of concern for you. Clearly, I am not. But I did think you had a right to know the current thinking among the Regents. Dowd, incidentally, is unaware of it.

MARTHA: As he is of so many things.

SPROUL: An odd man, David Dowd. I had no idea. Regent Pauley can't stand the sight of him.

MARTHA: So, the rumors go.

SPROUL: As to why he didn't get the Vice Chancellorship?

MARTHA: I try never to repeat gossip.

SPROUL: High-minded of you. Truly, Martha, it was never my intention to release the dogs of war upon you.

MARTHA: They descended upon me nonetheless.

SPROUL: Yes, they did. But they haven't been able to defeat you.

MARTHA: Why does it feel like you're patronizing me?

SPROUL: Because you don't trust me anymore.

MARTHA: Hoover and Nixon must be getting parched.

SPROUL: Thank you for your always gracious hospitality.

MARTHA: You know it would help me if you would stack that box over there.

SPROUL: My pleasure.

(*He moves the box with effort. It's heavier than it looked. Martha smiles.*)

MARTHA: Those, too. Thanks.

(*These two boxes are heavy, too, but Sproul moves them. When he's done, he grins a bit ruefully and holds out his hand for her to shake. Game over.*)

SPROUL: Goodbye, Martha.

MARTHA: Goodbye, Bob. (*He moves to exit.*) Be sure to give Ida my regards.

SPROUL: I will.

(*He exits.*)

SCENE NINE

(*Ruth sits at a desk doing paperwork, talking on the telephone. It's a nice office. She's doing well. Rosalind enters and watches her for a moment until Ruth looks up. It is early fall 1954.*)

ROSALIND: Hello, Ruth.

RUTH: Rosy. What a nice surprise.

(*They hug.*)

ROSALIND: You're looking well.

RUTH: So are you.

ROSALIND: You're lying, but I appreciate the thought. The hallowed halls are not a pleasant place to be these days, I am afraid.

RUTH: How's the program?

ROSALIND: Wobbly.

RUTH: I'm sorry to hear that.

ROSALIND: The insurance business, on the other hand, appears to be booming.

RUTH: Looks can be deceiving, but it's going well, Rosy.

ROSALIND: A mutual friend of ours always thought insurance would suit you.

RUTH: Well, the level of politics is considerably lower than in academia. I can work independently. And there's a reasonable correlation between effort and reward.

ROSALIND: Quite different from my line of work.

RUTH: How is our mutual friend?

ROSALIND: As you might expect, I suppose. And you?

RUTH: Me?

ROSALIND: You are well?

RUTH: Well enough.

ROSALIND: Still playing basketball?

RUTH: Every Saturday. A little golf now and then. And you would be proud of me, Rosy. I've joined the League of Women Voters.

ROSALIND: Ah, our mutual friend's influence?

RUTH: Let's just say I'm starting to see the world a little differently. Perhaps a bit less selfishly. But the main thing is I've bought a piece of land up on the Tiger Tail. That's taking all my extra time.

ROSALIND: Oh, I'm envious!

RUTH: A few acres. I'm going to build on it.

ROSALIND: I remember you always were handy.

RUTH: Has she been able to keep the house, our mutual friend? *(Rosalind shakes her head.)* She loves that house! Look, I would be happy to loan her —

ROSALIND: There's no point. Living there would always remind her of what she's lost.

RUTH: Is there any chance —?

ROSALIND: She'll win in court? *(She shakes her head no.)*

RUTH: My poor Martha.

ROSALIND: Mac says you can't win these kinds of cases. He thinks she should settle before the Regents pull their final offer. She's had it a few months now and they're running out of patience.

RUTH: Settling would be hard for her.

ROSALIND: She's successfully fought them to a draw — which in this case everyone knows is the same as a victory.

RUTH: Everyone but Martha.

ROSALIND: You know her well.

RUTH: Only Martha would —

ROSALIND: Would what? Jeopardize her entire future security on a matter of principle?

RUTH: She doesn't see it that way.

ROSALIND: Oh, you always take her side.

RUTH: She doesn't see it that way, either, I'm afraid. Why haven't I heard from her, Rosy?

ROSALIND: You walked out on her, Ruth, as I recall.

RUTH: Didn't she tell you —?

ROSALIND: No. What?

RUTH: The next day I realized what an ass I'd been, leaving her when she really needed me. I called her. The phone just rang and rang. I called her in the middle of the night, and even then, she never picked up. So I wrote. And wrote. But the letters just came back to me. Over and over I tried to reach her. Nothing. No response, Rosy. No damned response. I assumed she was so angry she never wanted to speak to me again.

ROSALIND: I wish you had told me. I just assumed, after a year or more —

RUTH: — fifteen and a half months —

ROSALIND: — I just assumed you had … gone on with your life.

RUTH: Well, that's true enough, I suppose. What was the alternative?

ROSALIND: To be honest, Ruth, I thought perhaps you'd met someone else.

RUTH: Met someone else! When would I have done that? In between crying and screaming and slamming basketballs against the floor?

ROSALIND: I'm sorry. I didn't know.

RUTH: Well, I'd be lying if I said that trying to meet someone else hadn't crossed my mind after a while.

ROSALIND: I don't know how that sort of thing works in your world.

RUTH: It works about as badly in my world as it does in yours, Rosy. Particularly if you're still in love with someone else.

ROSALIND: Yes, that can be a problem.

RUTH: I had dinner last month with a perfectly nice social worker from Van Nuys. Funny, kind, lovely, intelligent. From the Midwest, even. At the end of the evening she smiled and said I talked so much about Martha that she felt like she was dating her and not me.

ROSALIND: That would actually be something of an improvement over some of the dinners I've had with men. At least you were allowed a word in.

RUTH: So, is that why you're here, then? To see how I still feel about Martha?

ROSALIND: I wouldn't make a very good secret agent, would I?

RUTH: Is she sleeping much? *(Rosalind shakes her head.)* That was always the first thing to go with her.

ROSALIND: She barely eats. Some days she doesn't get out of bed.

RUTH: Oh, my God.

ROSALIND: Ruth, I wouldn't be here if it weren't important. Mac says they'll pull the offer on Monday if she doesn't take it. The rest of us have tried to talk to her, but I think you are the only person she'll listen to.

RUTH: She won't even talk to me, Rosy, why on earth would she take my advice?

ROSALIND: It's very simple, dear. She loves you. And no matter how hard she may try not to let you know, she always will.

(Beat. Ruth is too moved to speak.)

RUTH: It was lovely seeing you.

ROSALIND: You, too, Ruth. (She turns to exit.) Invite me to the groundbreaking.

(Rosalind exits.)

SCENE TEN

(Martha's patio, that evening. Martha sits drinking and staring out at her garden. The patio is bare now. Ruth enters.)

RUTH: Hello, Martha.

MARTHA: Ruth.

RUTH: Rosy suggested I come by.

(Beat.)

MARTHA: I finally had to give up on the fruit trees. I just couldn't seem to keep them going. I'm sorry. I know how much you loved them.

RUTH: I'd like to talk to you, Martha. But if you want me to leave, I'll go.

MARTHA: I never wanted you to leave, Ruthie.

RUTH: I never wanted to go.

MARTHA: It all seems so long ago now. A lifetime.

RUTH: I was wrong, Martha. I know that now.

MARTHA: No, no! You had to do what was right for you —

RUTH: I didn't understand. My feelings were hurt.

MARTHA: Of course, they were.

RUTH: Martha, you were courageous and brave and strong and all I saw was my own pain.

MARTHA: I put you through so much —

RUTH: I should have stood by you, taken my lumps —

MARTHA: Not everything's about justice.

RUTH: But this was. You were right to fight with everything you had.

MARTHA: Well, it didn't get me so very far, did it? All my rantings and ravings.

RUTH: You've fought them to a draw. No one else could have done that.

MARTHA: Well, now they've made me a final offer. They say a final-final.

RUTH: Rosy told me.

MARTHA: The neighbors are probably snapping photos right and left. Recording all those unspeakable acts.

RUTH: Do you want to take it?

MARTHA: I want my life back, I know that. My old life.

RUTH: It was a terrific life, Martha. Teaching, directing the program. You were loved and valued and respected. And you were very happy.

MARTHA: Yes, I was.

RUTH: So was I. *(Beat.)* I think you're supposed to ask how I'm doing these days.

MARTHA: Rosy already told me.

RUTH: She gets around, I see.

MARTHA: You bought some property up on the Tiger Tail. Several acres. You're going to build on it —

RUTH: Martha, it's too much space for one person.

MARTHA: Perhaps you'll find a roommate.

RUTH: Perhaps.

(Martha gets out her handkerchief and dabs her eyes.)

MARTHA: My allergies.

RUTH: You don't have allergies.

MARTHA: Can't you leave me any illusions?

RUTH: If I can't have them, neither can you.

MARTHA: They took away my life, damn it.

RUTH: They took your career. They took your money. They've even taken your house. But they did not take your life. You still get to wake up every morning and be Martha Deane, the most marvelous woman I have ever known.

MARTHA: Perhaps you should go now, Ruthie.

RUTH: Why? Because we're finally getting a chance to talk?

MARTHA: Because I'm too old to start over!

RUTH: Don't be ridiculous!

MARTHA: I am old, Ruth. Do you hear me? I am old and unemployed and cantankerous —

RUTH: — and stubborn —

MARTHA: — and you deserve someone who can make you happy.

RUTH: Damn it, Martha! Why didn't you return my calls, my letters —?

MARTHA: You left me!

RUTH: All right, I was wrong! But you wouldn't talk to me!

MARTHA: I couldn't think straight! I felt like I was being attacked on all sides. I stopped knowing who I was, much less who you were.

RUTH: We would be building the new house the first year or two. There really wouldn't be much time for you to think about being old or anything else, for that matter.

MARTHA: You're not listening to me!

RUTH: You've always wanted to spend more time with the League of Women Voters and do some acting again in

Pasadena. Travel more — you always wanted to go to Hawaii.

MARTHA: Damn you, stop it!

RUTH: Do you want me to leave, Martha?

> *(Beat. Ruth turns toward the door to exit.)*

MARTHA: I was tenured faculty, Ruthie!

> *(Ruth moves to her and they embrace.)*

RUTH: I know, baby, I know. … Take the offer, Martha. Start a new life.

MARTHA: How can you ever forgive me, sweetheart? I put you through so much over this.

RUTH: It's you who needs to forgive me.

MARTHA: I suppose we're both human, when you get down to it … As well as notorious lesbians, apparently.

RUTH: That's how we will live out our days, then. Notorious lesbians on the Tiger Tail, living lives of quiet dignity behind tall trees.

MARTHA: Very tall trees … Don't go, Ruth. Don't ever go again.

> *(They kiss.)*

SCENE ELEVEN

> *(David's office midmorning. It's early in 1955. David fusses busily with things on his desk. There's a knock at the door. Sproul enters.)*

SPROUL: Hello, Dave.

DAVID: Oh, Mr. President.

SPROUL: I just wanted to come by to thank you —

DAVID: A chair?

SPROUL: — no, thanks. To thank you personally for the hard work you did with the Martha Deane case. I know it was a long and difficult process. We've finally got all parties signed off and the papers filed.

DAVID: Thank you, sir. That means a lot.

SPROUL: Phyllis is well?

DAVID: Off to France.

SPROUL: France? You're meeting her there?

DAVID: No. No, indeed. She's off with a cousin. I encouraged her to go. So much going on here, you know.

SPROUL: Well, it's over now.

DAVID: There's always plenty to do here. I'm looking forward to getting back to my regular duties.

SPROUL: Oh, about that.

DAVID *(hopefully)*: Sir?

SPROUL: The Regents are very grateful for the role you've played. They're eager to see Ray Allen do well as the new Chancellor.

DAVID: Oh yes, Ray. I've known Ray for years.

SPROUL: It would be a big help if you could smooth the rails some for him if there's a problem.

DAVID *(deflated)*: Smooth the rails. Yes, of course.

SPROUL: He's a good man.

DAVID: So, it is over, then? The Deane case.

SPROUL: Yes. She's formally accepted the Regent's Counsel's final-final offer.

DAVID: Back pay?

SPROUL: Yes.

DAVID: Pension, of course.

SPROUL: At the level current at suspension. She'll miss the bump from last year. Bad timing for her.

DAVID: Yes. Too bad the whole thing couldn't have waited a year or two, you know. What will she do now?

SPROUL: I don't know. Mrs. Sproul is still in touch with her. Perhaps I'll ask. Is something troubling you, Dave?

DAVID: No, not really.

SPROUL: Good.

DAVID: It's just, we had that sworn statement from the neighbor. About what he'd seen. Yet I never could get Martha to admit she'd done anything, anything inappropriate.

SPROUL: Don't let it trouble you. You were just doing your job.

DAVID: Yes. A difficult one it was, you know. (*Sproul looks at his watch.*) I suppose we never will resolve it further now.

SPROUL: Resolve what, exactly?

90

DAVID: Oh, I don't know that it matters. What she did, what they were doing. Would you say the Regents won, Mr. President?

SPROUL: I hadn't thought about it all in quite those terms.

DAVID: But if you did?

SPROUL: Martha beat us, Dave. Between you and me, I don't think it's a bad outcome. Now, I can't guarantee you Martha agrees with me — she has a tremendous amount of pride. But my guess is in time she'll see it.

DAVID: Regent Pauley would agree with you, then?

SPROUL: Why the interest in Regent Pauley? Not much you can do about his opinion. I wouldn't worry too much about it. Life goes on.

DAVID: Thank you —

SPROUL: Interesting times we live in. The Senate finally voting to censure Joe McCarthy.

DAVID: End of an era. I wonder what happens to him now, do you suppose? Now that the tent's packed up and the circus is over.

SPROUL: I don't know, Dave. I really must go.

> *(Sproul exits. David picks up the telephone.)*

DAVID *(on telephone):* Oh, hello. Yes, I was hoping to call a number in Paris, in France. It's …

> *(Lights down.)*

SCENE TWELVE

MARTHA *(offstage)*: Ladies!

MARTHA *(continuing):* Thank you all for joining us today for the Tiger Tail ground-breaking ceremony. You'll find Polynesian drinks on the bar. Rosy will be doing that new dance craze, the hula, for us later. No? Oh, excuse me. Dr. Rosalind Cassidy will be doing a scholarly analysis of the hula for us. That should be fascinating.

I want to thank you all for the support you've given me over the last two and a half years. I have no words to express my gratitude. I am both happy and humbled to be able today to return to each of you the money you loaned me during that difficult time. I have checks for each of you, with interest and with my deepest thanks. It was the only income I had for many, many months.

For years I told my students at UCLA that becoming an instructor of Physical Education was a choice they would never regret. I still believe that, deeply. As you all know, it has been difficult for me to accept that the days of teaching are behind me now. You know that was not my choice. But I am proud of the program we built together and of every single young woman who passed through it on her road to her career. I celebrate them.

Indeed, life goes on. And so do I. As many of you know, Ruth and I recently returned from Hawaii. Thus, the party theme. While we must wait for Dr. Cassidy's scholarly analysis to fully understand the significance of hula, I thought we might begin with a demonstration for those new to it. As I used to tell my first-year Physical Education students in the Methodology of Teaching class, you've got to learn to listen to your body and hear what it's telling you. Mine tells me I am older, but not old. Wiser, but not yet wise. Happy, but not as happy as I will become. Lord knows I will undoubtedly hula until I drop. *(Hula music begins off stage.)* Imagine a pink sunset sky on an exotic island. You're with the person of your dreams. You have a drink in one hand and not a care in the world. The worst is behind you and you have your life ahead. Ah, imagination rules the world.

> (She begins to dance the hula, rather well as a matter of fact.)

We begin with the hips.

> (Spot slowly down on Martha. Hula music continues off stage.)

End of Play

IN CONVERSATION WITH THE PLAYWRIGHT

Maya: What inspired this play, **Unspeakable Acts***?*

Mary: My partner, an oral historian, made me aware of research on Martha Deane, a tenured UCLA professor in the 1950s who lost her position because of her lesbianism. Unlike many queer people during the McCarthy Era, however, she stood her ground and basically fought the University to a draw. I was intrigued by what led her to that choice. Through oral history transcripts at the Center for Oral History Research at UCLA I was able to piece together a narrative of events that I think does justice to the spirit of Martha Deane and the many others who were forced to make very difficult decisions in a time of great repression.

Maya: How would you distill this play in ten words or less?

Mary: Lesbian professor fights Red Scare homophobia to save her career.

Maya: Are there any formative moments for your development as a playwright, or this work, in particular, that you want to share—key research or "Ah ha" moments?

Mary: One of the most important aspects of my development as a playwright has come through working with dramaturg Jan Lewis. Her expertise was critical for me in finding the play's form, developing the characters, and refining (and *refining*) the piece. The process of working with her has always seemed a bit magical – I would sit down not sure what I was doing or where I was going. But after engaging in this mysterious dramaturgical process with her, I would come out knowing just what to do. It's been amazing!

Maya: What surprised you most in the research?

Mary: I was surprised to find how deeply buried Martha Deane's story had become. [...] Both Rosalind Cassidy and

Martha Deane have oral history transcripts on file at UCLA. Cassidy's interview, completed in the mid-1960's, was actually sealed to the public until everyone mentioned in it was dead, roughly forty years. By pre-arrangement with the interviewer, Deane's interview does not mention anything about the events surrounding her departure from UCLA. Interestingly, however, on the tape upon which the transcript is based, she blanks on the name of her nemesis and mutters that she can't stand him. The comment doesn't make it to the transcript.

Maya: Can you tell us a bit about your play **Women and Horses and a Shot Straight from the Bottle***, which was honored as a Jane Chambers Award Finalist in 2000?*

Mary: I grew up loving country music, cowgirls, and rodeo. *Women and Horses and a Shot Straight from the Bottle* is a kind of feminist deconstruction of the mythic western hero in the form of a rumination on loss. […] The play premiered in the most perfect venue imaginable – Echo Theatre in Dallas, Texas. Echo only produces work by women playwrights and Dallas is a prime spot for horses and cowboys.

Maya: When you consider your body of work, what themes, ideas or forms emerge as emblematic? Any key differences?

Mary: I often write about women and the American West. Although at first blush Martha Deane doesn't seem to have much in common with a bronc-riding cowgirl, in fact they are both at home in their physical selves and feisty as the day is long. In fighting the University of California, Martha knows she's drawn the toughest bronc in the chutes, but is determined to ride the full eight seconds.

In terms of form, *Unspeakable Acts* is a departure for me as I tend to envision plays as non-linear. And believe me, I did everything I could to make the piece behave that way! Ultimately, though, I realized that the play worked best utilizing a linear form, an approach which seemed to match the rather more traditional personality of its main character.

Maya: What led you to playwriting?

Mary: I grew up as the youngest child in a lively, highly verbal, story-telling family so I spent a good part of my childhood listening to other people talking. This was in a small, isolated town halfway between San Francisco and Eureka. We didn't have much in the way of theater so some friends and I made up plays and staged them for our families and classmates. Looking back, I realize it was probably my way of finding a "voice" in my family that didn't require interrupting someone.

Maya: How is your playwriting shaped by your other life or creative roles?

Mary: I'm a history geek. I recently completed my M.A. and hope to continue in a Ph.D. program. I loved doing the research for *Unspeakable Acts*, but my specialty is early American borderlands. History and playwriting are a natural combination for me: as a playwright, I find myself asking what motivated people in the past to do what they did; as a historian, I try to understand the social and cultural milieu in which my characters exist.

THE SIEGELS OF MONTAUK

by
Meryl Cohn

**Winner of the
2009 Jane Chambers Prize**

FIRST PRODUCTION

Directed by Rosemary Andress, at The Provincetown Theater, Provincetown, Massachusetts, produced by Counter Productions in Fall, 2008.

FLORENCE SIEGEL	Lynda Sturner
WENDY SIEGEL	Valerie Stanford
SARA SIEGEL	Braunwyn Jackett
JULIE SIEGEL	Sara Shatzel
JAKE SHILOWITZ	Ty Hewitt
LACEY MCMAHON	Nikki Wing

CAST OF CHARACTERS

WENDY	Oldest sister, 40. A psychologist. The sane one.
JULIE	Middle sister, 39. Doesn't know she's beautiful. Has an edge.
SARAH	Youngest sister, 33. Hugely pregnant.
FLORENCE	Mother of Wendy, Julie & Sarah. Turning 70.
JAKE	Rugged, earnest, 40.
LACEY	Physically hearty, 27.

SETTING

The living room, porch and bathroom of an old, somewhat run-down beach cottage in Montauk, New York, with painted plank floors and great light. The Siegel family has owned the house for forty years. The furnishings are worn but attractive. The cottage is utterly filled with clutter: fishing poles, guns, empty booze bottles, books and clothing scattered all around. The clutter is practically like another character.

TIME

The present.

SCENE ONE

(Noon. Wendy is on the porch of the cottage. Birds chirp. Temperature is sweltering. Wendy sets down a suitcase, a cooler and a cake box. She struggles with the door lock. She tries to make a phone call but there's no reception. She gives up. She cracks open a beer. A few moments later, Sarah enters with an overnight bag. Sarah is hugely, unbelievably, comically pregnant — about to burst.)

WENDY: Sarah! Oh, my God — look at you! You are so —

SARAH: Don't say it!

WENDY: — sweaty!

(They hug.)

SARAH: I was stuck in traffic on 27 for two hours. I had a nightmare last night about giving birth in a traffic jam. The baby's head came out while I was still driving, but I stuffed it back in. *(Beat.)* So … no dream interpretation?

WENDY: A dream about a traffic jam is about obstacles that you fear you can't overcome.

SARAH: That sounds like a fortune cookie. What about the head emerging from my —

WENDY: You stuffed her back in: That's ambivalence. *(Beat.)* Come, sit down! Put your feet up; have a beer — Oh. I guess not.

SARAH: It's four hundred degrees. Aren't we going inside?

WENDY: Would you like a sparkling water?

SARAH: I need food!

WENDY *(looks in the cooler)*: Apple?

SARAH: How about chocolate in a trough or bacon on a spit? I need to go in and wash up. *(Beat.)* We're locked out, aren't we?

WENDY: I tried calling the locksmith, but there was no answer. You look beautiful.

SARAH *(cheerfully)*: I can't wait to get the little motherfucker out of me.

WENDY: Don't say that to Julie!

(*Sarah looks through the window, into the cottage.*)

SARAH: Whoa. Have you looked in there? My next-door neighbor's place is neater, and he's running a meth lab.

WENDY: Mom needs us to clear it out this weekend so the realtor can start showing it.

SARAH: I thought we were coming for a celebration, not an excavation.

WENDY: She wants us to do it as her birthday present.

SARAH: I already bought her a sequined sweater.

WENDY: We should do whatever she wants. It's her first birthday alone.

SARAH: Whoopsy! I'm about to overflow! You don't mind …?

WENDY: Of course not.

> (*Sarah takes out her automatic breast pump, sits on the porch step and attaches the pump to her breasts. It makes a loud and rhythmic sound.*)

WENDY: Wow.

SARAH: Primitive, but it keeps you from exploding.

WENDY: I don't get how you nurse while you're pregnant. Doesn't the milk come in after you give birth?

SARAH: I never stopped pumping for Baby Number Two. Did I tell you they named him Hunter? Hunter's gay daddies pay me ten dollars for every three ounces of milk. Gas money.

WENDY: Barely.

> (*Wendy takes out the camera. Sarah poses, pump still attached. Wendy snaps a picture.*)

WENDY: I'm sure there's a very specific porn market that would appreciate this.

SARAH: Hey. Isn't that Dad's camera?

WENDY: He gave it to me two summers ago, along with some old psychiatry textbooks.

SARAH: We're not the kind of people who fight over possessions.

(*Wendy hands Sarah a wrapped package.*)

WENDY: Despite our superstitious heritage, here's a baby present before she's even born.

SARAH: That's sweet, but you have to give it to Julie.

WENDY: Oh, right. Sorry.

SARAH: She hasn't paid me yet. Not one dime. You were a witness to the conversation when she said she would pay me —

WENDY: I don't want to be in the middle.

SARAH: You're already in the middle because you encouraged me to do it!

WENDY: Julie seems so fragile lately.

SARAH (*disconnects the breast pump*): Well, she's had a couple more bad dates. The last guy referred to himself in the third person all through dinner. "Brian likes the moo shu pork. Brian hopes to be invited up to your apartment."

WENDY: Yuck.

SARAH (*confiding*): You do know that she still hasn't done it yet?

WENDY: *It ...? ?* You don't mean ...?

SARAH: It's become a *thing* for her. You can't tell her that I told you.

WENDY: But she's gone through IVF! How do you go through IVF if you haven't —

SARAH: She told them that she'd tried to get pregnant, but it wasn't even true! It's not like her hymen's intact. She's used tampons and sex toys.

WENDY: But, technically, she's still —?

SARAH: You can't use that word! Seriously. She'd kill you.

(Julie enters.)

JULIE: Hey, you two! Oh, my God, you popped! You are SO huge!

SARAH: Thanks.

WENDY: Hey, Julie. It's a porch party! You want a beer?

SARAH: Or, there's breast milk. Everyone says it's tasty.

(Wendy and Sarah hug Julie. Julie rubs Sarah's belly. She takes the bottle and squirts some milk into her mouth and makes a face.)

JULIE: How's my bambina?

SARAH: She's a healthy little kickboxer.

JULIE: Guess what? I stole a parking sticker from a Beemer and glued it to my windshield, just like we used to.

SARAH: Mom will kill you if you if you end up in the Montauk Sun crime blotter.

WENDY: It's normal to regress when you go back home. Full-grown adults often end up cursing, slamming doors and getting drunk in the bushes when they visit their parents.

SARAH: Were the birds always this noisy?

JULIE: Yes. I hate them. I have to pee.

(She tries the door.)

WENDY: We're locked out.

JULIE: Remember how often you lost the key when we were kids? You were the only one "responsible" enough to hold it because you were oldest, but you always lost it.

SARAH: We always had to wait in Mrs. Flomanhoff's yard for Mom to come home.

JULIE: Well, we can't just languish on the porch until Mom arrives tomorrow.

WENDY: More importantly, we can't just let the birthday cake melt.

SARAH *(singing, to the tune of "MacArthur Park," inspired by the Supremes):* Someone left the cake out in the rain.

JULIE *(singing):* I don't think that I can take it, because it took so long to bake it ...

SARAH and JULIE and WENDY *(singing):* And I'll never have that recipe again!

WENDY *(to Julie):* Oh! I have something for you.

> *(Wendy hands a wrapped present to Julie, who opens the package and takes out a little pink dress.)*

JULIE: Wow, that's so pretty and so ... feminine! Thank you! Mom keeps forgetting that she's mine. It means a lot to me that you always remember.

WENDY: Of course, I remember!

JULIE *(kneels and puts her face on Sarah's belly):* Are you there, Brianna? It's me again. I just want you to know that Mommy has wanted you for a very long time. Mommy is blowing you kisses!

(Julie kisses Sarah's belly repeatedly.)

SARAH: Do you really have to do that? *(Beat.)* Mom wants us to pack up Dad's crap so she can list the cottage with a realtor. That's what she wants for her seventieth birthday.

JULIE: That'll take all weekend!

SARAH: I still wish she wasn't selling it. Doesn't being here make you miss Daddy?

JULIE: I've always hated this place.

SARAH: We spent so many great summers here!

JULIE: It was always too hot. No central air, just those ancient window units. Too many bugs.

WENDY: I wish we still had the boat. I was on the boat with Dad the first time I smoked cigarettes.

JULIE: He never taught me to smoke.

SARAH *(rapturously):* We all drank our first drinks in the cottage and smoked our first weed and made out with the cute townie boys —

JULIE: I got crabs when I borrowed some guy's blanket for a bonfire on the beach. *(Beat.)* Why didn't Mom just hire someone to pack the place up?

WENDY: Getting rid of all the junk will help Mom feel better. Then, after Dad's estate settles, maybe we can hire someone to help her.

JULIE: Help? You mean, like a caretaker? She's not sick.

SARAH: She does fall a lot.

WENDY: It's not uncommon to be accident-prone when you're in mourning. What she really needs is therapy; she's still in denial about Dad.

SARAH: She's not "in denial." She just doesn't believe it's true.

WENDY: That's the definition of denial: if the thing you refuse to believe *is* true.

JULIE: Can you imagine spending forty years married to someone and then finding out that you didn't actually *know* him at all?

SARAH: Stop talking about it. It's over!

WENDY: It's not really over until we help Mom get over it.

JULIE: How exactly do you "get over" something so disturbing?

SARAH: Can we move on, please? *(To Julie.)* We need to talk about the *money*.

JULIE: I've covered the medical tests and prenatal vitamins —

SARAH: What about the monthly fee?

JULIE: I thought my screenplay would sell. My agent says it's a bad time for historical romance.

SARAH: Isn't it always a bad time for historical romance?

WENDY: Hey hey hey. Where's the love?

JULIE: Okay, Dalai Lama, why don't you front Sarah the money and I'll reimburse you later?

WENDY: I don't have any money.

JULIE: You've always saved every penny you ever made.

WENDY: I spent it on copayments for the treatment; I've never been able to catch up.

JULIE *(lightly):* You always know just the right moment to play the cancer card.

>   *(Sarah packs up her nursing pump and her bag.)*

WENDY: Don't go, Sarah. Julie can pay you out of her share of Dad's estate, right, Julie?

>   *(Julie looks at her iPhone and doesn't respond.)*

Julie? *(Beat.)* Hello? Julie?

>   *(Sarah gathers her things and stands up.)*

JULIE: Hey. Where are you going?

SARAH: I'm hot and I have to pee!

WENDY: Don't go! I'll figure out a way to get us in.

>   *(Sarah exits.)*

JULIE *(to Wendy):* She always leaves in a huff! *(To Sarah)* Wait! I'll go with you! *(Julie exits.)*

WENDY *(calling after them):* Don't go! I'll crawl through the window!

>   *(continuous to:)*

SCENE TWO

(Afternoon. Lights up on the sunny interior of the summer cottage. Fishing poles, fishing boots and gear and several rifles clutter the space. Piles of boxes and books are scattered throughout. A large striped bass is

mounted on the wall. Skin-care products, nail clippers, empty plates and a bottle of scotch cover the coffee table. Wendy enters awkwardly through the upstage window, dragging her overnight bag. She sprawls on the couch, pours a glass of scotch and begins to drink it. Jake enters from another room, wearing only a towel. They are both very startled.)

JAKE and WENDY: AAAAAGH!!!

JAKE: Oh, God! I didn't mean to scare you — I thought no one was here.

(Wendy picks up a shotgun and points it at him.)

WENDY: Get out!

JAKE: I'm sorry! I'm a friend of Fred's. It was so messy that I knew no one had been here since he died — I just came to hang out here. I love the claw-foot tub. I take a bath and then I lie on the couch —

WENDY *(disgusted):* Do you put on clothes before you lie on the couch? Or do you just let your … parts touch the fabric?

JAKE: What?

WENDY: How long have you been here?

JAKE: *(embarrassed beat)* About three weeks.

WENDY: What? You have nerve! You just break into your dead friend's house —

JAKE: I'm sorry! Can I help you with anything? Are your bags still in the car?

WENDY: Just get dressed and go!

JAKE (*still in a towel, puts on his socks*): I'm so sorry about what happened to Fred. I was in Spain when he died and nobody thought to call me. He was more of a dad to me than my own father was. I really feel for you; no matter how important you are to someone, you just can't have a meaningful public role when you're the other woman. Wait — that came out wrong. I feel like a douchebag. Can we start over?

(*He extends his hand, nearly dropping his towel.*)

I'm Jake.

WENDY (*stricken):* Wait a minute. Jake?

JAKE: He mentioned me, right? I grew up here during the summers with my family and now I rent a little cabin a couple miles down the road —

WENDY: Jake Shilowitz? Jake fucking Shilowitz? I'm not Fred's slutty girlfriend. I'm Fred's daughter Wendy!

JAKE: What? No way! Oh, my God! Wendy?

WENDY: Yep.

JAKE: You're kidding me! Wow! I can't believe it! Wow! You look great!

WENDY: Thank you! So do you!

JAKE: Now I feel really self-conscious! Let me go put my clothes on.

(*He leaves the room to get dressed.*)

JAKE (*offstage*): So, you must have lost like a hundred pounds since the last time —

WENDY: About thirty.

JAKE *(offstage):* I lost forty pounds my first year at Wesleyan. I didn't even diet; I just got this really persistent parasite — *(Beat.)* Why'd you let me think you were Fred's girlfriend?

WENDY: You're the one who broke into my dead father's house and took a three-week-long bath!

JAKE: And you let me stand there and apologize like an idiot with no pants!

WENDY: I didn't make you into a no-pants idiot; you came that way.

> *(Jake re-enters in boxers and a flannel shirt, carrying his jeans.)*

JAKE *(laughs):* This is like twenty years later and you still get the last word!

WENDY: Twenty-five years. *(Beat.)* Isn't that my father's shirt?

JAKE *(embarrassed):* I borrowed it. I'll give it back.

WENDY: Keep it. We'd probably give it away anyway.

JAKE: My mother said you're a lesbian. She ran into your mother, who was handing out pamphlets for Marriage Equality in front of Whole Foods. *(Beat.)* Listen, I stood by your father. I didn't believe any of that garbage in the news —

WENDY: Thanks.

JAKE: The stress of that whole thing must have been what killed him. He was in good shape … not the kind of guy you'd expect to have a heart attack.

WENDY: He did love his Camels —

JAKE: All that crap they said about him … One person starts it, then once it's in the press, it's fair game. The guy's a psychiatrist and no one considers that maybe some of his patients aren't all that well —

WENDY: Would you like something to drink? I was also just about to retrieve my father's secret stash of marijuana —

JAKE: I happen to have some excellent weed myself, actually.

> *(Wendy pours drinks. Jake brings a joint to the couch and lights it.)*

JAKE: I love this place. Did you ever feel like you're almost a different person when your location changes? Like you're not your right self in some places?

WENDY: I feel that way in my mother's house in Oyster Bay.

> *(They pass the joint back and forth.)*

JAKE: Don't take this the wrong way, but … you didn't seem like a lesbian back then.

WENDY: I used to think your sister Jackie was hot. *(Beat.)* I don't usually connect that way with men. You were different, the only man who found his way in.

JAKE: Really? Wow. Thanks.

> *(Wendy inhales deeply. She lies back on the couch.)*

JAKE: So … no kids?

WENDY: Nope.

JAKE: Me neither. *(Awkward pause.)* You don't say much, do you?

WENDY: You still talk a lot.

JAKE *(proudly)*: I am a communicator.

WENDY *(yawns and stretches out)*: Don't be offended if I fall asleep.

> *(Jake stretches out. They lie together awkwardly.)*

JAKE: Do you remember the mattress that we dragged down to my parents' basement? We'd lie on it and watch TV?

WENDY: *General Hospital* at three. Phil Donahue at four. It was dark when I got home; I always said I'd been at the library. Your mother was way cooler than mine.

JAKE: Do you remember the back rubs?

WENDY: Every day! And what about that first blow job? *(Laughs.)* I had no idea what I was doing.

JAKE: I didn't care. That was totally amazing!

WENDY: Even with all the teeth?

JAKE *(reconsiders)*: Oh, right … *(Beat.)* So, you wouldn't have recognized me?

WENDY: You looked like a kid. You don't anymore.

> *(Wendy breathes deeply and begins to doze. Jake lightly touches her hair.)*

JAKE: This is so weird, isn't it? Sometimes someone from your past holds a part of you that you can't reach until you see that person again. It's like my fifteen-year-old self disappeared a long time ago. But seeing you, it's like that part of myself is waking up. … So many people pass through your life and there's no way to know: "Will this person turn out to be someone who matters deeply in the big picture or is she just drifting by like a snowflake?"

> *(He takes the hair tie from Wendy's hair, holds it up to his face, then puts it in his shirt pocket.)*

(Beat.) Hey, Wendy?

WENDY *(half-asleep)*: Hmm?

JAKE: I was just wondering if you were awake.

WENDY: Shhh. Sometimes *not* talking is nice.

JAKE *(softly)*: I've been not feeling like myself lately. Maybe I'm depressed.

WENDY: Dusk is a sad time of day.

JAKE: Am I an overwhelming person?

WENDY: Just a very gabby one.

JAKE: I saw this psychic once. She told me to shut the fuck up. She said, "No one needs to know everything you're thinking."

WENDY: She was right.

JAKE: Do you want me to rub your back?

WENDY *(hesitates)*: Sure.

> *(Jake begins to rub Wendy's back and shoulders, gently.)*

WENDY: So, what's your sister Jackie doing these days?

JAKE: She's a commercial airline pilot.

WENDY: Wow. That's hot!

(Wendy kisses Jake and pulls him on top of her. They make out passionately. A few moments later, the door opens; they don't hear it. Florence enters, freezes for a moment, and then screams.)

FLORENCE: AAAAAGGGHHHHHHHH!!!

WENDY and JAKE: AAAGGGGHHHH!

(Florence quickly dials on her cell phone.)

FLORENCE *(frantically)*: Hello, Police? Please come right away. My daughter is being raped!

WENDY: Oh, my God! Mom, it's not that!

(Jake runs and retrieves his pants.)

FLORENCE *(on phone)*: Can't you tell where I am? Don't cell phones have a tracking thingy?

(Lacey enters.)

FLORENCE *(to Lacey)*: Thank God you're here! He's a rapist!

(Lacey punches Jake in the face. He falls; she pins him.)

WENDY: Mom! Hey, you! Get off him! Stop it!

FLORENCE *(on the phone)*: The address is 145 West Lake Drive. It's the ugly bungalow on the right.

WENDY: Mom, stop it! I told you, I'm not being raped! *(To Lacey)* Don't hurt him!

JAKE: Florence, it's me! Jake!

FLORENCE *(on the phone)*: My daughter claims she's not being raped. She's supposed to be a lesbian and yet there was a man on top of her. You can imagine my confusion. *(To Lacey)* I guess you can get off him.

(Lacey reluctantly climbs off Jake.)

FLORENCE *(to Wendy):* The police officer wants me to make sure it's not against your will.

(Wendy grabs the phone from Florence.)

WENDY: This is Wendy Siegel. I am not being raped. Yes, I'm sure! *(Beat.)* What? Who is this? Evan Horowitz? You're kidding! *(To Florence)* It's Evan Horowitz. He's a police officer.

FLORENCE: The one who bit you!

WENDY: Well, hi Evan Horowitz. *(Beat.)* Good for you. You sound lovely yourself. Okay. Bye.

FLORENCE: I've never heard of a Jewish police officer. *(To Lacey)* He bit her neck and drew blood. There's something wrong with that boy.

WENDY: Mom, that was thirty-five years ago.

FLORENCE: People don't change! *(To Lacey)* They say human bites are worse than animal bites —

LACEY: I think it depends on the person.

WENDY *(about Lacey):* Who is this? *(To Florence)* I thought you weren't coming until tomorrow.

FLORENCE: I thought it would be a nice surprise if I came early! Hello, Jake. You'll have to forgive me for not recognizing you from behind.

(Sarah and Julie enter.)

SARAH: What a pigsty!

JULIE: This place is still hotter than balls!

WENDY: The Sisters of Perpetual Cheer have arrived.

FLORENCE *(to Sarah):* Hooray! It's the beautiful Mommy of my very first granddaughter!

SARAH: *Julie* is the Mommy —

JULIE: — as we've discussed a thousand times!

WENDY: You guys remember Jake? *(Indicates Lacey.)* And who's this person?

SARAH: Of course. Jake was your chubby little boyfriend with the Jewfro —

JAKE *(interrupts):* It was a perm!

SARAH: — who failed to fulfill his academic promise and became a carpenter and then turned up years later and became Daddy's fishing buddy.

JAKE: You women all look so beautiful! It seems like hardly any time has passed.

JULIE: Thank you, Eddie Haskell.

FLORENCE *(to Julie and Sarah):* The craziest thing happened: I walked through the door and found Jake and Wendy about to do the bumpity-bump.

JULIE: Gross.

SARAH *(indicating Lacey):* Who's she?

FLORENCE: Oh. Julie, Wendy, Sarah, Jake, this is Lacey. She's my… Pilates instructor.

LACEY: Uh, I'm all about core strength.

(Lacey shakes hands heartily with Julie, Wendy and Sarah.)

(To Jake) Sorry if I was a little rough, Dude.

JAKE: I didn't feel right about hitting you back so I had to let you pin me.

SARAH: I miss Daddy. Being surrounded by all his stuff makes me miss him even more. Like, his hands held that fishing pole so many times … but they'll never hold it again. *(She begins to hyperventilate.)*

It's so hot! Could someone open a window? It's hard to breathe.

WENDY: Uh-oh. She's having a problem.

LACEY *(to Sarah)*: Okay, Big Girl, sit down and elevate your feet. Someone get her water.

> *(Lacey eases Sarah into a chair. Wendy gets her a glass of water.)*

SARAH: Did she just call me "Big Girl"?

FLORENCE: Should I call 911 again?

LACEY: No. *(To Sarah)* Just breathe into your hands. *(To Jake)* Let's get her legs up higher.

> *(Jake hoists her legs way up in the air.)*

WENDY *(amused)*: Whoa there, Lumberjack.

FLORENCE: So, you're a bisexual now?

WENDY: No.

LACEY *(to Florence)*: Sexuality is mutable in nature; it's as fluid as a river.

FLORENCE *(to Jake):* Wendy's obviously not in her right mind and you took advantage of her!

JAKE: It was her idea; we took a nap and then it just … progressed.

JULIE *(to herself):* Why do the lesbians get all the men?

FLORENCE *(concerned):* I hope the chemo didn't damage her brain.

JAKE *(worried):* Chemo? Is she okay now?

WENDY: Hello? I'm right here. *(To Florence)* You know perfectly well that I'm fine!

FLORENCE: Her treatment was horrible, but she's okay now, *kenahora*, except she'll never have babies.

JAKE *(to himself):* I'm not shallow. I could love a sterile woman.

SARAH *(whispers to Wendy):* What would Nina think about this?

WENDY: About what?

JULIE: You know — your little slip.

WENDY: We broke up.

SARAH: But Nina was so beautiful and nice!

FLORENCE: You didn't tell me that you and Nina broke up! *(Florence trips on a fishing rod.)* Goddamn it! This place is a pigsty! Am I going to have to break a hip to get any help?

JULIE: No injury required; everyone already knows about the Birthday Blackmail Cleanup.

FLORENCE: Blackmail? You're a very mean girl, Julie Siegel. I'm ashamed of you!

WENDY: Mom, could you please *not* do this —

FLORENCE: I'm ashamed of *you*, too!

WENDY *(to herself)*: Nothing changes. It's still horrifying.

FLORENCE *(to Wendy)*: You know what's horrifying? *You! YOU* are truly *horrifying*!

WENDY *(to Florence)*: Oh, really? I'm horrifying? What exactly horrifies you about me?

LACEY: Florence, let's take a couple of deep breaths like we practiced in the car —

FLORENCE *(raving at Wendy)*: What horrifies me? My beautiful gold-star lesbian daughter having sex with a sweaty grunty *MAN*! Twenty years ago, I bought all those books to try to understand you, and I believed the propaganda about two women being beautiful together, and I even grew to appreciate the word "cunt" at your insistence. Now… *THIS*!

WENDY *(angry)*: You know what, Ma? I don't need you ranting at me like a crazy person. I am an adult and I can fuck whoever I want!

JULIE: Whomever.

FLORENCE *(still ranting)*: Being gay wasn't special anymore so you had to outdo yourself by being a lesbian who screws men? I am a lifetime member of PFLAG! What am I supposed to tell my friends? That you're just too sophisticated for the rest of us, and you should be living in Paris?

JAKE *(to Wendy)*: Should I go?

WENDY: No.

LACEY: What about me?

WENDY: Please stay.

FLORENCE: I'm going to my room to rest. And when I get back up, I'm going to hope that order is restored and the heterosexuals are heterosexual and the gays are back to being gay. *(Calmly.)* Right now, I'm disappointed in all of you. What could be more important than being supportive during a difficult time, to someone you supposedly love?

LACEY: Uh —

FLORENCE: That's a rhetorical question, Bozo.

SCENE THREE

(Later afternoon. Living room. Julie types on her laptop and eats a sandwich. Sarah enters, also eating a sandwich.)

JULIE: Can you think of a word that describes being sexually aroused, other than "hot" or "wet"?

SARAH: *Tumescent?*

JULIE: That's fancy, but ... no.

SARAH: What are you writing?

JULIE: My agent has three clients who make a lot of money writing romance books.

SARAH: Sounds like porn to me.

JULIE: We in the biz like to call it erotica, actually.

(Wendy enters, followed by Lacey.)

SARAH *(to Wendy):* Did you know Julie was writing porn?

WENDY: Yep.

SARAH (to Julie): How come Wendy knew and I didn't?

JULIE: Wendy appreciates erotica.

LACEY: Don't you feel that porn exploits women?

JULIE: No, Pilates Instructor, I don't. I find it liberating.

LACEY: You guys need to do something wholesome. Go outside and look at the incredible clouds!

SARAH: Who are you again?

JULIE: She's Mom's gofer but she wears a unitard.

SARAH: *Gopher* as in buck-toothed mammal, or *gofer* as in personal fetcher?

JULIE: She's Mom's bitch.

　　　(Sarah laughs.)

WENDY: Be nice! You guys don't need to continue the family tradition of chewing up every new person who enters the house.

JULIE: Yes, we do.

LACEY: I'm Florence's *friend*, actually.

　　　(Jake enters.)

JAKE: Whoa. Did you guys just see that? Over there, in the bushes —

LACEY: Looks like a skinny dog with a huge bushy tail. It's a coyote!

JAKE: When they come out before nightfall, they're sometimes rabid.

JULIE: This place is like the set of a horror movie!

WENDY: The sky is purple. It's going to pour.

LACEY: Do you hear that high-pitched sound?

SARAH: It's those exasperating birds. Aren't they only supposed to chirp in the morning?

JAKE: Some birds are nocturnal, and some will stay up at night in order to protect their territory from predators. The birds with that distinctive sound —

(He imitates the song.)

— are cow birds, which are nest parasites. The female stalks the nest of a bird from another species and waits until nobody's home. Then she pushes one of the eggs out of the nest, and leaves her own egg for the mother to raise.

WENDY: The nest-napping must be an evolutionary adaptation to keep their species alive.

LACEY: I like the sound they make. It's peaceful.

SARAH *(to Jake):* The mother of the other species doesn't mind raising someone else's baby?

LACEY: It's free nanny care.

JULIE: Birds are filthy. They carry diseases.

JAKE: Probably only city birds carry diseases.

WENDY: Surely the Montauk birds are pristine.

SARAH: Guess who's susceptible to germs from birds? Babies, the elderly and *pregnant women.*

JULIE: Maybe we should remove that nest from the window.

WENDY: We can't; the babies would die.

JAKE: They'll only stay a couple of weeks. Once the babies grow strong enough, they fly away.

LACEY: Imagine knowing everything you'd need to know by the time you're a few weeks old, even though you're still bald and vulnerable.

JULIE: As I always say: nature is ugly.

>	*(Julie begins looking at her iPhone.)*

JAKE: I'm going to go build a bluebird box to keep out other species. I bet there's still wood in the shed.

LACEY: I'll help! I'm good with a saw.

>	*(Jake and Lacey exit.)*

JULIE *(looks at her iPhone):* Uh-oh.

SARAH: Do you ever stop playing with that thing? It's so rude.

JULIE: Suzanne Edelstein just filed a lawsuit against Dad.

SARAH: You can't sue a dead person.

>	*(Lacey enters, opens a drawer and pulls out a hammer.)*

JULIE: Apparently you can. She's going after Dad's estate.

SARAH: She's a liar! She already dragged him through the mud in the newspapers. What does she want now?

JULIE: Dad's money, apparently. The lawyer says *(reading)*, "You should be aware that the assets of your father's estate could be used to satisfy a judgment against your father."

WENDY: Let's just let the lawyer deal with it.

SARAH: Dad must have had malpractice insurance.

WENDY: Actually, I think that covers negligence, not "intentional acts."

LACEY: I do remember reading that your father may have diddled his patients.

SARAH: He did not!

LACEY: How do you know?

WENDY *(whispers to Lacey):* Don't go there.

LACEY: Can I just ask —

SARAH *(yells):* NO! Get lost, cretin!

> *(Lacey scurries out the door.)*

(To Wendy and Julie) Where's your sense of loyalty?

JULIE: Stay calm, Sarah. Stress hormones aren't good for the baby.

SARAH: Easy for you to say, Deadbeat. *(To Wendy)* I don't get it. Why aren't you upset?

WENDY: I *am* upset. I realize that ranting is the family tradition, but it's not my style.

SARAH: What exactly is your style? Making yourself disappear?

WENDY: I'm right here, Sarah.

SARAH: You're not angry that this woman ruined Dad's life and now she wants his money?

WENDY: What about the other women? If they're all saying the same thing, maybe it's true.

SARAH: They were just copycats; Suzanne Edelstein was the ringleader.

JULIE: There was no ringleader. Those women didn't know each other.

SARAH: Do you guys really think that we didn't know our own father?

WENDY *(carefully)*: I loved Dad as much as anyone, but how could I know anything for sure? I wasn't there.

SARAH: Are you fucking kidding me?

WENDY: I don't mean to upset you, Sarah. But there's no way to unequivocally know what he did or didn't do.

SARAH: Mom doesn't believe it's true.

WENDY: How would she know?

SARAH: Dad was devoted to his patients. He wouldn't have hurt them.

JULIE: Life must be very simple for you.

SARAH: You two are so shallow! Your loyalty goes out the window the minute Dad stops breathing.

WENDY: No one ever wants to believe it about their family member, but what if it is true? What if Dad was really a —

SARAH: Don't use that disgusting word!

WENDY: Perpetrator.

SARAH *(freaking):* I told you not to say it!

JULIE: It's not the *word* that's disgusting.

WENDY *(to Julie):* Maybe we shouldn't get her all riled up.

JULIE: If that woman is telling the truth and she wins the lawsuit, she could end up owning this cottage — or all the money from the sale of it.

WENDY: Don't mention that to Mom; we don't need to freak her out.

SARAH: That woman will not win! We don't even know if she's mentally stable!

WENDY: Why is your automatic response to question her sanity?

JULIE *(to Wendy):* What would you like us to do? Write her a check?

SARAH: She didn't sue for financial damages until he was dead and couldn't defend himself, which means it's bullshit. If he were guilty, the professional board would have taken his license.

WENDY: They didn't say he wasn't guilty; they just said there wasn't enough evidence to strip him of his license.

SARAH: In America, that means you're innocent!

WENDY: You're defending him based on your feelings about him, but what if it's true? What if he really did molest his patients?

SARAH: Daddy would never have done that!

JULIE: We don't know that.

SARAH *(to Julie):* What did you ever see him do that would make you doubt him?

JULIE: I was his daughter, not his patient. It's different.

WENDY: For what it's worth, everyone who knew Albert DeSalvo thought he was a very nice gentleman too.

JULIE: Who's Albert DeSalvo?

WENDY: The Boston Strangler.

SARAH: You're comparing Dad to a serial killer?

WENDY: The "self" that someone shows to the outside world doesn't necessarily align with his more secretive behavior. And the closer you are to someone, the less likely you are to see his faults.

JULIE: Okay, but can we leave the Boston Strangler out of it?

WENDY: Why am I the only one facing reality here? *(To Julie)* What if Suzanne Edelstein wins? Aren't you counting on your inheritance to pay Sarah?

JULIE: It's the only money I have.

WENDY: You don't actually have it yet.

SARAH *(to Julie):* This is bullshit. You'd better think of another way to pay me.

(Sarah gathers her things.)

JULIE: Sarah. Wait. Don't leave —

SARAH: I'm out of here.

(She exits.)

JULIE: There she goes.

(They go to the window and watch her leave.)

WENDY: She'll probably just walk on the beach until she cools off. *(Beat.)* Every time she storms out, it reminds me of how it used to be: the three of us, in the back of the station wagon.

JULIE: If anyone said anything she didn't like, she'd unlock her door and jump out.

WENDY *(laughs)*: Sometimes the car was still moving!

JULIE: And she'd go home and run up to her room and we'd have to go without her. *(Beat.)* I guess she's still more or less the same.

WENDY: Maybe we're all more or less the same.

SCENE FOUR

(Late afternoon. Lacey videotapes Florence.)

LACEY: Has anyone ever taken a test shot of you?

(Lacey shoots and then shows Florence the back of the camera.)

LACEY: Do you see how beautiful you are?

(Points the camera at Florence.)

The accusations must have been very upsetting to you. It's always hardest on the loved ones. *(Beat.)* Talk to me.

FLORENCE: I can't just speak on command, like a dog. *(Bursting.)* Did you know we were thrown out of Temple Beth-El? When Fred was still alive, the rabbi called to say that the other congregants were "uncomfortable" in our presence. Our daughters were all Bat Mitzvahed at that temple! They went to Hebrew school there. Fred participated in dozens of minyans.

LACEY *(puts down the camera):* I'm so sorry.

FLORENCE: You don't know what a minyan is, do you, Lacey McMahon?

LACEY: No.

FLORENCE: Write it down and Google it when you get home. *(Beat.)* My daughters are very suspicious people. You have to be careful not to let it slip that we just met.

LACEY *(laughs):* You already told me that forty-five times. I promise.

FLORENCE: How old are you?

LACEY: I'll be twenty-seven next month.

FLORENCE: I know who you are. I thought you might show up after he died.

LACEY: Really? I was so worried about intruding —

FLORENCE: You should be happy you weren't raised by him. It's like missing the plane that ends up crashing into the mountains.

LACEY: Metaphors are not my strong suit.

FLORENCE: After Fred died, the rabbi called to invite us to come back, but I couldn't imagine walking back in. All I could envision was Marjorie Stackman's extra-tight face, staring at me. (*Beat.*) Film me some more.

> (*Lacey turns the video camera back on and points it at Florence.*)

LACEY: Do you think, in general, a person must believe her spouse's innocence to stay with him?

FLORENCE: How should I know "in general"?

LACEY: Okay, here's an example: By the time Mary Jo Buttafuoco realized that she was shot in the head by Amy Fisher, she was probably pretty confident that Joey had done something wrong. And yet she didn't leave.

FLORENCE: Joey Buttafuoco was a moron. I wouldn't have stayed with *him*.

LACEY: Those who believe in Fred's innocence will know why you stayed with him until his unfortunate passing. But those who don't …

FLORENCE: Who cares what they think.

LACEY (*surprised*): Do you really not care?

FLORENCE: Actually… I care very much. (*Beat.*) That's off the record.

SCENE FIVE

> (*Late afternoon. Wendy reads on the porch. Jake enters.*)

JAKE: Hey.

WENDY: Hey.

JAKE: I rehung the wobbly mirror in the bathroom. I used a couple of bolts and I sunk it into a block of wood. If there's ever an earthquake, the one thing staying in place is that mirror.

WENDY: That's great. Thank you.

(She goes back to her book.)

JAKE: Wendy? What are you thinking?

WENDY: Don't ask me that.

JAKE: Why not? I'm just wondering what's going on in your head and I thought it would be best to, you know, just put it out there. *(Beat.)* I want to connect with you.

WENDY: Please. Don't act like that.

JAKE: Like what?

WENDY: Like … like a teenage girl.

JAKE: Why do you have to be so demeaning! If a person is interested in you, interested in your thoughts… Besides, why would you say something disparaging about women? I thought you like women! Not that I'm trying to be like a woman. *(Beat.)* You're making me feel like a freak for wanting to communicate!

WENDY: Communication is good. But that was an aberration for me and it's not happening again.

(She kisses Jake's cheek. Jake sulks.)

You're a great guy —

JAKE: Those are four words no man ever wants to hear.

WENDY: Sorry, Dude.

JAKE: You used me!

WENDY: Jake …

JAKE: I know, I know. Sorry.

>   *(As Jake leaves, he takes the hair tie from his shirt pocket and tosses it to Wendy. She ties back her hair.)*

SCENE SIX

>   *(Sunset. Living room. Wendy organizes the clutter. Florence reclines on the couch, napping. Julie reads from the* Smith Alumnae Quarterly.*)*

JULIE: Here's another one: "Bitsy Lazar Williams married a brain surgeon she met at Yale Medical and has two girls, ages seven and nine; both are musical prodigies. Bitsy is an oncologist at NYU Medical Center and has written a book on how to achieve a Zen state even when life is challenging."

WENDY: You have to stop reading those.

JULIE: I can't. How about this one: "Frieda Gaffney Remington owns a consulting company focused on environmental strategy for philanthropic clients. She teaches French cooking, salsa dancing and flute, and in her spare time flies to India to mentor young women in sustainable business practices."

WENDY: You can't compare yourself to other people, Julie. No one writes to the *Quarterly* about their kids' crack addiction, or their husbands' erectile dysfunction, but that doesn't mean you're the only one going through a rough patch. You've been focusing on your creative process for all these years. A lot of your classmates would envy that.

JULIE: Oh, I doubt it.

WENDY: You don't have go to your reunion if it makes you feel so bad.

JULIE: Did you know that a Smith alum discovered the ozone hole?

(Sarah enters.)

SARAH: Hey guys. What's happening?

JULIE: Sarah, I need to ask you something. I'm hoping you'll consider it before you just say no.

SARAH: What is it?

JULIE *(tentatively):* Well … I was hoping to bring the baby to my reunion.

WENDY *(incredulous):* Isn't your reunion at the end of this month?

SARAH: There's no way I'm being induced.

JULIE: I'm not asking you to be induced! *(Beat.)* What if I just feed you spicy foods and eggplant?

SARAH: No!

JULIE: Nothing good ever happens in time for a reunion! I'm at my heaviest weight, and the lowest point of my career. The *Quarterly* just published the results of this study about career success: Nineteen women in my graduating class make over $500,000 a year; fifty percent have two or more children; twenty-six women have creative jobs that I envy —

WENDY: Reunions are designed to make people feel bad about themselves. Everyone feels like they don't measure up.

JULIE *(to Sarah):* What if we just take a little power walk together?

SARAH: Sorry.

JULIE: I need that baby! *(To herself)* No one cares about my pain.

WENDY: I care.

SARAH: Uh-oh!

FLORENCE *(wakes up, alarmed):* What's wrong?

SARAH: Is this a tick?

FLORENCE: Oh, my God! Where?!!

SARAH: Here. On my head.

(*Wendy and Florence look at Sarah's head.*)

JULIE: I don't want my baby to get Lyme disease. It's a spirochetal illness, practically like syphilis!

WENDY: It does look all bloated …

JULIE: Jesus. This place is crawling. I hate it here! We should just stay at Gurney's instead of this dumpy cottage.

WENDY: Please try to calm down.

JULIE: The longer it stays attached, the more toxic it gets! Will somebody do something?

(*Lacey enters.*)

LACEY: Hey.

JULIE: Fitness Chick! Do you know how to remove a tick?

LACEY: Let me see.

(Lacey examines Sarah's head.)

LACEY: Can you get me a pair of tweezers?

(Wendy retrieves tweezers and gives them to Lacey.)

Come here, you little mother … I got her!

(Lacey holds up the tick and tweezers victoriously.)

JULIE: Thank you!

FLORENCE: Thank God!

LACEY: Good news: She's not a deer tick.

SARAH: How can you tell?

LACEY: Based upon her size, the shape of the mouthparts, the crenulations at the posterior margin and the ornamentation of the dorsal surface, this is obviously an adult dog tick.

WENDY *(impressed):* Whoa! What's all that?

LACEY: Entymology is my sideline.

JULIE *(to Sarah):* We have to sterilize your scalp. We don't want any nasty little microbes to remain on your body.

FLORENCE: I know where the first-aid kit is. I'll help with the sterilization!

(Sarah, Florence and Julie exit.)

LACEY: Well, I'm going for a swim.

WENDY: Wait. Thank you. That was great.

LACEY: It was nothing.

WENDY: Julie was about to work herself into a frenzy. And Mom would've called an ambulance, like she always does. How'd you get so … fearless?

LACEY: My dog runs in the woods and I've had to remove a lot of ticks from her. They go for her ears and her neck.

WENDY: I didn't mean just fearless around ticks. You seem so *un-neurotic*. *(Beat.)* If you don't mind my asking, what are you doing hanging out with my seventy-year-old mother?

LACEY: I enjoy her company and I think she's brave.

WENDY: She is.

LACEY *(intimately):* So, what do you think she believes?

WENDY: Uh … Spiritually?

LACEY: No.

WENDY: About my father? I don't know. Her style of expressing herself is complicated.

LACEY: What was he like?

WENDY: He was distracted, but once you got his attention, he made you feel important. He had a good sense of humor. Sometimes too desperate for people to like him. A little self-involved, I guess. He was a complex package; she seems a little adrift without him.

LACEY: I guess everyone needs an anchor. *(Beat.)* I like to pretend that I don't.

WENDY: Ah. Me too.

> *(A moment of connection.)*

LACEY: You have a compassionate face.

WENDY *(laughs)*: Thanks, I think.

LACEY *(awkwardly)*: Well, I'm pleased to be able to hang out with you guys. Thanks for letting me be here.

WENDY: Of course. *(Beat.)* But don't you have a girlfriend somewhere who misses you?

LACEY: Nope. No one misses me at the moment.

WENDY: That's surprising.

LACEY: Not really.

WENDY *(teasing)*: If you don't return from swimming, I'll miss you.

LACEY: Come with me then.

> *(Wendy stands; Lacey grabs her hand. They exit.)*

SCENE SEVEN

> *(Early evening. The porch. Florence picks up the video camera. She sets it up on the tripod and points it toward herself.)*

FLORENCE: My name is Florence Siegel. I am nearly seventy years old. I'm a Virgo, but not as organized as you'd imagine. I grew up in Brooklyn, New York. My father was a furrier. My first real winter coat when I was a toddler was made of raccoon.

When I was younger, I was an artist. I'd set my easel near the beach and paint a portrait of someone's kid. The parents would always buy the painting because they couldn't stand the thought of their kid's picture out in the world, in someone else's possession. I never painted anyone over forty. Older people don't like the way they look. They want you to feed into their delusion and paint them the way they looked twenty years ago, but it would be dishonest.

People reach a certain age and then they spend the rest of their lives trying to outwit nature and gravity. I'm a realist: If your knees fail, maybe it's time to stop walking so much. If your face gets set in a certain grim line, maybe it's a message: Maybe it shows the world something about the faces you've been making all your life.

> *(She makes a face.)*

That's a wrap.

> *(Julie enters. As Florence moves to turn off the camera, she stumbles.)*

JULIE: Hey.

FLORENCE: Oopsy.

JULIE: Are you okay? Is your balance off?

FLORENCE: It's getting dark.

JULIE: Wendy wanted to get someone, a person to help you, but I said you wouldn't like it.

FLORENCE: I'd rather shoot myself in the head than have a caretaker. Maybe I should write that down and keep it in my box of important papers?

JULIE: Maybe you should. *(Beat.)* What's that sound?

FLORENCE: Crickets. Don't you remember?

JULIE: Weird that we're really selling this place.

FLORENCE: After nearly forty years.

JULIE: Will you miss it?

FLORENCE: Only the aspects that don't exist anymore. The way it was when we were all together, before it became Daddy's fishing cottage. Remember how you girls loved camping under the stars in the station wagon on Sunday nights? We'd put you in your pajamas late at night and we'd lay blankets in the back and you'd sleep out there, just you three —

JULIE: When we'd see the first star, we'd each make a wish. Wendy's was always something huge, like ending world hunger. Sarah's wish was always about a new stereo or bicycle.

FLORENCE: What did you wish for?

JULIE *(lying):* I don't remember.

FLORENCE: And then Daddy and I would drive the station wagon home early Monday morning, before you were even awake. You girls were so cute!

JULIE: I can't believe you let us sleep in the car! It's lucky we weren't raped and murdered.

FLORENCE: It was a different time.

JULIE: It was right around the time of Charles Manson, actually. I remember scaring Sarah by telling her that he was trolling the streets of Montauk.

FLORENCE *(laughs):* You and Wendy told her that Mrs. Flomanhoff was really Squeaky Fromme. Oh, and then you put on those Manson Family puppet shows in the basement! You've always had a wonderful imagination.

JULIE *(vulnerable):* You know what I wished for on all of those stars? I wished that things between all of us would stay as they were, all of us together as a family. I didn't want to have to grow up and move out and not live with you and Dad.

FLORENCE: That's sweet.

JULIE: Somehow, I knew, even then, that I was going to be a failure. I could feel little pieces of failure start to attach themselves to me, like porcupine quills. *(Builds slowly to a rant.)* You gather pieces of loss the same way you accumulate physical injuries: You hurt your knee and it doesn't quite heal, then a nerve in your tooth doesn't settle down, and if you fall on your coccyx, you never sit comfortably again. Emotional disappointment is similar: When you're young, you think you're in charge of your life. But then you get bashed at work, and your friends all start to have babies, and the man you desperately want never looks your way and you can't even say hello to him … and your breasts start to sag … and you finally realize that you're no longer even in the running!

FLORENCE: You are not a failure! You're a creative person, and you're gorgeous. And you just wrote a screenplay!

JULIE: There is no screenplay! I tried and I tried, but then I got to page fourteen and I just stopped. I've been trying to get a real job, but no one hires me. They look at me and they just can tell that there's something wrong with me.

FLORENCE: There's nothing wrong with you! You're a wonderful, very special smart girl — the most compassionate of my children, which is why you've always been my favorite. You remember that, Julie Siegel!

JULIE *(grimly):* Thanks.

FLORENCE: Look, I've heard you compare yourself unfavorably to everyone. But just remember, at the end of the day, everyone takes off her clothes and takes down her hair. Once you strip naked, all that's left is your essence — and no one has anything on you, no matter how much money they make or how many Zumba classes and private yoga lessons they take.

(*Florence stands. She pulls off her wig and tosses it off the porch.*)

JULIE: Oh, my God. I didn't know you were wearing a wig.

FLORENCE: All that recent stress made my hair thin, but who cares?

(*Florence takes off her shirt and stands in her bra.*)

JULIE (*alarmed*): Mom! What are you doing?

FLORENCE: I am being myself! Either I am beautiful or not beautiful, but I am me! And who I am is okay! Am I right?

JULIE: Yes, you're right, but … don't take anything else off! Please!

FLORENCE: Stop stifling me!

JULIE: Just put your clothes back on and sit down!

FLORENCE: There are a couple of great equalizers in life. Do you know what they are? Death and diarrhea. No matter how much success or fame or money you have, you can't escape those two things. (*Beat.*) Julie, can you help me with something? Just between us? I don't want your sisters to know.

JULIE: Okay.

FLORENCE: How long does a respectable widow wait before dating?

JULIE: It's been three months. Life is short. You'd better get on it.

FLORENCE: You're the writer. Will you help me with a personal ad?

JULIE: Sure.

FLORENCE: Get the pencil and paper and let's go! I'm not getting any younger.

> (Julie fishes around in her bag and pulls out a scrap of paper and a pen.)

JULIE: Let's describe who you are and what you're looking for.

FLORENCE: Okay. How old am I?

JULIE *(concerned):* You don't remember?

FLORENCE: Don't be daft. How old am I for the sake of JDate? How about this: "Elegant fifty-five-year-old woman who offers and demands honesty —"

JULIE: Wait. Are you really saying "fifty-five" and "honesty" in the same sentence?

FLORENCE: "With high IQ and strong libido —"

JULIE: Don't mention your *libido*! You don't want a man who just wants you for sex!

FLORENCE: Maybe I do! My ladies' group had a discussion about this. Our children don't want to see us as sexual beings.

JULIE *(impatient):* Maybe Sarah should help you.

FLORENCE: Sarah has enough on her head. She's having a baby.

JULIE: I'm having a baby. Sarah is just carrying her.

FLORENCE: She's the one with the mood swings and the swollen ankles, but okay, whatever you say. Don't you think you should find a person for yourself? Man, woman, transperson. Whatever?

JULIE: It's just going to be me and Brianna, and that's okay for now.

FLORENCE: What about Jake?

JULIE: Jake? Jake Shilowitz?

FLORENCE: He makes a nice appearance and he has a good heart.

JULIE: If I recall correctly, you described him as a "sweaty grunty man."

FLORENCE: Unsuitable for my lesbian daughter, but very nice for you.

JULIE (flustered): I thought we were working on your ad.

FLORENCE: Okay, write this down: "Hot fifty-two-year-old woman seeks honest, kind man for hooking up and who knows what else?"

(Julie writes for a moment.)

JULIE: Got it.

SCENE EIGHT

(Late evening. Julie and Wendy in their pajamas. Julie throws clothes into a box. Wendy gathers fishing poles and shotguns.)

WENDY: I'm reading this book about mothers who drown their children. I think that's half the reason I never had a child: What if you just go crazy and do something horrible?

JULIE: That's a delightful thing to say to an expectant mother.

WENDY: I think it's brave to have children. Especially if you're smart or thoughtful enough to think about all the reasons it's insane, which you obviously are. I mean, children get bullied, they get hurt, they get abducted —

JULIE: A few more hours with you could undo seventeen years of therapy and all my efforts at self-soothing.

WENDY: Why did he have to buy a new fishing pole every season? He never caught anything.

(She points to the striped bass mounted on the wall.)

I don't think we're supposed to know, but Uncle Bruce caught that one.

JULIE: My back hurts.

WENDY: Let's take a break.

JULIE: You know what I resent? Here we are, just you and me, as usual.

WENDY: We can't expect her to help. She's too big, she's short of breath. She can't bend over.

JULIE: She could sit and be supportive instead of drinking virgin daiquiris in the yard with Mom.

WENDY: She needs her rest. And Mom can't deal.

JULIE: I can't believe she's only waiting a few months before the next one. That's a brutal way to treat your body.

WENDY: She must really need the money.

JULIE: Are you trying to make me feel worse?

WENDY: Sorry. Help me move this last box and then we'll stop.

JULIE: Listen, I need to tell you something: Nina called me this morning.

WENDY: She called you? Why?

JULIE: She told me you stopped seeing your clients.

WENDY: That's not her business.

JULIE: She cares about you, Wendy. What are you doing?

WENDY: I told them I had to go on leave.

JULIE: Don't they need you to be consistent?

WENDY: Sometimes things happen. Therapy is like life; sometimes there are interruptions.

JULIE: I don't think you could really believe that it's okay to dump your clients.

(Sarah enters with bags from Starbucks.)

SARAH: Take a break, everyone! Lacey got us pastries and coffee!

(Sarah hands out pastries and coffee and drinks from a huge cup of coffee.)

JULIE: Uh, Sarah? I thought you were caffeine-free?

SARAH: Not anymore.

JULIE: You promised —

SARAH: Oh well. You promised me $32,000.

WENDY: Sarah. She'll pay you.

JULIE: I wonder how much we'll actually get from Dad's estate. I hope it's enough so I can take time off from writing and just be a mother for a while.

SARAH: I hope it's enough so I can buy a house.

WENDY: I hope there's enough for Mom to be comfortable so she won't have to worry about anything as she gets older.

SARAH: What about you, Wendy? What do you want for yourself?

WENDY: I have what I need.

JULIE: It must be hard to be so much more evolved than everyone else.

WENDY: There's no harm in fantasizing about an inheritance, but I don't think we'll end up with anything. If that woman wins the lawsuit, she might get everything, including this house.

JULIE: You are such a downer. *(To Sarah)* Oh, my God! You're not using Splenda! Splenda is poison.

SARAH: Don't be so controlling! Just be thankful that you're not adopting a baby from a toothless drug addict who's turning tricks for Twinkies and crack.

WENDY *(to Sarah):* Remember when we used to get stoned and bake?

JULIE: Dad must have known that we squeezed the weed out of his joints until they were all paper.

WENDY: When was the last time the three of us got high together?

SARAH: My graduation from Bennington. Julie threw up on Joshua's pants and he broke up with me.

JULIE: I had a virus.

WENDY: Let's walk down to the beach and get high right now! I could excavate Dad's pot.

JULIE: No!

WENDY: Oh, right.

SARAH: Where *is* Dad's pot anyway?

WENDY: He made me promise never to tell.

SARAH: He didn't mean after he was *dead*.

JULIE: Why are you still the only one who knows? It's not fair — you're *still* the favorite.

> *(Jake enters.)*

JAKE: Hey! I'm back and better than ever!

WENDY: Hey, Jake. Do you have any weed?

JAKE: Nah. I ran out. But I was thinking maybe we could all just, you know … converse.

> *(Sarah walks to the door.)*

SARAH: I have to go lie down.

JULIE: Hang out for a while, Sarah. You just got here.

WENDY: Let her go. She needs her rest.

> *(Sarah exits.)*

JULIE *(to Wendy):* Now go get Dad's weed.

WENDY: You two go into the bathroom. You can't see the hiding spot.

JULIE: No. You're a ridiculous and secretive person.

> *(Wendy feels around for a hidden wall panel; she removes a shoebox from inside the wall and pulls out a monstrous bag of marijuana.)*

JAKE: Holy shit. It's the Mother Lode!

JULIE: Whoa, Daddy!

> *(Julie starts rolling joints. Jake pokes around in the wall.)*

JAKE: Hey. There's another box back here.

JULIE: Maybe that's where he keeps his heroin. Who has a lighter?

WENDY: Check the kitchen.

> *(Julie exits to offstage kitchen. Jake pulls the second box out from the wall and opens it.)*

JAKE: There's a book here. It's handwritten, like a journal. And an envelope … *(Jake opens it.)* Photographs.

WENDY: Of what?

JAKE *(stricken)*: Holy shit. It's really bad.

WENDY: What do you mean? Let me see!

JAKE *(nervously)*: What they said about your father … These are pictures of women —

WENDY: Give them to me!

JAKE: He's wearing no shirt. They're sucking on his —

WENDY: No!

JAKE: It's not his penis. It's his … It's like he's … nursing them.

WENDY: Nursing?

JAKE: Like a baby. He's holding them in his arms and they're —

(Wendy grabs the photos.)

WENDY: Ewww. It's his nipples. Why is he doing that?

(Julie enters.)

JAKE (loudly): Hi, Julie!

JULIE: I can't find the lighter. Are we going to have to rub two sticks together? I guess we could use the gas stove. (Beat.) Is something wrong?

WENDY: No! Everything is fine.

(Julie grabs a photograph and looks at it.)

JULIE: Oh, my God.

SCENE NINE

(Midnight. Wendy, Julie and Sarah are in the living room; Florence, alone on the porch, talks to the video camera. Wendy reads aloud from random pages of her father's red journal.)

WENDY: Listen to this.

JULIE: If that's Dad's journal, I don't want to hear it.

WENDY: Just listen. It's fascinating. *(Reads from the journal.)* "What we each have inside of us is an enormous untapped capacity to be nurturers. If you are a man, you've been taught to disown this part of yourself. There is a huge cost associated with this disownment, which may be more aptly described as dismemberment."

JULIE *(hands over her ears)*: La la la la la.

FLORENCE *(to the camera)*: My friends discuss their husbands' eccentricities and their habits and shortcomings. Some of these things I have not wanted to know. You don't want to envision certain things when you sit across the table from someone, sharing a meal.

WENDY *(reading)*: "If you are a male psychotherapist, you are encouraged to pathologize your patients and disavow any feelings for them, or to acknowledge counter-transference but to treat it as something about which to be 'extremely cautious.'"

SARAH: I didn't notice the effect that he had on other people until I was about eighteen. I was eating lunch on the outdoor patio of a cafe and I saw everyone around me crane their necks toward the entrance. He was walking in his tall lanky way, leaning forward, half-smiling. His hair was windswept, his face a bit craggy but still rugged and boyish. I saw that familiar motion of his head, moving from side to side, taking in everything and nothing as he walked. It was in that moment that I saw him the way other people see him: striking and hip. You look at him and wait for him to see you. You need for him to notice you; everyone does. It was an astounding experience, like waking up one day and realizing that your father is Mick Jagger.

WENDY *(reading)*: "It is not our maleness that we reject; we embrace our maleness. But we need to reject the paradigm that renders us mute, cold and ungenerous, when we are meant to be warm nurturers. The role of the male therapist is misunderstood not only in therapeutic practice, but in its depiction in literature and the cinema."

JULIE: Please stop.

FLORENCE *(to the camera):* Esther's husband, Larry, is the worst. He keeps a knife under the pillow because he's afraid someone will break in while he sleeps and hurt his wife. But sometimes Larry pretends that he climbed through the window and Esther has to fight him off. Larry likes it when she kicks and screams, and the more she fights, the easier it is for him to get off.

WENDY *(reading):* "Women who have never given birth are called 'nulliparous.' Note the word *null*. A man's inability to become pregnant makes him even less valuable in the matrocentric family system."

FLORENCE *(to the camera):* Pearl's husband has dirty underwear. When Pearl talks about it, you can tell she's not complaining that he doesn't change it often enough. She means shit stains.

SARAH: Then when he does see you, you feel like the most important person in the world. His attention is so full and clear. You drink in the feeling. You believe, for a moment, that you are cradled in love.

WENDY *(reading):* "Men's breasts are considered more or less to be vestigial, remnants of a time prior to sexual differentiation. But this view assumes that the only function of a breast is milk production, when in actuality breasts also provide comfort, support and bonding."

JULIE: Shut the fuck up!

FLORENCE *(to the camera):* Bernice's husband makes her call him "Daddy."

WENDY *(reading):* "Who am I to my patients? In my struggle to define my role, I must relinquish all obstacles, including gender. I imagine myself a healer, a Shaman, a Goddess, a mother; a metaphorical breast … giving and feeding and nurturing."

JULIE: That's disgusting.

SCENE TEN

(2 a.m. bathroom. Wendy takes a bath in a big claw-foot tub surrounded by lit candles. Lacey enters and is very startled to see Wendy there.)

LACEY: Oh! I'm sorry —

WENDY: It's okay. I forgot to lock it. Sometimes when I can't sleep I take a bath.

LACEY: I do that too! *(Awkwardly.)* I'll see you in the morning.

(Lacey turns to leave.)

WENDY: Wait. Do you want to hang out and talk?

LACEY: Uh, sure. *(Beat.)* Uh … have you read any good books lately?

WENDY *(laughs):* No.

LACEY *(embarrassed):* Should I just sit here on the edge?

WENDY: If you're comfortable. *(Beat.)* Or, you could come in, if you want to.

LACEY: Would I have to take off everything?

WENDY: You're in charge of what comes off.

(Lacey strips to her underwear and climbs into the opposite end of the tub.)

WENDY: I can't help but notice that when we went swimming, you were naked —

LACEY: It was dark out, and you were ten yards away.

WENDY *(laughs)*: Every time I swam in your direction, you swam away!

LACEY: My head wanted to be near you, but my arms kept swimming me away. *(Beat.)* So, what do you want to talk about?

WENDY: I was just ruminating about my practice. I don't know if I want to be a therapist anymore, but I don't know what I want to do with my life. Let's talk about something else.

    (They stare at each other.)

LACEY: Do you want me to just … wash your hair?

WENDY: That's a little more intimacy than I could tolerate right now.

LACEY: Okay. *(Beat.)* So, why don't you want to be a therapist anymore?

WENDY: I'm afraid I'll do more harm than good.

LACEY: Is that your foot?

WENDY: No.

LACEY *(embarrassed)*: Sorry. *(Beat.)* You don't seem like you'd hurt anyone —

WENDY: You don't really know me yet.

LACEY: I'd like to know you.

WENDY: Everyone assumed my father was good at what he did, but he was screwed up. We probably don't even know the half of it.

LACEY: If he was screwed up, I'm sure you're not like him.

WENDY: That's the thing: Maybe I am. And if there's any remote chance that I'm at all like him —

LACEY: He must be different from you in a thousand different ways.

WENDY: I don't know.

LACEY: Just so you know, if you were my therapist, I would trust you.

WENDY *(laughs):* That's sweet. But if I were your therapist, we wouldn't be taking a bath together.

LACEY: Oh, right. Then I'm glad you're not my therapist.

(They kiss. They wrap themselves around each other.)

SCENE ELEVEN

(Early morning. The porch. Florence, in her nightgown, videotapes herself, with the camera on a tripod.)

FLORENCE: The typical portrait of a woman who stays with her husband through a crisis is misleading. You have to be strong to endure media attention. People stare at you in the produce aisle. No one remembers to avert her eyes in the dressing room at Macy's.

At first you think it's sympathy, but maybe it's actually a way of feeling separate and superior, like it could never happen to them. Sometimes I run into acquaintances from the temple, and they pretend I've turned invisible. I saw

Marjorie Stackman in Whole Foods the other day, and she walked right by. I said, "Marjorie! Marjorie Stackman!" I said it three times; finally, she turned around. I said, "I just want you to know I'm still here. I'm still a person in the universe, which means you didn't obliterate me." She just cleared her throat and walked away. (Beat.) That's a wrap.

SCENE TWELVE

(Early morning. Birds chirp loudly. A decorated birthday cake sits on the table. A banner on the wall says "Happy Birthday, Mom!" The mess is gone; a few things remain, organized into piles and boxes. Guns are piled neatly. Wendy climbs onto the couch, exhausted. Jake and Julie enter.)

JULIE: Look what we got. A paper shredder. A really excellent one.

WENDY: We don't need a paper shredder.

JAKE: Let's make a list. A major to-do list that will guide us through the wilderness we're currently experiencing.

WENDY: We're not in the wilderness, Rambo.

JAKE: First, we should shred the journal and flush the pieces. No one will ever know about it but us —

WENDY: That's like believing you can just make the sick reality disappear. And I haven't finished reading it.

JULIE: But Mom is fragile and Sarah is prone to hysteria. (Beat.) Why didn't any of the women say anything about photos?

WENDY: They look candid. Maybe he used a hidden camera.

JULIE: That's so creepy!

JAKE: Couldn't there be an explanation? I mean, maybe some therapists —

WENDY: Maybe some therapists have their patients suck their nipples? No, I don't think there's much room for misinterpretation. *(Beat.)* But do you think we should have known? I mean, were there were any clues in our own lives that we ignored?

JULIE: Are you suggesting that we're supposed to remember some bizarrely inappropriate moment in which Dad did something? Because I don't think I do.

WENDY: Well, maybe his blatant failure to uphold boundaries only occurred when he was in the proscribed role of therapist, or so-called "nurturer."

JULIE: That sounds good to me. Let's go with that.

WENDY: What should we do about Mom's birthday? She'll be waking up soon.

JULIE: "Happy Birthday. We found pictures of your husband's titties."

(Florence and Lacey enter. Florence is totally speedy.)

FLORENCE *(singing maniacally):* Happy Birthday to me! Happy Birthday to me!

WENDY: Happy Birthday, Mom.

LACEY: Florence and I just went for a little trot on the beach. I could barely keep up.

FLORENCE *(hyper):* Are we eating breakfast out? Should I cook?

WENDY: Mom. What's going on? Are you back on the diet pills?

FLORENCE (*dancing as she talks*): They're herbal this time. Very gentle! The thing is, it makes me want to move! I have news: I spoke to the lawyer. I didn't want to tell you because I didn't want to upset you, but Suzanne Edelstein is trying to sue Dad's estate. The good news is that Suzanne Edelstein is not a reliable witness. She has problems. She's on medication for depression!

WENDY: Half the people we know are on meds for depression.

JAKE: I take Wellbutrin. No sexual side effects.

FLORENCE: Dad's attorney said he'll drag in everyone she knows to testify about her mental health, even her coworkers. Hopefully that will give her the incentive to drop the suit.

WENDY: Wouldn't that make you feel horrible?

FLORENCE: Horrible? Why?

LACEY: He'd be manipulating that poor woman into being afraid to testify.

FLORENCE: That's what lawyers do!

WENDY (*to Julie*): Maybe we should show her.

JULIE: Not a good idea.

FLORENCE: Show me what?

WENDY: We found Dad's hidden journal and photographs. They're very disturbing.

FLORENCE (*lightly*): I'm disturbed enough already.

WENDY: Just look at this before deciding to allow the lawyer to just pretend this woman is crazy.

FLORENCE: I said *no*.

LACEY *(to Florence)*: Do you want me to look at them first?

JULIE: What are you, her guardian?

(Lacey grabs the photos and looks at them.)

LACEY: Whoa. I can't believe he got so many women to do this.

FLORENCE *(yelling)*: What is wrong with you people? This is turning into the worst birthday ever!

JAKE *(to Florence)*: There's a journal too —

(Florence grabs the shotgun and points it at them. Jake puts his hands up and drops the journal. Everyone drops to the floor.)

JAKE: Jesus, Florence. Put that thing down!

FLORENCE: I want all of this crap put away now! I don't want to hear another word about it.

(Florence points the gun at the ceiling and fires it.)

JULIE: Oh, my God. Mom!

LACEY: I don't feel safe in this house.

JULIE: No one does.

(Florence drops the gun and exits.)

WENDY: Wow. She really can't handle it.

JAKE: Maybe we should have sung "Happy Birthday."

JULIE: Let's put this stuff away right now.

(Sarah enters. Everyone freezes. Bird sounds become very loud.)

SARAH: Hi guys!

JAKE: Hi, Sarah!

LACEY: Top of the morning.

JULIE *(feigned cheerfulness)*: Hey, Sarah! How'd you sleep?

SARAH: Those Goddamn birds woke me up at five, rude as ever. *(Beat.)* What's going on?

JAKE: Nothing!

WENDY: Let's make pancakes! Remember when we made pancakes for Mother's Day, but we didn't know they had to be cooked?

SARAH: Why is it that when I come in, everyone stops talking? Is something wrong?

JULIE: No.

SARAH: Is something on my face?

WENDY: No. You're beautiful.

(Jake surreptitiously takes the photos from Julie.)

SARAH *(to Jake)*: What's in your hand?

JAKE: Uh … Nothing.

JULIE: Don't let her —!

(Sarah grabs the photos away from him and begins to flip through them.)

WENDY: Sarah —

SARAH: What the hell? Holy shit. (*Laughing hysterically.*) Oh, my God. Are those his —?

JULIE: Yes.

(*Sarah continues to laugh; it reaches an hysterical pitch.*)

SARAH (*still laughing*): You were keeping this from me!

WENDY: We didn't want to upset you.

SARAH: I'm not upset, but I might poke my eyes out. I mean, do you see the size of his nipples?

JAKE: His areolas are rather shocking.

JULIE: Maybe he used a breast pump. I read something on the internet about that, about how even men can make their milk ducts work.

WENDY: He may even have tried to produce milk for his clients.

SARAH: That's disgusting! Why would he do that?

WENDY: He did write about "mothering" his clients. He created a theory —

SARAH: Mothering? Well, it would be the least horrible interpretation.

JULIE: Do you really believe that he wasn't doing it for his own sexual pleasure?

SARAH: It's not about sexual pleasure. It's obviously about nurturance!

JULIE: Are you kidding? Look again.

SARAH: They're sucking his nipples, not his … wiener.

LACEY: Maybe he had an erection while he nursed them.

SARAH *(deeply disturbed):* Eeeww!

WENDY: Men do get sexual pleasure from their nipples.

SARAH: How would *you* know? You're a lesbian.

JAKE *(mutters to himself):* Sort of.

LACEY *(to Jake):* It's true, isn't it? Men's nipples are a locus of sexual pleasure.

JAKE: Uh, I can't really speak for all men …

JULIE: Speak for yourself: Do you or do you not derive sexual pleasure from your nipples?

>   *(They all stare at Jake.)*

JAKE: Uh —

WENDY: Maybe it's too personal.

JAKE *(beat, courageously):* No, I'm not afraid to say it: I do have sexual feelings in my nipples.

SARAH: Okay, fine. Jake is a freak. That doesn't mean Daddy was.

JAKE *(to Sarah):* Why so ḥarsh, Dude?

SARAH: Don't call me "Dude," you nipple-loving freak!

WENDY *(to Jake):* All parts of the body are pleasurable, and that's okay.

LACEY: I read *Our Bodies, Ourselves* too, but I don't think that's the question on the table.

JULIE *(to Sarah):* Do you really think you can tell if someone is a creepy pervert just by looking?

WENDY: They actually do everything they can to hide it and make it look like something else.

JULIE: They say, "Hi, I'm a warm and nurturing man. Just pop this in your mouth —"

SARAH: Stop! Daddy was *not* a pervert!

JULIE: If you google "sexual perpetrator" and "professional," you'll see that every sleazebag who's caught fondling someone has an excuse. Teachers say that their students made it up. Clergy people say they were teaching their parishioners to find God. Doctors say they were researching sexual lubrication — or looking for their missing sandwich.

SARAH: Stop it!

JAKE *(amused):* Plumbers say they're cleaning your pipes; mailmen say they're stuffing your box —

SARAH *(losing it):* It's not funny! That's not what Daddy did!

> *(Sarah grabs the birthday cake from the table.)*

WENDY: Please don't wreck Mom's eighty-dollar cake! We can't replace it. The bakery is closed today.

SARAH: You people make me sick!

> *(Julie grabs the cake from Sarah.)*

WENDY: Daddy loved you, Sarah.

SARAH: Don't say that!

> *(Bird chirping becomes louder. Sarah freaks out.)*

I can't stand the sound — everything is so noisy. *(Yells.)* I don't want to hear those little motherfuckers anymore!

> *(Sarah grabs a broom, rushes to the window. Jake tries to block it.)*

SARAH: Out of my way, freak!

JAKE: Wait —

> *(Sarah kicks Jake in the crotch and pushes the nest out of the window with the broom. The chirps stop abruptly.)*

JULIE *(beat)*: We could have called the wildlife organization.

SARAH: I hate you all!

> *(Sarah storms out. Wendy follows her out.)*

JULIE *(to Jake)*: Is there anything we can do to save them?

JAKE: Even if they survived the fall, the mother won't come back.

LACEY *(bereft)*: Oh … that poor mother. Those poor babies. *(Beat.)* I'd better go bury them.

SCENE THIRTEEN

> *(Florence enters the empty living room. She collapses onto the couch and looks through the photos slowly. She is devastated. She takes the photos and leaves.)*

SCENE FOURTEEN

> *(Sarah sits on the porch, pumping breast milk. Wendy drinks whiskey from a bottle. Lacey enters carrying an elaborately decorated wooden box.)*

LACEY: I couldn't find a shovel, so I built a little mausoleum for the birds. I'll put it in a tree so that the other animals can't get at them.

WENDY: It's beautiful.

LACEY *(to Sarah):* I also wanted to make sure you were okay.

SARAH: Thanks.

LACEY: Don't torment yourself too much. Everybody does something crazy at some point. *(Beat.)* I slept with my mother's boyfriend once.

SARAH: Oh, man. How old were you?

LACEY: Fifteen.

SARAH: Fifteen! The guy must have been a total creep.

LACEY: He was pretty nice, actually. I wanted it to happen.

SARAH: He was the adult. He's the one who should have stopped it.

LACEY: I got him to do it; I didn't know why it felt so important, but it was this *urge* — almost physical, like the need to pee when you wake up in the morning. I couldn't rest until it happened. Right after, he called me and I wouldn't call him back. He felt guilty about what happened between us and he hated himself, so he broke up with my mother and never told her why. And then my mother cried for a year and had to go on antidepressants. *(Beat.)* We've never really been close since then.

WENDY: That's pretty heavy.

LACEY: It's not the only crazy thing I've done.

WENDY: I've done crazy things too.

SARAH: No, you haven't. You're the perfect one.

WENDY: That's bullshit.

SARAH: I don't believe you've ever stepped out of the lines, Wendy Elizabeth Siegel.

LACEY (amused): Wendy Elizabeth.

WENDY: Shut up, Sarah Naomi Siegel. It's not true; I've "stepped out of the lines" plenty.

SARAH: For example?

WENDY: I broke up with Nina because our relationship began badly; I could never get over it.

LACEY: She was already with someone else and you stole her away? Or — I know! — she was straight and you flipped her?

WENDY: Worse. (Beat.) When I first met her, she was my client.

SARAH: I thought you met her at the dentist.

LACEY (excited): You started sleeping with her while she was your client? Did you get her to lie down on the couch and you got on top of her?

WENDY: I saw her for a couple of months and then realized we were really attracted to each other, so I referred her to a friend and decided to forget her. But then a few weeks later, we ended up at the same dentist. We both got our teeth cleaned; she walked me out to the parking lot.

LACEY: And then you did it right there? You had sex in your car in the parking lot?

WENDY: Don't be ridiculous. *(Beat.)* We had a date that night and then she moved in.

LACEY *(awed)*: Wow.

SARAH: You broke up with her because of Dad?

WENDY: We were together for two years; even though I did what I thought was right, I could never stop feeling like I was doing something wrong. We broke up three weeks ago.

LACEY: Maybe you two were meant to be together. Maybe your love is bigger than the rules.

WENDY: There's no way to get totally right with something like that.

LACEY: Maybe there are exceptions.

WENDY: People always want to believe that.

SARAH: Nina always had dirt under her fingernails.

WENDY: It was paint.

SARAH: She was bossy and critical and she always wore that ugly brown sweat suit.

WENDY: She was my *client.*

SARAH: At least you guys didn't kill anyone.

SCENE FIFTEEN

(Early afternoon. Jake sits on the porch, drinking beer. He picks up Sarah's breast pump and tinkers with it. He

166

attaches it to his nipple. It makes a rhythmic pumping sound. After a few moments Julie enters. She watches him, amused. Then he notices her.)

JULIE *(amused):* Hey.

JAKE: Oh, hi! *(He quickly removes the breast pump.)*

I made something for you.

(He reaches under the chair, pulls something out and hands it to her.)

JULIE: A bassinet! Thank you. That's so sweet.

JAKE: That's just the way I roll. I need to get you a baby mattress that fits inside. *(Awkwardly.)* So … you must be excited?

JULIE: Terrified, really.

JAKE: I can't exactly talk you out of that.

JULIE: Birdhouses, baby houses. You've got a theme going.

JAKE: Shelter. I didn't even think of that. I was reading this book to my niece about animal fathers and their babies. There's a frog species called Darwin's Frogs where the father guards the eggs and then carries the babies around in his mouth after they're born.

JULIE: In his mouth? That's disgusting.

JAKE: Seahorse dads carry the babies in a pouch. I was thinking that's the kind of thing I'd contribute, if I ever had a baby. I could build a nest. Or I could be like those male penguins that sit on the eggs half the time. I wouldn't mind.

JULIE: I don't know how I could think about bringing a baby into this world. The oceans are sick; the air is toxic; seals have viruses; honeybees are becoming extinct —

JAKE: It'll be okay, Julie.

JULIE: People abuse kids and get away with it; the world is at war; I'm totally preoccupied with thoughts about terrorism; just when you think you know someone, you find out that he's a different person than you ever imagined. Everything is so fucked up!

JAKE *(calmly):* That's true. It's also true that right in this moment, right here and now, everything is okay.

JULIE: Maybe.

> *(Julie rests her head lightly on Jake's shoulder. After a moment, she sits up.)*

JULIE: Are you a Buddhist, Jake Shilowitz?

JAKE: Just a regular guy.

SCENE SIXTEEN

> *(Wendy and Florence are in the living room.)*

FLORENCE: I have something I want to give you, Honey.

WENDY: What is it?

FLORENCE: This ring that I bought in Italy.

> *(Florence takes her ring off and hands it to Wendy.)*

WENDY: It's beautiful, but you still wear it —

FLORENCE: I'd rather give it to you while I'm still alive.

168

WENDY: You're not dying, Mom.

FLORENCE: I have some things for Julie and Sarah too. Nothing as valuable as this ring, but I'll give them something at the same time so they don't get resentful that you're my favorite. *(Beat.)* I'm concerned about you and Lacey. She's not the right person for you.

WENDY: You don't need to be concerned about who's the right person for me. Anyway, I thought you wanted to ensure my sacred commitment to pussy.

FLORENCE: I have something important to tell you, but you can't tell your sisters.

WENDY: I hate when you do that.

FLORENCE: Can I trust you or not?

WENDY: No. I don't want to be the one to hold all the family craziness.

FLORENCE *(confidentially):* A long time ago, when I was in my teens, I fell in love with someone that I wasn't supposed to be with.

WENDY: Who?

FLORENCE: It was a person who was considered taboo.

WENDY: So, you're saying "this person" was, what? A drug addict? A person of a different race? A woman? You were with a woman!

FLORENCE: No, but I'm sure if I was, I'd stick with it. I wouldn't flop back and forth like a fish.

WENDY: So, what was so taboo? You were with a cross-dresser. Wait: He was a *goy*!

FLORENCE: He was a nice Jewish boy.

WENDY: Okay, I'll bite: What was the problem?

FLORENCE *(whispers):* My mother and his mother were sisters.

WENDY: What? You're telling me you had a relationship with Uncle Bruce?

FLORENCE: No! God forbid. Uncle Ruby.

WENDY: The one with polio?

FLORENCE: Well, he didn't have polio at the time. But it wouldn't have mattered to me. I was crazy about him.

WENDY: He was your first cousin.

FLORENCE: We didn't care; we were in love. Anyway, he joined the Air Force and we wrote to each other every day. But when he came back on leave that first time, I could tell he was a different person. He didn't say much anymore.

WENDY: Why? What happened to him?

FLORENCE: He wouldn't tell me. He just went silent. Anyway, I happened to meet your father on the same day that I realized that I wouldn't be happy with Uncle Ruby. Your father was very chatty and charming and I knew he'd never stop talking. I'm glad that I didn't stay with Ruby; I don't think our family would ever have gotten over the … incest. On the other hand, my love for your father was never quite as profound.

WENDY: Why are you telling me this?

FLORENCE: Because I've seen what's going on, and you can't be with Lacey.

WENDY: Sorry, but if there's a connection, I don't get it.

FLORENCE: Early in our marriage, your father had some affairs. He was what we then called "gregarious," but now might be called a sex addict. *(Beat.)* Anyway, he once told me that he had a rendezvous at a pharmaceutical conference —

WENDY: Mom, do you think I really want to know this?

FLORENCE: I didn't find out about it until many years later. His daughter from what he referred to as "The Quaalude Incident" contacted him about five years ago and he asked me how I felt about him meeting her. I encouraged him to see her, but so far as I know, he didn't. Then, when Lacey showed up, I knew it was her.

WENDY: So Lacey — You're saying that Lacey is —?

FLORENCE: Yes, that's what I'm saying. You can't go around humping your half-sister!

WENDY: Get out! You said she was your —

FLORENCE: Do I *look* like I've been doing Pilates?

WENDY: I don't believe you.

FLORENCE: She stalked me! She must have wanted to meet her relatives.

WENDY: I'll ask her myself.

FLORENCE: Fine. Go ahead.

(Wendy walks to the door, then turns around.)

WENDY: Mom. I need to ask you something. *(Beat.)* Did you believe Daddy?

FLORENCE: Your father could make anything he did sound selfless. He could justify anything.

WENDY: So you're saying you knew he was guilty?

FLORENCE: I did not say that.

WENDY *(gently):* Let's just speak hypothetically: Why would a person stay with someone who they knew wasn't innocent?

FLORENCE: Your father said his work was groundbreaking and that people wouldn't understand. What did I know?

WENDY: You never let yourself imagine that he did something wrong?

FLORENCE: Of course, I did. *(Beat.)* What if someone you love is sick, only the illness isn't cancer, it's something else, something in their mind? If you found out that someone you love had done something wrong and you knew that he wasn't an evil person, you would think it was his sickness that was responsible. You would hope that he would get help.

WENDY: But could such a person actually get better?

FLORENCE: How should I know?

WENDY: I'm not saying you know. I'm just wondering what you think.

FLORENCE: If he had love and support, if his family stood by him, maybe he could get better. *(Beat.)* The question in such a case is not whether or not you believe him. The question is, How do you go on?

SCENE SEVENTEEN

(Late afternoon. Lights up on the porch and the living room simultaneously. Jake and Julie kiss in the living room. Wendy and Lacey stand on the porch, kissing. The two scenes are entirely separate.)

JAKE: The thing is, I feel like we've known each other for a long time.

JULIE *(giddy):* Well, we have!

WENDY: I just want you to know: My mother told me.

LACEY: She did?

WENDY: And I know I should care, but I'm not sure I do. I mean, it's not like we grew up in the same family…

    (They kiss.)

JAKE: I've known your family forever.

JULIE: I had a huge crush on you when we were kids.

JAKE : I always thought you were beautiful.

    (They kiss.)

LACEY: You're not mad?

WENDY: How could I be mad? I mean, I don't think you intended for this to happen, did you?

LACEY: No. I was surprised that your mother welcomed me; I really wanted to get to know you guys, but I wasn't sure she'd allow it.

WENDY: You know, it's not uncommon for relatives who grew up apart to meet late in life and be incredibly attracted to one another. I mean, the blood-relative thing is a little freaky, and I guess it would be a serious problem if we were straight and wanted kids …

LACEY: "Blood relative"? *(Beat.)* What are you talking about?

WENDY *(alarmed):* What? Mom said you knew —

JAKE: I was a little afraid of you.

JULIE: Me? You were afraid of *me*?

JAKE: You seem so confident and so powerful.

JULIE: *Me?*

JAKE: I really *love* children.

JULIE: The only thing I feel badly about is that this one wasn't created from your body.

JAKE: I could get beyond that.

JULIE: Really? It's not apparent at first, but you really are cool!

>   *(Julie and Jake kiss.)*

LACEY: Your mom said we were *related*?

WENDY: She said you're Fred's daughter from an affair. She'd better not be fucking with me …

LACEY: I'm not Fred's daughter.

WENDY: Thank you, Jesus!

>   *(Wendy kisses Lacey passionately.)*

JAKE: I think you're really cool too.

JULIE: I guess I should tell you: My sexual experience with men is pretty limited.

JAKE: That can't be true. I mean, I believe you if you say so, but you're so … beautiful.

(Julie and Jake kiss.)

LACEY: I thought your mother knew: I was Fred's patient.

WENDY: You were his what?!

LACEY: You just said you knew! I thought Florence knew —

(Wendy breaks away from the embrace.)

WENDY: Do you really think she would have invited you here if she knew you were his patient?

LACEY: Yes! Well, I didn't know what to think; I felt so upset and confused after what happened, and then he was gone, and I realized that I didn't even know anyone who knew him. At first, I thought I wanted something that belonged to him, some little object, like a pen or a rock, but then I realized that I needed to know people who had a *connection* to him —

WENDY: I think you should leave.

LACEY *(incredulous):* You're kicking me out?

WENDY: You were his *patient*!

LACEY: I'm not his patient anymore!

WENDY: Don't you realize how fucked up this is? I'm a therapist!

LACEY: But you're not *my* therapist. And anyway, you're not even practicing anymore.

WENDY: At least I know when I've done something wrong.

LACEY: But you just walked away from your patients—

WENDY: And now I'm walking away from you.

(Wendy exits.)

JAKE: We are so cool together!

JULIE: So cool!

SCENE EIGHTEEN

(Living room. Several suitcases lean against the walls of the cottage, packed and ready to go. A few pieces of furniture remain, but all of the clutter is gone. Florence sits organizing a photo album. Sarah enters.)

FLORENCE: There you are! My favorite! You know what you should do, Honey?

SARAH: If it involves going back to school, I'm still not interested.

FLORENCE: Having babies is nice, but someday your body won't cooperate.

SARAH: Don't waste your breath. I've already decided that I'm not going to be a surrogate anymore. And I'm keeping this baby.

FLORENCE *(delighted):* You're keeping Julie's baby!

SARAH: *NOW* you're calling her Julie's baby? At precisely the moment I decide to keep her?

FLORENCE: I'm dancing as fast as I can.

SARAH: I don't want to just crank out babies anymore; I actually want to be a mother. I woke up this morning thinking, "I am good enough. I am a good enough mother."

FLORENCE: Mazel Tov, Honey! I prayed about this; I don't know if I believe in God, but sometimes I pray just in case, and it works! I hope Julie won't think I'm taking sides, but she needs time to sort things out. She should start off with something easy … like a cat.

(Wendy enters.)

WENDY: Mom, I need to talk to you.

FLORENCE: Perfect timing! Sarah just announced that she's keeping Julie's baby!

WENDY: Oh, my God! Julie will kill you.

SARAH: Julie and Jake are rolling around upstairs. I frankly don't think she'd notice if I gave birth on the living room floor. And Lacey would just mop up and make a placenta stew.

FLORENCE *(to Wendy)*: It's a healthy choice, isn't it? She wouldn't have been paid, anyway.

WENDY: I'm sure it's more about Sarah's need for *integration:* needing to integrate her reproductive abilities with her total self —

SARAH *(dryly)*: Or maybe I'm just traumatized by seeing Dad's boobs.

WENDY: Maybe it comes down to the same thing: The need to escape from an employment situation — even though you chose it — that doesn't recognize you as a whole person, as more than just a uterus and breasts, is probably somehow related to having been stuck in the role of Daddy's Little Girl, where you also weren't appreciated for your whole self —

SARAH: I don't know much about psychology, but I'm pretty sure you're not supposed to psychoanalyze your relatives.

FLORENCE: That's exactly what I told your father!

WENDY: Mom, how could you not have told me that Lacey was Dad's patient?

FLORENCE *(confused)*: But she's *not* his patient; she's his daughter.

SARAH *(to Wendy)*: His daughter? You're saying she's our *sister*?

(Lacey enters.)

LACEY: I just wanted to say goodbye. I'm catching the noon train back to the city.

FLORENCE *(to Lacey)*: Is it true? Were you Fred's *patient*?

LACEY: Yes.

FLORENCE *(outraged)*: Why didn't you tell me that?

LACEY: I thought you knew. You said, "I know who you are." I thought that meant you knew I was his patient.

FLORENCE: That's ridiculous, and it's not what you led me to believe.

LACEY *(to herself)*: Maybe everyone believes what they want to believe.

(Julie and Jake enter, looking rumpled and sex drunk.)

JAKE: Good morning, beautiful women!

SARAH: Oh, my God, Julie finally did it!

FLORENCE: Mazel Tov, Honey! Now I hope you feel better about going to your reunion!

WENDY: Why? Because she found a man? That's the antifeminist comment of the decade.

FLORENCE: Not because she found a man; because she feels happy! Isn't that what matters?

WENDY: Doesn't the source of the happiness matter?

JULIE: I'm happy because I finally realized I don't actually have anything to prove. *(To Florence)* You helped me to believe that.

SARAH: Julie, we need to talk. I want to keep the baby.

JULIE: You can't do that! We made a deal!

SARAH: The deal is off. It's my life and it's my body, and I'm keeping her. Sorry.

JULIE: That's not fair. … I was planning to pay you!

SARAH: It's not about the money.

JULIE: We signed a legal document that requires you to give me that baby. *(To Florence)* Mom! Tell her she has to give her to me!

WENDY: It's not up to Mom, Julie. You're not five.

FLORENCE: I'm not getting in the middle.

JULIE *(to Sarah):* If you're not giving me my baby, I'm not speaking to you anymore.

LACEY: Uh, I think I'll go wait outside for my taxi.

SARAH *(to Julie):* Did you hear the news? Lacey was Dad's patient.

JULIE: Oh, my God.

(Lacey goes toward the door.)

JULIE: Wait. Lacey, do you have the pictures?

LACEY: No. There weren't any of me. I checked.

JULIE: We can't let her leave until we find them.

WENDY: What are you going to do — Hold her hostage?

FLORENCE: I have the photographs.

JULIE *(to Florence):* What about the video? Did she get you to confess?

FLORENCE: What would I confess? I'm not a criminal.

JULIE: I *knew* she didn't know Pilates. *(Whispers.)* She does not have abs of steel.

FLORENCE *(to Lacey):* Don't listen to her, Honey. We know it's not your fault.

SARAH *(to Lacey, earnestly):* So, is it true? What he did?

LACEY: You saw the pictures.

SARAH *(gently):* I mean, did he do it to you, Lacey?

WENDY: Lacey, can I ask? How did he convince you that what he was doing was okay?

LACEY: Do you really want to know? *(Beat.)* I thought I was special. I thought he was re-creating me; in some ways, he was actually pretty maternal. *(Beat.)* Even after he was gone, I thought he gave me something that I could use … to reinvent myself, maybe start over from a different place. But maybe there's no such thing as becoming someone else, someone with a happier story.

FLORENCE: I'm sorry, Lacey.

SARAH: Give the photographs to Lacey.

LACEY: I don't want them.

WENDY: You should take them.

LACEY: What would I do with them?

SARAH: You can cut them up ... or make a man-boob collage ...

JULIE: No way! We can't let those photos out of our control. Did you people forget there's a lawsuit out there that could directly threaten our inheritance?

SARAH: Fuck the money.

WENDY: I agree.

JULIE: Even beyond the money, what about Mom? It's humiliating!

FLORENCE: I have done nothing wrong. I have nothing to be ashamed of.

> (Florence tries to hand the photos to Lacey.)

LACEY: I really don't need a souvenir.

> (Sound of a car horn.)

I gotta go.

> (Florence goes to the window.)

FLORENCE: It's a Volkswagen Beetle. A lady is standing in the driveway.

LACEY (embarrassed): It's not actually a taxi. It's my mother.

FLORENCE: Oh. *(Beat.)* Does she want to come in?

LACEY: No, she's just picking me up. She said I could stay with her for a while if I need to. We made up. *(Awkwardly, to Wendy)* So ... I'll see you around.

WENDY: Okay. Take care.

> *(They look at each other. They move to hug each other, but it's awkward and they don't. Lacey exits. Wendy, Julie, Jake and Sarah stand at the window and watch her go.)*

JAKE: I hope she'll be okay.

JULIE: I kind of liked her by the end.

WENDY: Nice way to show it.

FLORENCE: She was an odd bird, but I'll miss her.

SARAH: Please don't say the word *bird*.

JULIE: So, do we really have another sister out there?

WENDY: Good question ... In case I ever have another date.

FLORENCE: I don't know. Your father said so ... He said a lot of things.

JAKE *(whispers to Julie)*: Do you want to give Sarah the bassinet?

JULIE: No! You made it. I love it.

JAKE: I can make you another one.

JULIE: Stop being such a people pleaser, Jake.

SARAH: I'll get my own Goddamn bassinet. *(Beat.)* Are you really not speaking to me?

JULIE: You can't just take the baby away and expect me to instantly bounce back.

FLORENCE: Listen, girls: I didn't speak to Aunt Audrey for three years —

WENDY and JULIE and SARAH *(in unison):* — and then she died!

FLORENCE: Feel free to ridicule me, but at least I can tell you've been listening.

JULIE *(to Sarah):* Try not to die before I start talking to you again.

SARAH: Okay, but try not to take too long.

FLORENCE: Isn't anyone walking me out to the car?

JAKE: Of course, Mrs. Siegel.

> *(Jake helps Florence carry her suitcase out the door.)*

SARAH: Do you think Dad was more nurturing than Mom?

JULIE: In some ways.

WENDY: Can I make a suggestion? Let's not talk about him right now. Let's just be present for a moment to say goodbye to the house.

JULIE: That seems silly.

WENDY: It's important to feel complete when you leave a place. You know the way we used to have a ritual for when we got here, when we'd run to our rooms and put on our swimsuits and jump in the lake —

SARAH: No matter how cold it was!

WENDY: I wish there was a ritual for leaving a place.

JULIE: We don't need a ritual. Besides, Mom's waiting for us in the driveway.

SARAH: We could sing a song.

WENDY: What song?

SARAH: I don't know. A camp song?

JULIE *(to Wendy):* I hope she's joking.

WENDY: Hard to tell with her. Maybe we should just say a few words?

SARAH: Goodbye, Sweet House. Goodbye, old windows that let in so much light.

WENDY: Goodbye, lovely thin walls through which we heard so much gossip.

SARAH: Goodbye, worn-out plank floors that creaked every time we tried to sneak out.

WENDY: Goodbye, little oasis on the beach.

(Sarah and Wendy look at Julie.)

JULIE: Okay, fine: Goodbye, dumpy house, place of my nightmares and unfulfilled dreams.

WENDY: That's right, Julie, let it all out.

JULIE: Goodbye, haunted ramshackle hoarder house.

SARAH: Go for it!

JULIE: You know what? *(Beat.)* I think I might actually miss this vermin-filled dump.

> *(Julie, Wendy and Sarah take a final look around; they walk to the door.)*

WENDY: Wait.

> *(Wendy takes a big crayon out of her bag. She writes, in large letters, on the living room wall:* THE SIEGELS WERE HERE. *They all stand back and look at the wall. They exit together.)*
>
> *(Lights down.)*

End of Play

IN CONVERSATION WITH THE PLAYWRIGHT

Maya: What inspired your play, **The Siegels of Montauk***?*

Meryl: In part, the play was inspired by an acquaintance who believed what she needed to believe about a loved one despite and against all evidence… I often write about families, and in this play I wanted to explore the idea of various family members having very different narratives, despite having grown up together. The play (and family) took on new shape when a stranger was introduced. That idea sparked my imagination while I was writing the play.

Maya: How would you distill this play in ten words or less?

Meryl: Siblings struggle to learn the truth about their deceased father.

Maya: When you think about your body of work, what themes, images, ideas or forms emerge as emblematic?

Meryl: Much of my work turns to be about finding or creating a home in the world, which I guess is really about identity and self-discovery. My plays often ride the line between tragedy and humor, how one is often embedded in the other. Despite being funny, my plays often involve ethical quandaries and loss. In *The Siegels of Montauk,* some of the questions asked are: How is it possible to understand and cope with the idea that someone you love might have done something terrible? What are the consequences of such betrayal?

Maya: What are this play's possibilities and pitfalls in performance? When has it worked best —and why?

Meryl: Performing this play requires striking a light-handed balance between comedy and drama. The first director focused on comedic pacing and tone, letting the drama come through naturally without overplaying it. I thought that was the perfect approach.

Maya: Why engage taboo themes via comedy? Or, why is comedy the form this play took shape?

Meryl: I […] write about dark themes in a comedic way. I don't set out to do it; maybe the comedy makes the tragedy more tolerable, both for me as a writer and for audiences. This play might be hard to take without the humor, but it would also be a very different play if it weren't funny. It's the most-often commented-on aspect of my work — the blending of comedy with difficult topics, ranging from sexual transgressions to the loss of a child to caring for a parent who's in a coma. I often start out thinking, "Okay, this play is going to be serious." And then the humor naturally comes through. […] I think humor has been a survival technique for me in my own life, as a way of making the intolerable more tolerable.

Maya: Yes... How might this play register differently, perhaps more explosively or expansively, amid today's Me Too moment?

Meryl: That's a great question and one that I've been thinking about. Though the Me Too movement has had an impressive impact on public spaces, I'm not sure how much it has crossed over into private spaces, like families and home life. I think family denial is such that the differences might still be subtle for some of the characters, although I think Wendy would be galvanized by the Me Too movement in such a way that her reaction might be quite a bit bigger. The character at the center of the play who's never seen, the father, is the subject of the ethical dilemma, and the media reaction to him, within the play, would probably also have a larger impact now.

Maya: Let's hone in on home communities. You've developed much of your work in Provincetown, an LGBTQ haven, and also had work presented by TOSOS (New York's oldest LGBTQ theatre). Can you talk some about how that shapes the experience in the room with artists and/or audiences? Have your LGBTQ plays notably changed in different contexts? If so, how?

Meryl: My work has been received differently by audiences in different locales, although it's equally true that an audience response in the same location can vary by the night. In Provincetown, in particular, where there's often a stream of visitors, the composition of the audience changes a lot. […] So many factors determine what makes a good performance one night into a magical one the next.

I've found mainstream theaters, at least the ones that produce my work, to be open to the themes and characters I present. What's been much more surprising is occasional divisiveness in the LGBTQ community. For example, a theater in Canada had offered to produce one of my plays, *Almost Home,* but rescinded their offer because a lesbian board member decided that my play was offensive. She essentially felt that one of my characters was the wrong kind of lesbian and would give lesbians a bad name. The artistic director said her objection was that they had selected a play that portrayed lesbians as a bunch of dysfunctional people who were only interested in indiscriminate sleeping around. The play is actually about something entirely different: How a stepmother and daughter figure out who they are to each other after the daughter's biological mother leaves. […]

Maya: What do you see as artists' key roles in the world today?

Meryl: Hopefully, artists make people think, comfort them AND make them uncomfortable. Bring new understanding, change viewpoints, and open doors to worlds that might otherwise be invisible.

A LIVE DRESS

by
MJ Kaufman

**Winner of the
2010 Jane Chambers Prize**

CAST OF CHARACTERS

GRANDMOTHER	The only place she feels at home is at the theater.
SABINA	16 years old. Actress, performer. Enjoys secrets and does not like following rules.
EMMA	16 years old. Actress. Very ambitious. Desperately wants to be famous, mysterious and save the world.
RUDOLPH	30 years old. An actor. Everything is a performance.
LOUISE	25 years old. Dressmaker and costumer. She sees through everyone and everything.
IVAN	30. He witnesses the spiritual inner workings of the universe and sometimes understands them.
VOICES OF SPIRITS	They might be recorded or might be played by the actor playing IVAN.

The voices of Manke and Rivkele in Act One, Scene Five should be played by two women-identified actors. Probably Louise and Grandmother.

In Act One, Scene Five, Emma and Sabina go to see the play *God of Vengeance* by Sholem Asch (*Got fun nekomeh* / Sholem Ash. Varsha: Tsentral, 1913). The text used from that piece here is my own free adaptation of the translation

190

by Joseph C. Landis (Applause Theatre Book Publishers, 1986). In Act One, Scenes Six and Thirteen Grandmother is watching the play *The Dybbuk* by S. Anski (*Tsvishn tsvey veltn (Der dibek): a dramatishe legende in fir akin / Sh. An-ski. Dramen, Gezamlte shrift*: Vilna-Warsaw-New York, 1920–1925, vol. 2, pp1–105). The text used from that piece here is my own free adaptation of the translation by Joseph C. Landis (Applause Theatre Book Publishers, 1986).

SETTING

An apartment on the Lower East Side, a Yiddish theater, an English theater, a jail, State Street, a bar on State Street.

TIME

New York City, 1923.

ACT ONE

SCENE ONE

(New York City 1923. An apartment on the Lower East Side. It is small and claustrophobic with too many old things. The wallpaper is peeling. There are probably mice.)

(Grandmother wears her wedding dress.)

GRANDMOTHER:
This is a dead dress.

There's no smell in the armpits, for instance.
No rips in the usual places.
The skirt wouldn't rustle
even if there was a breeze.

Bad things can happen if a dress doesn't get worn.

It might become a rag, for instance, or a curtain.
Do you know what happens if you get married in a dress
that hasn't been worn in two hundred years?
A dead dress?

My aunt Esther got married in a dead dress. Everyone
knew how dead it was. And it was bad luck. Her husband
turned out to be as stupid as a horse.

My granddaughter doesn't understand how a dress needs
to be worn and full of smells. She's always putting on
brand-new American dresses.

That's dangerous too.

Dresses with no dust are empty dresses. They have that
new, empty dress smell. It's dangerous to wear them out.
Fatal to get married in them.

> (She leans in closer or shifts her eye contact. Now she's
> getting to the real business.)

I'm keeping this dress alive for my granddaughter. It was
my wedding dress that my mother dressed me in on my
wedding day, and hers before that and her mother's before
that. I'm going to wear it every day from two to four p.m.
Even if I'm just sitting in the apartment. Dresses have to
collect smells and dirt to stay alive. I'm going to keep
wearing this dress. Just in case.

SCENE TWO

> (A Yiddish theater. Emma and Sabina perform their
> weekly comedy routine that is a prelude to a longer
> show. Grandmother is in the audience. This time they're
> really on. The audience is packed.)

> (Emma is dressed like a girl. Sabina is dressed like a boy.
> Emma begins to stroll as though she is walking down the

street. Sabina follows her, she tugs on the back of her skirt. Emma turns around.)

EMMA: Excuse me?

SABINA: What a lovely face you've got, miss! What's your name?

EMMA: Have you been following me?

SABINA: No ma'am, no I haven't! But I must say your eyes are as blue as the ocean!

EMMA: I say! Do you always talk to strangers like that?

SABINA: Yes, but never ones as beautiful as you!

> *(Lights shift. Emma and Sabina quickly undress and exchange clothes. Lights come back up again. Now Sabina is a girl and Emma is a boy. Emma presents Sabina with a bouquet of roses.)*

SABINA: Really! A whole bouquet of roses just for me! Why, how kind!

EMMA: I couldn't help it. Their bright color reminded me of your rosy cheeks and I just had to.

SABINA: Stop flattering me so, you'll make my cheeks even redder!

> *(Emma leans forward and kisses Sabina on the cheek. We hear the audience laugh. Emma looks the other way quickly, Sabina leans over and kisses her on the cheek and then looks away quickly. The audience laughs harder this time.)*

> *(Lights shift. They quickly undress and trade clothes. They help each other.)*

> *(Lights up again. Emma and Sabina are both dressed*

as girls.)

EMMA: The matchmaker told me she'd found a fine husband for me.

SABINA: Me too.

EMMA: She told me to meet him right here.

SABINA: Well that's funny. She told me to meet my suitor right here!

> *(They look around. Their eyes slowly land on each other.)*

EMMA: Do you think …

SABINA: She's matched us up with the same man?

EMMA: Or with each other by mistake!

> *(Grandmother laughs and claps ecstatically.)*

> *(Lights down.)*

SCENE THREE

> *(Emma and Sabina are changing out of their costumes.)*

EMMA: Tomorrow's our last chance to see the show at the Apollo again. Everyone says it's going to get shut down.

SABINA: Shut down? By who?

EMMA: By the police.

SABINA: I told my Grandmother I'd go to the theater with her. I've left her alone the last two times.

EMMA: But it's our last chance to see it! Did you hear what happened? Five more dresses hanging in the air down on State Street.

SABINA: Five more?

EMMA: Been one or two every day the whole last month.

SABINA: Can't be. It's not even in the papers.

EMMA: The news doesn't report it. Not worth it to them.

SABINA: What'd they look like?

EMMA: One of them was green and white striped. And they think it belongs to Bessie Steinman who used to live next door.

SABINA: Really? Bessie?

EMMA: Uh-huh. She went missing and her mother said it was definitely her green striped dress on State and Second Street. I saw it myself.

SABINA: You went down there?

EMMA: Of course, I wanted to see. Don't tell anyone.

SABINA: I have to get home.

EMMA: Wait, are you coming to the show tomorrow?

SABINA: Yes, I'll be there.

EMMA: Meet me at the fire escape?

SABINA: Of course.

SCENE FOUR

(The apartment. Sabina and Grandmother.

Grandmother wears the wedding dress.)

SABINA: That dress doesn't fit you.

GRANDMOTHER: I'm keeping it alive for you.

SABINA: It's hideous.

GRANDMOTHER: It's hideous now but I'll make it attractive by wearing it. Did you hear what I just said? I'm keeping it alive for you. Just in case. I promised your mother on her deathbed …

SABINA: Stop.

GRANDMOTHER: I didn't promise her you would get married … but I did promise her you'd always be well dressed. I'd hate to show her what you wear these days. Did we come all the way to New York so you could run around in torn-up sundresses? What, you didn't get your fill of bad fashion in the old country?

SABINA: Why now all of a sudden, why today are you suddenly possessed to do this?

GRANDMOTHER: You know, Sabina, I'm getting old! And I see what you're wearing these days and I don't like it.

SABINA: Did you hear what happened? Five more dresses hanging in the air on State Street.

GRANDMOTHER: Five more dresses?

SABINA: The same way it's been happening all year. A girl disappears during the night and in the morning her dress is hanging above State Street.

GRANDMOTHER: It's dangerous to wear a dead dress.

SABINA: That's not why it happens.

GRANDMOTHER: Trust me. I know from dead dresses.

SABINA: Now it's happened to almost thirty girls in the last month but it's not in the news.

GRANDMOTHER: It's what I've always been telling you. Look smart. Don't wear a dead dress. Well, are you ready to go to the theater?

SABINA: I'm not going today.

GRANDMOTHER: You're abandoning me?

SABINA: I have to go see another play instead.

GRANDMOTHER: You're disgracing me. Only widows walk into that theater alone. How could you do this to your grandmother? I never abandoned you anywhere, Sabina.

SABINA: Just wear your dark brown scarf and slip in behind the lighting booth, no one will notice. They'll think you've stayed home with a cold.

GRANDMOTHER: Can't you go see this other play tomorrow? What if I'm sitting alone today in the theater and I croak, you'd sure feel bad about that, wouldn't you?

SABINA: Today's the last day to see this show, it's going to get shut down tomorrow. By the police.

GRANDMOTHER: What kind of play gets shut down by the police?

SABINA: It's getting shut down for obscenity.

GRANDMOTHER: Well. Why don't you invite me to see this obscene play with you?

SABINA: It's in English. You wouldn't understand it. And anyways its uptown on 42nd Street, it's too far for you with your bad leg. Plus, we have to sneak in by climbing up the fire escape.

GRANDMOTHER: English will make your brain dry out. Those plays in English are duller than watching the wallpaper for two hours.

SABINA: That's because you don't speak English.

GRANDMOTHER: No, it's because *goyim* have no stage presence or sense of humor.

SABINA: Well this play isn't *goyish*. It came from our theater.

GRANDMOTHER: They're putting on one of our plays in English and calling it obscene?

SABINA: I'm late, Grandmother.

GRANDMOTHER: You know the English theater is no place for you. It's full of dull *goyim* in dead dresses. I hope you don't become a rock sitting there. My grandfather became a rock at the theater, did I tell you?

SCENE FIVE

(A secluded corner of a balcony at the Apollo Theatre. Fancy. Warm. Lots of red velvet. It smells of old women's perfume. Emma and Sabina have snuck into the play.)

EMMA: I'd take off her dress first.

SABINA: I'd start with her shoes. Then stockings. Work my way up.

EMMA: This scene is the best. When it starts to rain.

SABINA: Nah. The light makes her hair look like a soggy blintz.

EMMA: Shh. It's getting to the best part.

(We hear the sounds of wind and rain.)

MANKE (VOICE-OVER): Your hair smells like the spring rain. Like grass in the meadow. Could I fix your hair like a bride? With two long braids?

RIVKELE (VOICE-OVER): Oh, please!

MANKE (VOICE-OVER): You'll be the bride, at the Sabbath table with your family, a young beautiful bride, and I'll be your lover, soon to be your husband, come to visit you!

EMMA: Listen to the audience, they're so quiet.

SABINA: Mmm. That's because they're *Goyish*. I wish we could do this play at your brother's theater.

EMMA: You mean, with us acting those parts?

SABINA: Of course. Wouldn't it be so great to do that onstage?

EMMA: Do what onstage?

SABINA: What ... they do ... you know? In the rain?

EMMA: You mean get all romantic?

(Sabina nods.)

EMMA: We do that. In every comedy act.

SABINA: But it's not like that. One of us is always dressed like a boy. Wouldn't it be great to do it ... like they do?

199

EMMA: What do you mean? Wearing those nice dresses? I love that blue one. We couldn't do what they're doing. We'd get in such bad trouble! Just think what's already happened to them. Everyone says they're going to get shut down by the police.

SABINA: They're getting shut down because they're doing it in a big theater. We'd do it downtown at your brother's theater. For people like us. And anyways, like you just said, it's basically what we do all the time. All we do is love stories.

EMMA: But one of us is always dressed like a boy.

SABINA: Everyone knows we're both girls.

EMMA: Sabina. I have to tell you something. It's the most important secret I've ever had to tell anyone. Do you want to hear it?

SABINA: How'd you get such an important secret?

EMMA: You promise not to tell anyone?

SABINA: Maybe if I can borrow your blue stockings for a week —

EMMA: Sabina.

SABINA: Fine.

EMMA: Fingl asked me to marry him.

SABINA: Fingl? Old Fingl with the white hair who smokes those disgusting cigars?

EMMA: Yes. And I want to marry him. I think I'm in love.

SABINA: You're not!

EMMA: No, I really think I am.

SABINA: Emma. You are not in love with Fingl.

EMMA: I know I am.

SABINA: Fingl is old. He was married once already, and Emma you're too young to get married. He smokes disgusting cigars and once I even saw him with a prostitute. A woman dressed like that.

(She points to the stage.)

EMMA: So? What's wrong with them? Didn't you just say you wanted to wear one of those dresses? You wanted to undress that girl … starting with the shoes?

SABINA: But I still wouldn't marry a man who slept with prostitutes!

EMMA: Shh. Please don't say that. I'm going to marry him. And I'm going to start acting with him.

SABINA: What about our comedy act? I thought we would keep doing it together … at least for another few years … I thought you liked it.

EMMA: Sabina. I told you. I'm in love with him. And our comedy act is so silly.

SABINA: This is a joke. Anyways, you've been in love with Reuben since the first grade. And seriously, you're sixteen, you want to be a widow with a wig at twenty?

EMMA: Who's saying I would wear a wig?

SABINA: All widows wear wigs.

EMMA: Look Sabina, I like our comedy act, but I don't want to do it forever.

SABINA: What does that mean?

EMMA: It means … I don't know, I want to really act someday, and I might get to if I marry Fingl, if I start acting with him. I want to act in a theater like this one, where the people sit quietly and listen and it's real serious drama and … it's in English … you know?

SABINA: What, your brother's theater isn't good enough? What am I supposed to do if you leave with Fingl — I can't do the comedy act alone!

EMMA: You know how it is, it's so noisy and distracting. And we don't do real plays there.

(Sabina looks away.)

EMMA: You won't tell anyone?

(Sabina watches the play intently.)

Please?

MANKE (VOICE-OVER): Rivkele. Run away with me! We could spend all our time together, from morning 'til night! Just the two of us! Would you like that?

RIVKELE (VOICE-OVER): My father wouldn't know?

MANKE (VOICE-OVER): No. We'll leave tonight. Can't you hear your father snoring? He sleeps so deeply, he'll never wake.

EMMA: Sabina? I need to go … the ushers will start patrolling soon, if we leave now we can get out the stage door before they see that we were here.

SABINA: We can wait until the very end like last time, remember? 'Til after the actors leave and everyone's gone.

EMMA: I have to be home to help my mother, it's going to be *Shabbes* … don't you have to go home to your Grandmother? I'm sorry Sabina.

(She exits. Sabina does not take her eyes off the stage.)

SCENE SIX

(Grandmother at the theater. A Yiddish Theater. She sits. We don't see the performers. We only hear them.)

KHONNEN (VOICE-OVER):
I want to search the earth for the most beautiful gem!
I want to find it and then sit weeping for centuries 'til I dissolve it in my tears.
I want to absorb my soul in this ocean.
I must remember to find two barrels of gold coins.
For the one who can only count coins.

HENEKH (VOICE-OVER): You frighten me, Khonnen. I'm afraid you won't get what you want through holy means.

GRANDMOTHER: Usually Sabina would be sitting next to me, right here. But not today. She'll learn. Those *goyim* only tell burnt-out stories. They tell the same ones over and over again and forget they've heard them before. Our stories make your arm hairs prickle.

The stories from my village are particularly good. Because my village was full of fools. It was an accident. We weren't supposed to have so many fools. We got more than our allotted dose.

You want to hear the story? When the Creator of all things created the heavens and the universe he … or was it she? Some of us wonder … in any case, the Creator, sent all the angels out to go fly around and drop souls into all the villages. There was one angel responsible for dropping a fool or two into each village. Well, when he got to our village, he got caught on a tree branch and spilled a whole bucket of fools out in one place. So we were a village of fools. And because we were fools we made very good theater.

Here is the thing about fools: We are foolish but we are honest. We tell the truth. We see the reality of every situation, and we are foolish enough to laugh at it.

SCENE SEVEN

(The Apollo Theater. Backstage. Rudolph is very upset. He has just finished crying. He hopes no one has heard him. He is wearing a dressing gown. It occurs to him that he might as well get a head start on cleaning out the space. He opens a drawer. He unloads piles of jewelry and makeup. He looks for a box to put it in. Sabina enters.)

SABINA: Hello?

RUDOLPH: I know you're lying and I'll piss on you if you say one more word! Tell Boris I'd like to make his balls melt off.

SABINA: Excuse me?

RUDOLPH: Who're you?

SABINA: I just came to tell you how much I liked the play. And I … wondered if you might need any other performers.

RUDOLPH: What's your name?

SABINA: My name is Sabina Weinblatt. I just watched this afternoon's performance.

RUDOLPH: I see. I'm glad you liked it.

SABINA: Is everything all right?

RUDOLPH: What?

SABINA: You look upset.

RUDOLPH: Didn't you just see me have a tantrum onstage? I was sobbing. One's makeup is always smeared after a tantrum onstage.

SABINA: It's very convincing. Are you sure there's not something wrong?

RUDOLPH: I'm an actor, I have to get into it, after all.

SABINA: What are you doing with all those things?

RUDOLPH: Vacating. We're being shut down.

SABINA: I heard.

RUDOLPH: Who did you hear from?

SABINA: I don't know. I can't remember.

RUDOLPH: It's very important! Who did you hear from?

SABINA: Are you from Vienna? Your accent sounds like you're from Vienna.

RUDOLPH: I'm from outside of Vienna.

SABINA: I grew up on Alser Street.

RUDOLPH: I used to live on Floriani Square!

SABINA: That's not far! Only a few blocks …

RUDOLPH: What's your last name?

SABINA: Weinblatt. Yours?

RUDOLPH: Schildkraut — I knew Weinblatts! Perla, Golde …

SABINA: Perla! My grandmother's name is Perla!

RUDOLPH: Your grandmother! I think I knew her! She wore fancy dresses? Has reddish hair?

SABINA: Well, when she was younger maybe. Her hair's been gray my whole life.

RUDOLPH: Did she have a twin sister named Golde?

SABINA: No.

RUDOLPH: Oh.

SABINA: We're not from Vienna originally, anyway.

RUDOLPH: Me neither.

(He turns around and continues to pack up boxes.)

SABINA: Well anyways, I was wondering if your troupe needed another —

RUDOLPH: Yes, I heard you the first time. We do, in fact, probably need someone. Probably a girl just your age. Could you help me with this? We need to empty those drawers over there. These are our props and makeup. Our most important possessions. We don't have anywhere else to keep them. Come on now, quickly, quickly, the police might come at any minute.

SABINA: I don't think they'll come today.

RUDOLPH: Anything's possible. We need to get it all out just in case. These are very important instruments. Good, that's the last of it. Can you take this box somewhere?

SABINA: Me?

RUDOLPH: Just this box? It's too much for me to carry and we need to protect it, just take care of it for tonight, we can find each other again tomorrow.

SABINA: Where will we find each other tomorrow?

RUDOLPH: In the alley behind the Thalia Theater at three p.m., I'll pick it up from you. And then we'll talk about your new job. In our company. Can you do that?

SABINA: I suppose.

RUDOLPH: Good. I'll see you then.

(He exits quickly. Sabina stands holding the box.)

SCENE EIGHT

(The apartment. Sabina and her Grandmother are on stage. The box is on the ground between them.)

GRANDMOTHER: No one cares what sewer rats do, so long as they stay down in the sewer while they do it. That's what *The New York Times* said about that play you saw.

SABINA: You can't read English.

GRANDMOTHER: Freyde translated for me. See for yourself.

(She passes the newspaper to Sabina.)

And now you're telling me you're going to leave our theater and join them? No. The English theater is no place for us. They shut it down. The whole cast was arrested.

SABINA: Well how will I make a living otherwise? We have to eat, don't we?

GRANDMOTHER: What was so wrong with the comedy act you do with Emma —

SABINA: We can't do it anymore. It's over.

GRANDMOTHER: Over? So suddenly?

SABINA: I don't want to talk about it.

GRANDMOTHER: Then go tomorrow and ask for a job at the cigar factory.

SABINA: Smells so awful there.

GRANDMOTHER: We have to eat, Sabina, and your Grandmother is old and sick.

SABINA: That's why I've got this new job —

GRANDMOTHER: Anyways, what's this box?

SABINA: It's nothing.

GRANDMOTHER: Not only does she go to the English theater but she brings home their detritus!

SABINA: Can't be any worse than what you've got stored up in this apartment.

GRANDMOTHER: There are lots of reasons why someone would want to get rid of a box. It might be filled with something no one wants in their life.

SABINA: It's just a box. It's just costumes and things.

GRANDMOTHER: What does it feel like? Is it heavy?

   (Grandmother picks it up.)

It's light for its size.

SABINA: If you're so afraid, why don't you open it up?

GRANDMOTHER: You open it up.

> *(There is a knock at the door. They look at each other for a moment. Sabina answers. It's Emma.)*

EMMA: Hello?

GRANDMOTHER: Hello! Good *Shabbes*.

EMMA: Where did that box come from?

GRANDMOTHER: Sabina took it from some stranger —

SABINA: Grandmother it's time for your bath.

> *(It's not.)*

GRANDMOTHER: Whatever you say, Sabina. Good night Emma.

EMMA: Good night.

> *(Grandmother exits.)*

I was coming to see if I could borrow back that blue dress of mine.

SABINA: Sure. Take all your dresses. I don't want them.

EMMA: You can keep borrowing the rest of them, I just want that blue one.

SABINA: Take them all. You can take all your old dolls too, they're over there in the bottom drawer of the dresser. … Ugh, what's that awful stench of cigars? Do people smell you on the street and run away?

EMMA: All right, Sabina. I just want to take the dress and go.

SABINA: When's the wedding going to be? Will it be big? Oh, wait, I forgot, Fingl doesn't have any family.

EMMA: Where's my dress?

SABINA: Here.

> (Emma goes to take the dress. She stops in front of the box.)

EMMA: What's in this box?

SABINA: It's the costumes for the new company I'm in.

EMMA: You're in a new company?

SABINA: 'Course. If our comedy act was going to stop I had to find a job.

EMMA: You already found a new one, just like that?

SABINA: Just yesterday. I went backstage and asked. Now I'll be working with a company that does real, serious drama.

EMMA: They gave you their costumes?

SABINA: Just to hold onto. For tonight.

EMMA: Can I see?

SABINA: I don't think so.

> (Emma opens the box.)

SABINA: Emma!

EMMA: Wow. Really nice dress-up clothes.

SABINA: Emma don't go through that box, I'm just taking care of it for tonight.

EMMA: Oh! Look at this dress. Oh. This dress. This dress is mine. This was my dress! Where did this box come from? It has my dress in it!

SABINA: What are you talking about?

(Emma holds up a dress.)

EMMA: This dress is my dress. It's my dress from when I was a kid, back at home. My mom made it for me, out of this material that used to be our curtains.

SABINA: I don't think it's your dress.

EMMA: It is my dress. It used to be my favorite dress. Once I wore it to the fair on Purim and we stayed up dancing all night — it looks like it would still fit me!

(She picks the dress up and slips it over her head.)

It fits. It smells like our turnip field after the rain. How did you know? This is what I needed! Where did you find it?

SABINA: Someone gave me that box to take care of. But that's not your dress and you can't have it.

EMMA: Who gave you the box? Someone found this dress and brought it over for me. I thought it was burned in the fire.

SABINA: No one brought it for you. It doesn't even fit you right — it's too small around the back.

EMMA: It fits me perfectly — that's just the style. It was always too big before, I couldn't wait to get bigger so that it would fit me. Especially here …

(She gestures to her chest.)

SABINA: Emma it's not mine to give you.

EMMA: I was supposed to find this dress. I've been thinking about it for years. Whose box was this anyways? What else is in here? *(She starts to rummage through the box.)*

SABINA: Emma, Stop!

EMMA: Oh god Sabina, what's the big deal?

SABINA: Just stop looking through it and take off the dress!

EMMA: No. It's my dress and I'm taking it home.

SABINA: It's not your dress!

EMMA: I need to go now.

SABINA: Take off that dress.

EMMA: I need to leave now. You can keep borrowing all my dresses, I don't need them. *(She goes to get her bag.)*

SABINA: Emma! Stop!

EMMA: I have to get home. Fingl and I are leaving tomorrow.

SABINA: What's going on?

EMMA: Goodbye, Sabina.

SCENE NINE

(The apartment. The box is there. Grandmother enters. She sees the box. She approaches it. She opens it.)

212

GRANDMOTHER: Anyone could tell this was more than a box. You may think that the things around you are solid, quiet, dead, but they're not. There's spirits in the smallest pebbles.

(She rummages around the box.)

Yes, these clothes are very alive. Dangerously alive.

(Suddenly Sabina enters and she closes the box quickly.)

SABINA: Were you looking in the box?

GRANDMOTHER: 'Course not.

SABINA: It's not ours to go rummaging through.

GRANDMOTHER: Whose is it then?

SABINA: Who cares? I'm taking it back tomorrow. What's that in your hand?

GRANDMOTHER: Nothing. Just a skirt.

SABINA: Did you get it from the box?

GRANDMOTHER: Enough already about the box!

SABINA: Put it back. You got it from the box.

GRANDMOTHER: All right, all right. Sabina, tell me something, do you think you'll wear this dress someday?

(She means the wedding dress.)

SABINA: I prefer not to look like the ghost of the *Shabbes* bride.

GRANDMOTHER: It's very important to me, Sabina. Think of this as a nice thing you're doing for your grandmother.

SABINA: How about I make you some nice kugel instead?

GRANDMOTHER: Soon you'll need it. Trust me.

SABINA: Sure. Next time I'm desperate to dress up in disintegrating tablecloth I'll be knocking on your door.

(But Grandmother knows she can't afford to wait.)

GRANDMOTHER: Sabina. I won't put this skirt back into the box until you promise me you'll wear this dress.

SABINA: What do you mean? Wear this dress tomorrow? Wear it on my wedding day that's never going to happen?

GRANDMOTHER: Wear it when I tell you it's alive enough. I first wore it on my wedding day, my mother dressed me in it. But just in case that doesn't happen to you, I want you to promise me you'll wear it when it's alive enough.

SABINA: Sure. Fine. I promise.

GRANDMOTHER: Good. Then I can go to sleep.

SABINA: Put the skirt back in the box.

GRANDMOTHER: I know!

(She slowly opens the box. She puts the skirt back inside. She does not close the box.)

SABINA: Close the box.

GRANDMOTHER: Look at all those things inside.

SABINA: Close the box!

GRANDMOTHER: All right, all right.

(She closes the box. She moves to her bed.)

You need a good live dress here.

SABINA: You're not going to take a bath?

GRANDMOTHER: I can't take off the dress. Not yet.

SABINA: You should really —

GRANDMOTHER: Please Sabina, I know what I'm doing.

SABINA: But it's been three days. You haven't bathed.

GRANDMOTHER: This is far more important than bathing.

SCENE TEN

(Rudolph is in jail. He sits down in the corner of his cell and faces the wall. He begins to cry. Sabina enters carrying the box. He doesn't see her.)

RUDOLPH: Leave me alone! I told you not to disturb me. It might be time for dinner but I'm going on a hunger strike.

SABINA: It's me again.

(He looks up suddenly.)

RUDOLPH: You're interrupting. I was rehearsing.

SABINA: I'm sorry. I waited for you at the Thalia theater — the newspaper said you'd been arrested. So I came here.

RUDOLPH: I was rehearsing gloom, and it wasn't simple gloom either: It was a very difficult sort. The sort that requires dust of this exact shade and one to two cobwebs. I've been perfecting the ingredients for this sort of gloom for years. I might be able to evoke something similar but never this exact quality. Not this century.

SABINA: I'm very, very sorry.

RUDOLPH: Why did you come find me here? Were you looking for a clown that you could mock? You might think that performers aren't susceptible to the pain of indignity but you're wrong.

SABINA: I was just bringing you your box like you asked me to, and also, you said you had a job for me and I need to bring home some money tomorrow night or else my Grandmother will make me get a job at the cigar factory.

But anyways, I'll just leave the box and go now.

RUDOLPH: Don't! I can't keep it here, they'll take it away!

SABINA: Well what do you want me to do?

RUDOLPH: Can you hang onto it for a little longer?

SABINA: It's getting to be a bother.

RUDOLPH: It's very important. It's the only important thing I have.

SABINA: My apartment has mice.

RUDOLPH: You're my only option. Please. I need to know you're reliable. If I'm going to employ you.

SABINA: I know you. You look like the brother of a girl I knew in Vienna.

RUDOLPH: In Vienna, I was a sad clown. Every evening I would emerge with a violinist and we would sit in the street and weep for several hours. Maybe that's where you know me from.

SABINA: No, I don't think I ever saw that.

RUDOLPH: No? Too bad. I ate well in Vienna, people had a taste for it there. We could always attract an audience. In New York you can't make a living with misery. You have to resort to obscenity instead. Even then you starve.

SABINA: You look like my friend's older brother. Did you have a sister?

RUDOLPH: No. I had a brother. He died of too much theater.

SABINA: What?

RUDOLPH: It's true. He spent too many days in the theater and a *dybbuk* entered his body. You know what a *dybbuk* is, don't you? A restless spirit. A soul of a dead person that comes to occupy the body of someone living.

(Enter Ivan from another part of the stage.)

IVAN: RUDOLPH! RUDOLPH! It's that thing again, come help, bring the heavy blanket.

(Rudolph approaches him. He carries a heavy blanket.)

RUDOLPH: Don't worry. Remember to breathe normally. Stand up so I can wrap you in the blanket.

(Ivan stands.)

IVAN: That feeling like a swarm of bees in my chest and someone else was using my voice and my eyes. For a moment I was only in my fingernails and even they were growing numb — was I crying, do I look like I was crying? I don't remember crying. Who used my eyes to cry while I was gone?

RUDOLPH: You weren't gone.

IVAN: My cheek is wet, feel, my cheek is wet! Taste it, tell me if it's saltwater.

RUDOLPH: Does it matter?

IVAN: Yes! Taste it or I'll jump in the river tomorrow.

> *(Slowly Rudolph leans over. He licks Ivan's cheek. Ivan exhales deeply.)*

RUDOLPH: Salt.

IVAN: Sweat or tears?

RUDOLPH: Tears.

IVAN: Let me taste it.

RUDOLPH *(to Sabina):* Ivan and I were not brothers in the traditional sense. We didn't have the same parents, for instance. We were a different kind of brothers.

> *(He slips his arm around Ivan. He kisses him deeply.)*

IVAN: Tears.

RUDOLPH: Tears.

IVAN: I know I cried. But I can't ever remember crying. I haven't cried since I was a baby.

RUDOLPH: It's true. You don't cry often.

IVAN: Someone else was in my body.

RUDOLPH: Shh. Try to go back to sleep.

(Ivan exits. Rudolph turns to Sabina.)

RUDOLPH: But someone else was in his body. It became very messy.

SABINA: What happened to him?

RUDOLPH: He died of it.

SABINA: How?

RUDOLPH: I won't give you details.

SABINA: I wouldn't mind hearing them.

RUDOLPH: I'd rather not. I wouldn't usually tell all this to a stranger, but you're from home. Could you do me a favor, actually?

SABINA: I don't know.

RUDOLPH: It's the first part of your job. I'll pay you upon completion. I'll pay you tomorrow, in fact. Just come back here. There's a wig in that box. It's a very nice wig. Made with real hair. Can you take it somewhere for me?

SABINA: I suppose.

RUDOLPH: Take it to 127 State Street under the bridge, but only between midnight and three a.m..

SABINA: State Street's dangerous.

RUDOLPH: You're right. State Street's dangerous. You're thinking of the dresses, right? But you've got a scar on your shoulder so nothing will happen to you.

SABINA: How did you know about my scar?

RUDOLPH: I saw it yesterday in the theater.

SABINA: And why would a scar keep me safe?

RUDOLPH: Just trust me, it will. Fifteen dollars.

SABINA: A whole fifteen dollars just for that?

RUDOLPH: I swear to it.

SABINA: All right. 127 State Street. Who should I give it to?

RUDOLPH: Ask for Esther. Good. Thank you. Thanks a lot. Can you leave me alone now?

(Sabina nods. She exits. Ivan enters again.)

IVAN: Rudolph? Did you speak to me yesterday? Did we have a conversation yesterday?

RUDOLPH: You slept all day yesterday.

IVAN: I know I didn't. That someone else was in my body again yesterday and you spoke to it, I know.

RUDOLPH: I didn't.

IVAN: You did. I heard you from my fingertips, which is the only part of my body where I still was. You and that other one on the beach — did you go to the beach yesterday? Did you go to the beach with me when I was not in my body?

RUDOLPH: No, Ivan. There was a performance yesterday. I played Hamlet, you sat in the front row. You fainted during the play within a play and the usher had to carry you out to the lobby.

IVAN: That's true. You're not lying. You gave the speech on to be or not to be wearing that silken shirt.

RUDOLPH: See? You remember. C'mon now let's go to sleep.

(He puts Ivan to bed as though he's a small child.)

SCENE ELEVEN

(State Street. Sabina walks down it looking for 127. It is dark out, and smells strongly of cigarettes. Voice calls out to her.)

VOICE: Where's all the girls tonight? I heard them down on Seventh Street. Ain't any girls gonna come down this way? Look over that way, issat one a them? Hey Gorgeous in the white dress, you free? Look at that nice tight dress, hey missy where're you going in such a hurry?

(Voice grabs Sabina's arm, she tries to get free. Her dress rips. Louise enters.)

SABINA: Hey, let go of me!

LOUISE: Hey Charlie get the hell off of her.

(Sabina's arm is released.)

LOUISE: Sorry he ripped your dress, mind if I take a look?

VOICE: Hope you come down this way later, Louise.

LOUISE: Don't talk to me, Charlie. *(To Sabina)* Come with me.
(They walk away from the Voice. Louise fingers the shoulder of Sabina's dress.)

LOUISE: Not too much damage done. I could mend it for you. If you wanted.

SABINA: My grandmother will mend it.

LOUISE: Are you sure? I'm a dressmaker by profession. It would only take me a minute.

SABINA: It's not necessary.

LOUISE: I'd enjoy it. It's a nice dress and I could put some lace down here, a ruffle there — I usually charge five dollars for something like this —

SABINA: I can't afford it.

LOUISE: But for you I'd do it for free.

Hey. You've got a gorgeous scar on your shoulder.

(Sabina quickly adjusts her dress to hide her scar.)

What, you ashamed or something? I said it was beautiful.

SABINA: I'm in a hurry. I've got to go.

LOUISE: Hey, where'd you get that box? I know that box.

SABINA: I have to go.

LOUISE: Where you taking it?

(Sabina turns away.)

Hey, come back with that! That's not your box!

(Sabina exits.)

SCENE TWELVE

(127 State Street. It's a bar. It's empty. Sabina knocks. Louise answers.)

LOUISE: Oh. Hello. Why didn't you tell me you were coming here? We could've walked together. By the way, who did you say made that dress of yours? Your grandmother? Can I touch it?

SABINA: I'm looking for Esther.

LOUISE: That's funny. Which Esther?

SABINA: I don't know … is there more than one?

LOUISE: We have five Esthers.

SABINA: Oh. I was just told to bring this to Esther.

(She pulls out the wig.)

LOUISE: Yup. Nicest wig. Haven't seen it since we got arrested.

SABINA: Who should I give it to?

LOUISE: Me, for now. Someone different plays Esther every night of the week. Tonight it's me. Where'd you get that box? Thought we lost it. Did you see Rudolph? Ain't he in jail?

SABINA: I went and found him there.

LOUISE: Hmm. How'd he look?

SABINA: Not well.

LOUISE: Yeah, didn't think so. He owes me ten dollars, the shmuck.

Want to stay and watch the show? We're not sure if there's going to be any more audience. I'm going to be Esther. It's a special show because it's just me. Usually we have Rudolph and some others but tonight it's just me.

SABINA: It's pretty late. I need to get home. Can I leave the box here?

LOUISE: What's the harm, you snuck out anyways, didn't you? Have a drink. It'll be a nice little *Purimshpiel*.

SABINA: It's not Purim, it's August. Anyways, can I leave the box here?

LOUISE: It's Purim every night here. And on Purim God commands that you get drunk.

Sure. You can leave the box here. You can go home.

(*Sabina realizes she doesn't want to leave the box.*)

It's fine. Go home. Leave the box here.

SABINA: I can ... keep it if you want. I don't mind. Maybe I should. Rudolph didn't say to leave it here.

LOUISE: Leave it here. This is where it lives. Didn't you just ask twice if you could leave it here?

SABINA: What do you use it for? *Purimspiels*?

LOUISE: And other stuff.

SABINA: Can I ... see what's in the box? I been carrying it around for a long time

LOUISE: Did you open it?

SABINA: No.

(*Louise opens the box.*)

LOUISE: Oh good. Here's this vest. I always used to wear it when I played the king. We missed it. And this nightgown.

SABINA: The nightgown was in the play! *God of Vengeance.* You were in the play!

LOUISE: You saw it?

SABINA: Just before it got shut down. I thought the whole cast got arrested?

LOUISE: We got released. Just Rudolph had to stay.

SABINA: Can I … try them on?

LOUISE: No. Only we get to wear the costumes.

SABINA: But Rudolph said I could be in the company.

LOUISE: Oh, did he now? I'll have to check with him about that. These costumes are tricky. You have to get trained on how to wear them. And you can only wear them in shows. Can't just wear them around for fun.

Someone opened this up, huh? Thought you said you didn't open it.

SABINA: I didn't.

LOUISE: Then who did?

SABINA: No one.

(*Louise closes up the box.*)

LOUISE: Think I could mend your dress now? I'd like to alter it for you … make you something really pretty.

SABINA: My grandmother would never let me. She likes to repair the dresses herself. She made it.

LOUISE: Your Grandmother. That's right. She's a dressmaker? And where is she from? You never see a dress like this around here.

SABINA: I don't really know. She said a village of fools, or something.

LOUISE: Village of fools?

SABINA: That's what she says.

LOUISE: Wise fools?

SABINA: What's that mean?

LOUISE: Never mind. Where's the village of fools?

(*Sabina shrugs.*)

SABINA: Not sure it's there anymore. Near Vienna, I guess.

LOUISE: Where's your grandmother now?

SABINA: I don't know. Probably at the theater.

LOUISE: Thalia Theater?

(*Sabina nods.*)

Seems like the kind of place a wise fool'd hang out.

Wouldn't your grandmother be pleased to know you gave it to a professional dressmaker to fix? I could give you something real nice to wear home. This dress for instance. Look. It's nice, right?

(*She shows Sabina a dress. It is nice.*)

SABINA: Okay.

(*Louise unzips a dress for Sabina. She holds it out for her. Sabina pulls her other dress over her head. The scar again. Louise looks at it. Sabina knows she's looking at it.*)

SABINA: I fell.

(Louise moves closer.)

LOUISE: Can I … touch it?

(Sabina nods. Louise touches it.)

It's so perfectly round and dark. Like a stone or something.

Put this on. All right. Goodnight then, walk home safe.

(She walks Sabina to the door.)

Careful around State Street, you know.

SABINA: Yes.

LOUISE: I could walk with you, if you wanted.

SABINA: I'll be fine.

LOUISE: Just don't look toward the voice.

SCENE THIRTEEN

(State Street.)

(Emma enters wearing the dress from the box. She is in love with herself in it. She keeps stopping to look at herself in it. She brushes it off. It is truly lovely.)

VOICE: Nice dress.

EMMA: I know, isn't it lovely?

VOICE: Lovely.

EMMA: It's new but it's also old. It used to be mine a long time ago.

VOICE: It's got a nice color.

EMMA: I know. And a nice smell. And it's so light and fresh feeling. I could do anything in this dress.

VOICE: Where are you going?

EMMA: To meet my boyfriend. We're going to be married.

VOICE: Going to be married, huh? Who's your boyfriend? Is he the one with the cigars?

EMMA: How come I can't see you?

VOICE: I don't have a body.

EMMA: Why not?

VOICE: Listen, will you do something for me?

EMMA: Maybe. Depends what.

VOICE: Just stand right there where you're standing. For a moment. I'll give you a prize at the end.

EMMA: What kind of prize?

VOICE: A good one. You'll see. Are you in?

EMMA: First tell me why you don't have a body.

VOICE: It's a long story. Too hard to explain. You wouldn't understand.

EMMA: And what do you want to do to me?

VOICE: Something harmless. And you'll get a very good prize. Something that will make everyone pay attention to you. It'll be over in a minute.

EMMA: All right.

(Lights down on them.)

(Lights up on Grandmother at the theater. She sits, paying attention, leaning in. Again, we hear the actors but do not see them.)

LEAH (VOICE-OVER): Grandmother, you mustn't abandon a bride before a wedding. Demons might come and take her away.

FRADE (VOICE-OVER): Leah! You mustn't call on those spirits by their forbidden names. Don't you know they're waiting in every nook and cranny for someone to utter those words and release them?

(Louise enters. She sits down next to her.)

LOUISE: Psst.

PSSST!

Ahem!!

GRANDMOTHER: Cough a little louder, why don't you.

LOUISE: AHEM.

GRANDMOTHER: Go ahead. Make a racket. Keep us all from hearing the ending.

LOUISE: I'm trying to get your attention.

GRANDMOTHER: Well congratulations. Now let's watch the play.

LOUISE: I want to show you something.

GRANDMOTHER: How about you show me your *tuches* headed out the door?

LOUISE: Would you like to see a really good play?

GRANDMOTHER: What? You calling this one mediocre?

LOUISE: I'm talking about a really, really good play.

GRANDMOTHER: Watch what you say — that actor's my good friend.

LOUISE: I'm talkin' about a play we're making just for you. You're the only that can fully appreciate it.

> *(Grandmother ignores her.)*

Can I touch your dress? I'm a dressmaker by profession. Some dresses really beg me to touch them. Tell you whole stories, you know? *(She touches Grandmother's dress.)* ... You're from the village of fools, aren't you?

GRANDMOTHER: Yes.

LOUISE: Would you like to come see a play that's being made just for you?

> *(Lights down on them. Lights up again on Emma. There is a big gust of wind. Two cigars land on the floor next to her. A dress falls from the sky. She catches it.)*

ACT TWO

SCENE ONE

> *(Sabina arrives home in the middle of the night. Emma is waiting at the door. She's been waiting for quite some time.)*

SABINA: Emma?

EMMA: Oh, thank goodness, Sabina, I thought you'd never come. Let's go inside, it's cold out here and it's about to start raining.

SABINA: Why are you here so late?

EMMA: I was waiting for you! Why were you out so late?

SABINA: I had things to do.

EMMA: At four A.M.?

SABINA: What are you doing here at four A.M.?

EMMA: I came … to say goodbye. And to give you something.

SABINA: I sure hope you're returning that dress.

EMMA: It's my dress and I'm going to keep it. Listen. Fingl and I are running away in the morning.

SABINA: Running away?

EMMA: I think my parents might come here in the morning. Don't tell them you've seen me or that you know anything about me leaving. Can you do that?

SABINA: We were supposed to run away together. We were supposed to catch the midnight train to Coney Island and only bring one tiny knapsack for both of us.

EMMA: Sabina, this is different.

SABINA: We were supposed to take a tiny sailboat that only fits the two of us and sail for days until we washed up somewhere like Paris or Casablanca!

EMMA: Sabina … running away isn't romantic. It's terrifying. I need your help.

SABINA: I still think you don't have to. I still don't believe you love him.

EMMA: Well believe whatever you want to then.

So … I have something to give you.

SABINA: Fine.

EMMA: You'll never believe it. I went down to that spot, where all the girls are disappearing? On State Street?

SABINA: Yeah, I know, I been down there.

EMMA: You been down there? How come?

SABINA: How come you been down there?

EMMA: Because I … oh never mind. Listen, wearing this dress everything's totally different.

SABINA: What are you talking about?

EMMA: I feel like I could do anything. And I know things. For instance, I knew that even though that voice down on State Street was scary nothing was going to happen to me because I was wearing this dress.

SABINA: So …?

EMMA: So, I listened to it. I stood in front of it just like it asked me to and there was this big gust of wind and then … I got this.

(She holds out a dress.)

SABINA: What is it?

EMMA: It's Bessie Steinman's dress. The one she was wearing the day she disappeared.

(*She hands the dress to Sabina. Sabina studies it.*)

SABINA: This was her dress?

EMMA: Uh-huh.

SABINA: Where was it?

EMMA: Fell right into my hands.

(*They hold the dress. It is much heavier than any dress should be.*)

Listen, I'm leaving in the morning but I need you to bring it to her mother, all right?

SABINA: To her mother?

EMMA: The funeral's tomorrow. They don't have a body to bury but at least now they have a dress.

SCENE TWO

(*127 State Street. Grandmother and Louise enter.*)

GRANDMOTHER: What, it wasn't enough to do this play in the middle of the night? You had to drag me to this godforsaken hole in the wall too?

LOUISE: Whoa, whoa, watch the complainin' I'm afraid your tongue's gonna fall out. I'll walk you home after.

(*Louise turns to set up.*)

GRANDMOTHER: And to think I was in the middle of an excellent play. That I paid for.

(Louise finishes setting up.)

LOUISE: Listen up. This'll be a one-of-a-kind show. Never before seen piece-a-theater. Witnessed only by a single audience member in the history of the universe. You're the only one who'll ever see it.

GRANDMOTHER: Where's the cast?

LOUISE: It's just me.

GRANDMOTHER: Where's the set?

LOUISE: Just this room. Allow me to welcome you to a village of fools! Over there is the baker. He's selling dough today because he couldn't figure out how to heat up the oven. Over there's the matchmaker matching up a man with a horse. On that corner, a young merchant's trying to sell his left shoe.

(Louise reaches into the box looking for a dress.)

It's a lovely spring morning with the scent of cows in the air.

(Louise puts on a dress from the box. She looks straight at Grandmother. She stops for a minute. Breathes in. She speaks to someone not present.)

LOUISE: That was my chicken! Did you hear what I said? No, did you hear what I said? That was my chicken! I've had enough. You know what? I hope you get a pimple the size of an egg. That's right. I hope something horrible happens to your face. I hope you have eight straight weeks of diarrhea.

(She turns toward Grandmother.)

Moishe's gonna be the death of me. How many times did I tell him that was my chicken?

Let's see, if we open the window we'll have the smell of lilacs but we'll also have the smell of cow manure. So you can take your pick. What'll it be? Cows and lilacs? No cows and lilacs?

You know, aside from the strong stench of cow manure, and the stifling heat, you've really been blessed with a beautiful wedding day. Your wig needs some help though. Are you trying to look like something the cat coughed up? Stand so I can fix it. Stand up so I can fix your wig. Perla. Stand up.

(Slowly Grandmother rises.)

LOUISE (DYBBUK): Give or take a few pounds you look just as I did on my wedding day. All right, I suppose you've got a nicer figure. All right, I won't sugarcoat anything. I was bursting out of this dress at the seams. That rip's from me. Stand up a little straighter.

(Grandmother does.)

LOUISE (DYBBUK): Good. I should've hemmed the bottom before, it's too long on you, look. God forbid you should trip on your way to the *huppah* like that *khazzer* Sheyna, remember how she face-planted in the mud? She had it coming.

(Louise [Dybbuk] works on the dress.)

Look at you, we should all be so gorgeous. I'll bring it in a bit here to flatter your figure.

GRANDMOTHER (tentative): We … don't have time for that, mother. The ceremony's in an hour.

LOUISE (DYBBUK): We can dream, can't we?

GRANDMOTHER: I don't want you to change it. I want to wear it exactly as you wore it on your wedding day. And your mother before you and her mother before —

LOUISE (DYBBUK): Don't be so ridiculous, when my grandmother wore that dress it was still white! The lace was brand-new from Moscow and it was the most coveted dress in the village. Now it's grayish yellow, the lace on the neck is scratchy, the armpits smell. Like old milk. No matter how many times you wash them.

GRANDMOTHER: This lace is from Moscow?

LOUISE (DYBBUK): Trust me, you don't want to look the way I did on my wedding day — I was a real lobster. Two feet taller than the groom with sunburnt cheeks and a peeling forehead. But you know I think you look perfect, don't you? Just the way you are today.

>   *(Louise [Dybbuk] stops and looks at Grandmother.)*

LOUISE (DYBBUK): You've been wearing this dress long enough. It's Sabina's turn now. You have to give it to her if you want the dresses back.

>   *(She goes back to hemming the dress as though nothing's happened. She's suddenly angry and impatient.)*

Why do you always bother me with questions, we never get anything done. It's nearly dark and I told your father I'd be ready with the flowers in an hour. We still have to visit the *mikveh*.

GRANDMOTHER: How do you know Sabina? You died before she was born.

LOUISE (DYBBUK): Try keeping your mouth shut for once in your life, I can't concentrate. Your father will be here any moment. You know how the mikveh fills up. You know how your father reacts when we're late.

GRANDMOTHER: Mother I'll never have another chance to ask you —

LOUISE (DYBBUK): I'm tired of your insolence. Act your age. You're about to be married. I'll go get the flowers.

GRANDMOTHER: Wait —

LOUISE (DYBBUK): Can't.

> *(Louise takes off the dress. She looks at Grandmother. Grandmother understands that she is Louise again.)*

LOUISE: Like the play?

GRANDMOTHER: Put on the dress again.

LOUISE: She won't come again. Not tonight.

> *(Grandmother takes the dress Louise was wearing out of Louise's hands. She studies it. Louise moves away or sits down, lights a cigarette, anything to shake off what just happened.)*

GRANDMOTHER: Will she come again another night?

LOUISE: Perhaps. Look. We need your help. We found you and brought you here and showed you that play for a reason. Your granddaughter told us you're a wise fool? We're good to pay you. In money or cigarettes. See, we're in desperate need of a wise fool. These costumes got us into a bad pickle. You understand what's going on? With these costumes? Awful consequences. Rudolph got arrested …

> *(Grandmother is not paying attention.)*

GRANDMOTHER: I haven't seen a stitch like this in years. They don't make dresses like this here. No one uses this fabric.

LOUISE: Did you hear what I was sayin'? 'Bout the costumes?

GRANDMOTHER: Where did this come from?

LOUISE: I dunno. Somewhere near Vienna, I guess. Rudolph brought 'em all.

(Grandmother looks over the dress.)

GRANDMOTHER: That's not good for you what you just did. You're stealing the dead from their rest. Keep going and you'll turn paler than you already are. Keep going and they'll grow very angry with you. You'll be cursed. Illness, early death, blindness in one eye ... don't test them. They're creative.

LOUISE: Listen, what we're actually worried about is these dresses on State Street. You heard about that?

GRANDMOTHER: Don't wear a dead dress.

LOUISE: We're a bit afraid that's our fault.

GRANDMOTHER: I'm sorry but I can't help you.

LOUISE: We've never found someone else who could talk to them.

GRANDMOTHER: Well, thank you for dragging me down here and thank you for the show but I don't like what you're up to. And it's long past my bedtime. Goodnight.

(She leaves.)

SCENE THREE

(The apartment. Morning. Sabina holds Bessie Steinman's dress. Grandmother enters.)

SABINA: Where were you all night? I was about to go out looking for you!

GRANDMOTHER: What is that? The deadest dress in New York? You hold it any longer and the blood in your veins goes still.

SABINA: Where were you?

GRANDMOTHER: Put the dress down. I was with your box-people from the English theater. Apparently, a little bird told them I was a wise fool and they decided to steal me away in the middle of the night. They've got that box-demon that's tearing apart the neighborhood with the costumes.

SABINA: They showed you those costumes?

GRANDMOTHER: They thought I would know how to fix their disaster. What do I know? All I know is they've got a box-demon that's released something evil on State Street. After they went to the English theater. I told you it's no place for us.

SABINA: That's not why —

GRANDMOTHER: What did I tell you about dead dresses? Those girls disappeared. And what did I tell you about the English theater? They got arrested. And still you never listen to your grandmother. What is that thing you've drudged up?

SABINA: It's Bessie Steinman's dress.

GRANDMOTHER: Where did you get that?

SABINA: It's … I don't know, Emma gave it to me, she found it down on State Street.

GRANDMOTHER: And what? She had the brilliant idea of schlepping the thing all the way back up here? Is this some kind of birthday present?

SABINA: She wanted me to give it to Bessie's mother. The funeral's today.

GRANDMOTHER: So?

SABINA: She said … now at least we have it to bury. We have to dress the dead in something, right?

GRANDMOTHER: There's no dead to bury.

SABINA: There's Bessie. There's no body, but there's still Bessie. There's the thought of her. We can't bury her naked.

GRANDMOTHER: Sabina, it's time for you to wear this.

SABINA: The wedding dress?

GRANDMOTHER: As long as you're lugging around that heavy one. I want you to wear this dress to the funeral today. You're right about dressing the dead. Even when there's no body. Can you do that, please?

SABINA: Grandmother, it's hideous. And it's not appropriate to wear to a funeral.

GRANDMOTHER: Trust me. You said you'd put it on and you need it now. If you're going to keep hanging around those box-people.

> (Grandmother takes off the dress. She hands it to Sabina. Sabina takes the dress. She takes off her other one and puts it on.)

GRANDMOTHER: Well. Let's see you.

SABINA: It's got stains all over it.

GRANDMOTHER: It was once white. The lace was once new.

Well! You don't have to get married just because you have a beautiful dress, but aren't you glad you have such a marvelous, beautiful dress!

SABINA: It's a little big on me.

GRANDMOTHER: Every woman in our family is inside that dress with you. Doesn't it feel wonderful? Does it feel like anything it all?

SABINA: I guess it feels warm.

GRANDMOTHER: Good. It's perfect. For a funeral that's not quite a funeral. Since we're burying a dress instead of a body.

> (She touches Bessie's dress.)

A dress that weighs as much as a body.

SCENE FOUR

> (Bessie's funeral.)

> (Sabina, Grandmother and others dressed in black gather around.)

GRANDMOTHER: I've always known this Rabbi's head was full of goat shit. He should know not to do this when there's no body. How do we know she's really dead? She could be frolicking around New Jersey.

SABINA: They haven't been able to find her for weeks. They know she's gone.

GRANDMOTHER: This is worse luck than getting married in a dead dress. A body should be buried within the first two days. Why is everyone going along with this? Are they all stuffed shirts?

SABINA: No. We all know the circumstances.

GRANDMOTHER: Where's Emma, shouldn't she be here? Her parents are standing over there all alone.

SABINA: How should I know?

GRANDMOTHER: She brought you the dress, didn't she? She knew about the funeral.

SABINA: I'm supposed to know where she is all the time?

GRANDMOTHER: You used to.

SABINA: I have to go now, I'm late to meet someone.

GRANDMOTHER: But you haven't even given your condolences to the family!

SABINA: I'll stop by later.

GRANDMOTHER: And I'll go alone?

(Emma approaches.)

EMMA: Sabina.

GRANDMOTHER: Oh, hello Emma! We were just talking about you. You know you've missed the service.

EMMA: I know. Thank you.

GRANDMOTHER: The family's just headed back to the house, if you want to go and give your condolences.

EMMA: Thank you. I will. *(To Sabina)* Can I talk to you alone?

SABINA: Grandmother, could you excuse us?

GRANDMOTHER: All right but only for a moment.

EMMA: Of course.

(Grandmother steps away from Emma and Sabina.
 She moves toward the grave.)

SABINA: I thought you were leaving.

EMMA: I was. I still might be.

SABINA: Why're you here?

EMMA: Because of that dress. And that box. Because of you. Why are you wearing your grandmother's wedding dress?

SABINA: Why does it matter?

EMMA: Will you tell me about the box?

SABINA: It's over now, I gave it back.

EMMA: Gave it back to who? Did they notice that the dress was missing?

SABINA: I don't know.

EMMA: Where did you meet this someone who gave you the box, anyways? It was at the Apollo Theater, right? Can I meet this person?

SABINA: No.

EMMA: Why not?

SABINA: Because they're my friend. From home.

EMMA: It's someone from home?

SABINA: Enough, I don't want to talk about it anymore.

EMMA: Wait, Sabina. I came back because I'm going back down to State Street. I'm going to speak to that voice again and I don't want to go alone. I wanted to see if you'd come with me. Will you? It's scary, but I know I have to go and you're the only one who could go with me.

SABINA: Why do you have to go?

EMMA: Because! I got Bessie's dress back last time, who knows what else I could get from them.

SABINA: What good is it to get Bessie's dress back? Doesn't really do any good to bury a dress. It's bad luck.

EMMA: No. I think it helps. I think getting that dress back made it weaker. No one else disappeared last night. Not after I got that dress. I'll go back there but not alone. I'm too afraid.

SABINA: I'll go with you.

EMMA: Oh, thank you! Tonight, then?

SABINA: Yes. Tonight.

EMMA: I'll meet you at your house at seven?

SABINA: My house at seven

SCENE FIVE

(Jail. Rudolph is rehearsing the part of Hamlet. Ivan is watching.)

(Sabina enters quietly. She is still wearing the wedding dress. She watches. She tries not to let Rudolph notice her.)

IVAN: Do it again, from the beginning. This time don't break character.

RUDOLPH: These costumes make me forget everything. I'm in a trance while I'm playing, but the moment I remove my shirt, I'm starving. I'm weak, I can't continue.

IVAN: Shall we stop for the night?

RUDOLPH: No. Let's continue. One more time. Then we'll eat and sleep.

(He pulls on the shirt again.)

(Rudolph turns around. He sees Sabina.)

RUDOLPH: What are you doing here? I was rehearsing.

(Ivan exits quietly.)

SABINA: I … was just watching.

RUDOLPH: I see that. I asked you, what are you doing here? Really, that was rude. Invasive. You could at least tell me what you're doing here.

SABINA: I came to get paid. You said you'd pay me.

RUDOLPH: Did I?

SABINA: Yes.

RUDOLPH: But I'm in jail now. I haven't got any money now. I'll pay you when I get out.

SABINA: When will that be?

RUDOLPH: Tomorrow, I hope.

SABINA: Well I also came to ask you more.

RUDOLPH: More what?

SABINA: More about the box. And your brother. Where did you get those costumes?

RUDOLPH: Why?

SABINA: Just curious.

RUDOLPH: Did you open the box? You did, didn't you? You didn't wear any of the clothes, did you?

SABINA: I'm just curious!

RUDOLPH: I didn't tell you there were costumes in it, you wouldn't know unless you opened the box!

SABINA: I saw you pack the boxes, don't you remember? And I know the costumes are special because I saw the show! I saw how well you perform in them. I wanted to know more about them.

RUDOLPH: You're talking about our acting.

SABINA: Yes, of course, but also the costumes. You did say if I came back you'd tell me more.

RUDOLPH: Another day.

SABINA: But I'm here now.

RUDOLPH: I'm not up for telling stories today. I'm in the middle of something.

SABINA: You could just show me what you were rehearsing.

RUDOLPH: I already told you, that was private. I can't share this with just anyone.

SABINA: I'm not just anyone, I'm from home, remember? And I took care of the box for you. Can't you trust me?

RUDOLPH: I'll need a secret from you.

SABINA: What kind of secret?

RUDOLPH: Something bad.

SABINA: I snuck into the Apollo Theater to see your play.

RUDOLPH: That's good but not good enough. Something you don't want anybody to know ever.

SABINA: I once stole a whole pound of sugar from the grocery store. One time I left a chair sitting out on the street and my neighbor who uses a cane tripped on it and had to go to the hospital. My friend and I kissed each other pretending one of us was the boy.

RUDOLPH: Excellent. That's enough.

    (He turns away, prepares himself.)

It starts on the banks of a river. On a sweaty afternoon in August.

    (Ivan enters running. Rudolph starts to run behind him. They're twenty years old. It's hot out, they're sweaty. They arrive at the banks of a river. They take off their shirts and roll up their pants to go swimming. They check each other out. First Rudoph jumps in the water. Then Ivan jumps in the water. They get out and lie in the sun to dry.)

RUDOLPH: Now will you tell me what happened when you went to see the rabbi?

IVAN: I went to the shul in the morning. The rabbi had been praying all night. When I walked in he stared at me because I was wearing all black and, you know, it was the Day of Atonement. I should have been wearing all white.

RUDOLPH: Did he ask you about it?

IVAN: Yes. And I said to him, "Rabbi, why should I wear white if my thoughts are not pure?"

RUDOLPH: Did he answer?

IVAN: No. So I said, "Why should I refrain from bathing, on this Day of Atonement, if my desires are never clean?" When he did not answer I said, "Why should I fast, if I will not give up the one thing I am truly hungry for?"

He was quiet.

(Rudolph listens to the flies buzzing.)

RUDOLPH: You're his favorite student. He'll be so disappointed to lose you.

IVAN: I'm going to study Kabbalah. That's much better.

RUDOLPH: Who will teach you?

IVAN: Reb Shimsky in the next village. I've already made arrangements.

RUDOLPH: Will you stay there a long time?

IVAN: Yes. For a year at least.

RUDOLPH: Have you told your grandmother?

IVAN: Yes and she disapproves.

RUDOLPH: You'd leave her alone for a year?

IVAN: My uncle will take care of her.

RUDOLPH: Will you … write me letters?

IVAN: Perhaps. If I'm not too busy.

(Lights shift.)

RUDOLPH: Many years later. When he was a learned man and I an actor …

(Ivan enters. Rudolph sits with a jug before him. He's been drinking.)

IVAN: Stop now. You'll drink yourself into a stupor.

RUDOLPH: Who cares if I do? I'll starve to death anyways. Our plays are terrible. Last night my own mother fell asleep in the front row.

IVAN: You're just going through a bad period.

RUDOLPH: It's time to face it. We can't act. We'll starve this way.

IVAN: No. You won't. I've got an idea. Let's go to the cemetery.

RUDOLPH *(to Sabina):* We went that night.

IVAN: I've invited your dead uncle.

RUDOLPH: I wonder if he still has bad breath.

IVAN: Mark it on the map. We're calling him using this gray vest.

RUDOLPH: Who's next?

IVAN: Isaac that drunk who used to threaten us.

RUDOLPH: Remember when he saw us up at the railroad tracks? Let's do it.

(Rudolph turns to Sabina.)

RUDOLPH: He invited the dead through a piece of clothing. Each article was for a different member of the village cemetery. And then we would wear one of the garments in performance and the dead would enter our bodies. Our performances were so real the audience would weep because we were letting the dead speak through us.

(He turns to Ivan.)

RUDOLPH: Did you notice, in our last performance, the whole first row was weeping?

IVAN: Yes. So?

RUDOLPH: So … it's a little frightening.

IVAN: What's frightening? Your work is real now.

RUDOLPH: Ida came to me afterward. She wanted to speak to her mother. She said she could feel the ghost of her mother in the theater. She asked me to do it again, whatever I did there, she said, there was something she wanted to tell her mother.

IVAN: What did you do? You didn't tell her, did you?

RUDOLPH: I told her I couldn't do it again … it was only the magic of theater.

(Louise enters.)

LOUISE: RUDOLPH!!!

RUDOLPH: You don't have to shout I'm right here. How many times have I told you not to disturb me when I'm rehearsing? And this time I have an audience.

(He gestures toward Sabina.)

LOUISE: Trust me, this time it's worth it. We got problems on our hands.

RUDOLPH: What's happened?

LOUISE: We got the box back but the blue dress is missing.

SCENE SIX

(Louise and Sabina arrive at Sabina's apartment. Emma is there.)

SABINA: This is it.

EMMA: Sabina, where've you been, I've been waiting for you for hours!

SABINA: For goodness sakes, Emma, you scared me. Sorry. I got held up.

EMMA: Who's this?

LOUISE: I'm Louise. I see you're wearing one of our dresses.

EMMA: This is my dress.

LOUISE: Ain't yours. Came from our box. Hand it over.

EMMA: Let's go inside.

LOUISE: Hand over the dress. No monkey business.

EMMA: I'm here to talk to Sabina.

LOUISE: And I'm here to collect that dress you're trying to stretch around your gigantic shoulders. The thing's too small for you. Take it off.

EMMA: Let's just go inside, I can't very well get undressed on the street, now can I?

(Sabina opens the door. They enter the apartment.)

EMMA: Sabina, aren't we going to go down to State Street?

LOUISE: Not so fast. Take off the dress.

EMMA: Okay. I know it's yours but I need it for something.

LOUISE: You need it for something?

EMMA: Something important.

LOUISE: What?

EMMA: All right, well you know down on State Street, where the girls have been disappearing?

LOUISE: Oh do I.

EMMA : Well I go down there and I hear this —

LOUISE : Voice.

EMMA : Uh-huh. And it tells me to —

LOUISE: I know what it tells you to do, get to the punch line.

EMMA: Well the point is, I do it and I don't disappear. Others do, but I don't. And I'm sure it's 'cuz I'm wearing this dress.

LOUISE: So?

EMMA: So, that's all. It's special when I wear it.

LOUISE: Honey I got news for you, it's special whoever wears it.

EMMA: What's special about it?

LOUISE: None-a your beeswax. Hand it over.

EMMA: It's just … I don't want to give it up just yet. Can I talk to Sabina alone for a minute?

LOUISE: For a minute. I'll be waiting over here for my dress. *(Louise walks away.)*

SABINA: You're being ridiculous.

EMMA: Listen, Sabina I gotta explain something to you.

SABINA: Make it quick.

EMMA: We have to go down to State Street together.

SABINA: I don't want to anymore.

EMMA: I told Fingl I couldn't run away.

SABINA: Why not?

EMMA: I needed to go visit that voice again. You said you'd go with me.

SABINA: Well I changed my mind. What's the big deal about that voice?

EMMA: I have an idea about them. Will you listen to it?

SABINA: What's your idea?

EMMA: It's not trying to make girls disappear … it's looking for something.

SABINA: What are you talking about?

EMMA: I just think, it wants something from us, and when I'm wearing this dress, I can talk to it and find out what it is. Maybe I can find a way to give it to it.

SABINA: This is disgusting, why do you care about what the voice wants?

EMMA: Because I think we could put an end to all this. If I just gave it something it could live inside, something really special.

SABINA: Like what, this dress?

(She touches the dress Emma is wearing.)

EMMA: No. This one.

(She touches the wedding dress.)

LOUISE: All right enough. If you don't hand over the dress this instant I'm going to rip it off you.

EMMA: What are you talking about?

LOUISE: Hey, you know how many times I repaired that dress already? I can rip it if I want to.

EMMA: Sabina get her away from me!

SABINA: Emma it was never your dress. You have to give it back.

EMMA: Look at her, Sabina, she looks like she's going to hurt me!

SABINA: I don't know what you want me to do.

LOUISE: All right. That's it.

(She rips the dress off Emma.)

LOUISE: Got it. *(She turns to leave.)*

You coming?

EMMA: Sabina, don't leave.

LOUISE: Seriously, Sabina, you coming?

EMMA: I need the dress. I can't go without that dress. You said you'd go with me, remember?

SABINA: Bye, Emma.

(Sabina exits.)

SCENE SEVEN

(The street outside. Louise walks briskly. Sabina follows her.)

SABINA: Where are you going now?

LOUISE: 127 State Street, of course.

SABINA: Why?

LOUISE: We gotta get all the clothes in the box and stop performing.

SABINA: And then?

LOUISE: That's all I know. How'm I supposed to figure out what's next? Your Grandmother doesn't know, Rudolph doesn't know or won't tell us. All I know is, I gotta get the clothes in one place and stop performing.

SABINA: But what about the voice? The girls who disappear? I thought you said it was your fault?

LOUISE: Maybe it is, maybe it isn't. How should I know what to do about it? If I don't stop performing I'll get a *dybbuk* that won't leave. That's what I care about. You wouldn't understand, you're not losing your body like me. You gotta nice scar.

(She starts to walk. Sabina does not follow.)

LOUISE: Come on.

SABINA: I just … I don't know how we're supposed to make it better.

(Louise stops and looks at Sabina.)

LOUISE: We just have to put the clothes away. Stop talking about it for godsakes. And you got that dress too. Can't believe this.

SABINA: What's the dress got to do with it?

LOUISE: No one would care about any of this if they had a dress like that. With a dress like that anyone would pay attention to you. No one's going to bother you. You're safe.

(She reaches out to touch Sabina's dress. She grips it.)

SABINA: Hey.

LOUISE: What?

SABINA: Let go.

LOUISE: Why?

SABINA: It's my dress.

LOUISE: So? I'm not hurting you or anything. It's just a dress. You should share it with me. You got this nice scar, this safe dress, why won't you share it with me?

(She grips a hold more violently.)

SABINA: Stop it. Let go!

(Louise drops the dress.)

LOUISE: Sorry.

SABINA: I have to go.

LOUISE: Sure you don't want to come to State Street with me? Your dress is there, the one I mended for you. We could start to … make a plan about all this.

SABINA: I have to go somewhere first.

LOUISE: Well, come by later, all right?

SABINA: Maybe. I gotta go now.

(Sabina turns and exits.)

LOUISE: Remember to be careful!

SCENE EIGHT

(Jail. Rudolph sits at Ivan's bedside.)

RUDOLPH: One time we stole cigarettes from the corner store, remember? The manager chased us down the street shouting absurdities.

IVAN: I remember. We spent all summer at the abandoned train junction.

RUDOLPH: You wore eyeliner and blue nylons. You always won the prize for best Esther at the *Purimspiel*.

(Sabina enters quietly. She moves to watch.)

IVAN: Listen. Pack up all the ghosts and take them to another place. When you get there bury them.

RUDOLPH: Please stay with me this time, please don't disappear again.

IVAN: You'll still know where I am. I've loved you since the world was created. That won't disappear.

(Rudolph turns around. He sees Sabina.)

RUDOLPH: What could it be now? Haven't you disturbed me enough?

SABINA: I'm sorry. I couldn't stop watching you.

RUDOLPH: That was a rehearsal, it wasn't meant for anyone else's eyes.

SABINA: What are you rehearsing for?

RUDOLPH: Really, I've had enough of this.

SABINA: When are you going to perform this?

RUDOLPH: What did you actually come to bother me about? I know it's not this.

SABINA: What happened to the *dybbuk*?

RUDOLPH: Ivan died. I already told you.

SABINA: But, the *dybbuk*. What happened to the *dybbuk*?

RUDOLPH: Ivan's body was destroyed, please don't make me relive it.

SABINA: I'm very sorry. What I want to know is, did you accidentally bring that *dybbuk* here?

RUDOLPH: Why are you making us out to be criminals? You came from somewhere else too. Who knows what you brought by accident. Anyways, all the souls in the box are *dybbuks.* They're all restless and that's all a *dybbuk* is anyways. Could you leave me in peace?

SABINA: What about the voice on State Street?

RUDOLPH: What about it?

SABINA: Is that your *dybbuk*?

RUDOLPH: How should I know?

SABINA: And why didn't you bury them?

RUDOLPH: What?

SABINA: Ivan said to bury the costumes when you got here. Why didn't you?

RUDOLPH: We're actors. We had to make a living somehow.

SABINA: That's not why.

RUDOLPH: Look, what are you doing here? You know the real reason, don't you? We didn't bury the clothing because the spirits got mixed up in us. Burying them would mean burying part of ourselves. Is that enough for you?

SABINA: It's just that we don't know what to do. We don't know how to get rid of the *dybbuk*.

RUDOLPH: We can't.

SABINA: We can't?

RUDOLPH: It's not going to go away.

SABINA: But then what do we do?

RUDOLPH: We just have to make sure it doesn't take over completely.

SABINA: How do you do that?

RUDOLPH: You practice. What do you think I've been rehearsing for?

SCENE NINE

(Outside the Thalia Theater. Grandmother stands waiting. It's a hot night. Others smoke cigars.)

GRANDMOTHER: Keep your smoke to yourself. Can't you tell how old I am?

(She coughs loudly.)

You'll be the death of me.

(Louise enters.)

LOUISE: Hey loudmouths over there, put a cap on your chimney, why don't you? You want a poor *bubbe* to cough to death?

(The sound of people in the background stops. We hear them shuffling away.)

There. They're gone.

(Grandmother still coughs.)

GRANDMOTHER: Can't leave an old woman alone, can you? You don't have to ask. I don't have the dress anymore. My granddaughter's wearing it, go look for her.

LOUISE: I know. Vodka?

(She holds out a flask. Grandmother takes it and sips

some.)

GRANDMOTHER: Might as well.

(Grandmother stumbles.)

LOUISE: Can I offer you an arm? Into the theater?

GRANDMOTHER: Sure, but let's hear it, why're you here? What do you want from me?

LOUISE: I just came looking for you. That's all.

GRANDMOTHER: Which of your many problems do you need me to solve?

LOUISE: You already told me you didn't know how.

GRANDMOTHER: Are you the angel of death? Is that what this is?

LOUISE: No.

GRANDMOTHER: You are, aren't you? Come here to bring my mother to me, now come to take me — will it be painful?

LOUISE: That's not who I am.

Theater's pretty empty tonight, huh?

GRANDMOTHER: Usually my granddaughter would be with me here but not today. ... She hasn't been to the theater with me in some time. You're to blame for that.

LOUISE: S'pose so.

GRANDMOTHER: She should have been performing tonight. Heading up the show. She should have been doing her fine comedy act with her friend. They both have such excellent voices. They should be performing right now. But they're not. What are we supposed to do? Just sit here? In the silence?

LOUISE: Guess so. Hey listen, what are we supposed to do with this box of costumes? Now I've got them all back in one place.

GRANDMOTHER: You're a worse liar than a sack of potatoes. I thought you didn't want anything from me.

LOUISE: Okay, I guess I want that one thing.

GRANDMOTHER: I already told you I've got no answers.

LOUISE: Should we stop performing?

GRANDMOTHER: Perhaps. Perhaps not.

LOUISE: Isn't that how this all started?

GRANDMOTHER: Put them away. Every once in a while, you'll take out a costume to perform with.

LOUISE: Every once in a while?

GRANDMOTHER: Look, you won't use them all the time. But you won't forget about them either. You should come to the theater more often. It's good medicine. For things like this, whatever it is that's making you so pale.

> (They both turn toward the theater. They watch. But the play hasn't started, so there is still nothing to watch.)

SCENE TEN

(State Street. Emma is standing talking to the Voice.)

EMMA: No, I won't. I'm waiting for someone.

VOICE: Why not?

EMMA: Because I don't have that dress anymore. I might disappear.

(Sabina enters.)

SABINA: Emma?

EMMA: Oh, thank goodness. I thought you'd never come.

SABINA: I came. I knew you'd be here.

EMMA: I don't … want to go too close to them, you know? Now that I don't have that dress.

SABINA: Yeah.

EMMA: You think you'll be okay, cuz of the scar and all?

SABINA: Maybe. I don't know.

EMMA: Or, because of your dress.

> *(She takes Emma's hand. They move closer to the Voice.)*

VOICE: That's a gorgeous dress you've got on. Come a little closer. Right there, maybe?

SABINA: I can't do that.

VOICE: Just a little closer?

EMMA: Don't.

SABINA: I know. *(Sabina takes off the wedding dress. She holds it out in front of her.)*

SABINA: Here.

VOICE: What is it?

SABINA: A dress for you.

EMMA: Try it on.

VOICE: Is this some kind of a trick? It feels like a trick.

EMMA: Take it!

VOICE: All right.

(*There is a gust of wind. The dress rustles. All remaining dresses fall from the sky.*)

(*Emma and Sabina look at each other.*)

EMMA: You think it's gone?

(*Sabina nods.*)

EMMA: Where do you think it went? Is it in the dress now?

(*Sabina touches the dress.*)

SABINA: I don't know. I don't know if it's safe to wear.

EMMA: Let's go.

SABINA: Wait. We need to take all the dresses.

(*She and Emma bend down and begin to pick up all the dresses that have fallen.*)

EMMA: What should we do with these? Bury them?

SABINA: I don't know.

EMMA: Let's ask your grandmother. She'll be at the theater now? C'mon.

(*Emma reaches for Sabina's hand.*)

(Sabina takes it.)

(They exit.)

End of Play

IN CONVERSATION WITH THE PLAYWRIGHT

Maya: You wrote this play early in your life as a playwright.

MJ: It was so long ago! My first serious full-length play.

Maya: What inspired **A Live Dress***?*

MJ: In 2008 when I was a senior at Wesleyan University, I found an archived *New York Times* review of the play, *God of Vengeance.* The first line was something like, "No one cares what sewer rats do as long as they stay down in the sewer while they do it." The play, originally written in Yiddish and featuring a lesbian relationship, was being performed in English on Broadway. The production was promptly shut down and the cast arrested and tried on obscenity charges. A few years later when I met Paula Vogel, she told me she was also working on a play about this too; hers became *Indecent* which went on to a Broadway Production.

When I came across this review in 2008 I was instantly captivated. Was the author referring to the theater artists as "sewer rats" because they were Jews? Because the play contained a lesbian relationship? Through researching the play and the worlds it came from, I learned that many of these ideas were interrelated. Stereotypes for Ashkenazi Jews emphasized weak, feminine men and grotesque, hairy, overbearing women. Was the cast being referred to as sewer rats because the play raised serious questions about the agency, independence and options for women in Jewish society? Because it dared to realistically portray the desolation of a home destroyed by manipulation and domestic violence? I wrote *A Live Dress* in order to understand the world of these sewer rats. If such was the climate in which they were performing *God of Vengeance*, what empowered them to so? I wanted to imagine their world as they saw it: How did they experience and negotiate melding their cultural memory of Europe with expectations of American-ness? In particular, how were expressions of gender norms and expectations in direct conflict and how did that violence play out for individuals and across generations? […] I learned a lot about structure, character and theme through writing it. Looking back at it now I see how it led me to later work.

Maya: How would you distill this play in ten words or less?

MJ: Love, death, ghosts, journeys.

Maya: The fall after you won this Award, you headed to Yale's MFA, led by Paula Vogel. Now you are one of NYC's most visible trans playwrights. When you think about your body of work over time, what themes or forms emerge as emblematic?

MJ: Themes of death, ghosts, ancestors, gender identity, queerness.

Maya: Can you share a few words about this play in performance? What are its possibilities and pitfalls?

This play has never been produced so I don't know!

Maya: Before you decided to become a playwright, how many women playwrights had you read or studied?

MJ: It is hard to pinpoint when I became a playwright! I am fairly certain that the first woman playwright I was introduced to was Paula Vogel with her play *How I Learned to Drive*. I don't think I found many others until I began writing plays and came to be a part of playwriting communities. I remember discovering Suzan-Lori Parks, Cherrie Moraga, and Naomi Wallace the summer between High School and College and feeling like something had cracked open for me. Something about the way these writers told stories centering women's experiences, full of ghosts and magic, felt like my universe. I was discovering the work I needed to make.

Maya: How do you define feminism today? And how does your work fit within a feminist framework?

267

Feminism is a social and political movement aiming to dismantle […] gender-based oppression for everyone with a specific emphasis on women and transfolk; also fighting racism, classism, ableism, because these are all connected.

This play centers the experiences of women, giving us a new perspective on history. I also try to expose and subvert patriarchal systems of dominance in all my work. And I'm interested in expressing gender fluidity onstage: how are we all different genders in different spaces? This strikes me as an inherently feminist concern — throughout time women and transfolk have always had to transform their gender presentations as they've moved through the world. Patriarchy wants us to understand gender as fixed and essential so that some people are powerful and others are not. But that's not actually how gender works.

Maya: Do you identify as a feminist playwright? A lesbian, queer or trans playwright?

MJ: Yes. I am feminist and I am trans. And queer.

Maya: What advice do you have for women or trans artists writing their first play or wanting their work seen? Would it be different for lesbian playwrights or writers of color?

MJ: I would say write without fear! Write exactly what you have to write, what only you can write, write unapologetically! And then produce your own work. Don't wait for anyone to tell you you're a playwright.

F U L L / S E L F

by
Claire Chafee

**Winner of the
2013 Jane Chambers Prize**

CAST OF CHARACTERS

LOUISE
14 years old. Feisty but inward, just got her first period, confides in few. A thinker. Her mother has taught her very little about her past, in her effort to bring them both onward and upward. (Also called Lu.)

CELIA
Louise's mother, 46. A highly accomplished lawyer, elegantly dressed, originally from outside of Denver, but has severed those ties and lives in New York City. Practical about her emotions, not always successfully. A lesbian, a bit quiet about it.

MAGGIE
Celia's mother, 68. Deceased but still around, living in the After Life. A rural person with a lightning-quick humor. Pragmatic. Warm but low on patience. Misses her daughter, has never met her granddaughter Louise.

OLIVIA
A geologist, 42. Lives and teaches in Golden, Colorado, but is currently in the After Life, temporarily, driving around with Maggie in a state of puzzlement. Lovely, a lesbian in repair from a disaster of heartbreak and a botched overdose of pills.

ECKERT
A rancher, 48. Louise's father, deceased and in the After Life. Quiet. Sorrowful. Avoidant. Not the least bit sentimental. Has never met Louise. (Doubles as Dr. Eckert.)

DR. ECKERT
A psychiatrist, 48, in New York City. Freudian. Wearer of corduroy jackets. A good listener.

270

SETTING

Manhattan, an apartment in the Upper West Side with
high end features, and the desert lands in Colorado.

TIME

Manhattan: current time. Desert: the Afterlife.

ACT ONE

LOUISE (*on her knees, on her bed, fully clothed in her pleated
corduroy skirt, looking out her window through binoculars*): I
like to watch the psychiatrists' wives. Jogging around the
track.

(*She takes down some notes.*)

Some people bird-watch. I wonder what it's like to get in a
really big fight with a psychiatrist.

(*Brings the binoculars back up to her eyes.*)

I see them in their padded headphones. Lumbering around
the oval in orange tracksuits. I know it might be rude to
watch their faces when they're thinking it's a private
moment. I like to think of God that way. Watching us
when we think we are having a private moment. There are
lots of ways to create privacy. My wardrobe, for example.
(*Motions to her outfit*) Corduroy, for instance. People leave
you alone if you wear this. They know you aren't fishing
for compliments. My mother doesn't dress this way. My
mother is a looker.

(*Lights up on Celia in an elegant gray suit shot through
with silver thread. She throws down a case file as she
starts to speak.*)

271

CELIA: That's precisely why I'd emphasize that this is utterly consistent with my clients' recollection of events. The timeline is unclear, the motive has yet to be determined and the evidence was collected by a deranged night clerk who admittedly has had mental problems that he's medicated for. I request on behalf of my client full and nonbinding dismissal of this entire case.

LOUISE: My mother never loses. She says she's driven to defend the first amendment. I think she's learned the art of lying with the truth. Believe me, I have tried this and I cannot get it right like she does. That's what makes me not respect her and respect her at the same time.

CELIA *(calling out to her):* Are you packing?

LOUISE *(calling back):* Yes!! *(To us)* I am packing for music camp. Viola. I have been playing the viola for eleven years. I know. As if. That's ridiculous, I think. I would know by now if I was good. I'm not that good. *(Confides)* I think my mother's lonely, but I'm not an expert on the subject.

> *(Lights up on a marble kitchen island, a designer pendant light hangs above. Two tall stools facing in. Celia is depressing a plunger in a tiny coffee press.)*

CELIA: Lu? Louise? If I come in there am I going to find you packing?

LOUISE: I am going for three weeks so my mother can get back on the dating scene. That's not exactly how she put it, but I know. She's hoping it will "slenderize" me to jump in and out of a lake all day and then go back to playing the viola. In the Rocky Mountains.

> *(Calling out to Lu, aggravated but controlled.)*

CELIA: I'm standing by the island with the list. *(Pause.)* This is where I have spent a lot of your childhood. *(Pause.)* Making lists. *(Pause.)* Things you should remember to do,

Louise? (*Pause.*) And things to remember not to do. Remember? (*Listens.*) Lotta lists.

> (*Lights up on Louise standing by a roller suitcase, a boarding pass in her hand.*)

LOUISE: I know. The lists.

CELIA: Clothing list: asthma meds, pair of shoes, running, one pair: nice, one pair: casual. Sandals. One sweater vest. Five cotton T shirts, one pair shorts, a blouse. Five pair pink-and-white striped cotton underwear, two bras: training. A bathing suit. Dark blue. Gum (*hands it to her*), Kleenex (*she hands it to her*) and a clementine (*hands her an orange*). Someone from Camp Kanoah is going to meet your plane. Outside the baggage claim. A couple of girls are flying in from New York, only from different airports. One of these days, you're going to have to think for yourself. One of these days, these things are going to bother you without me having to tell you. Now: Things are different in the West.

Sit up straight. Clip your nails. Create opportunities. And don't always ask people what their sayings mean out there: There is no direct translation.

LU: O.K.

> (*They stare each other in the eye.*)

CELIA: Every time you just do what I tell you, Louise, it's like a miracle.

> (*Lights up on Maggie, Celia's mother, standing near a car with its door open. A sweater is draped around her shoulders. She is looking at the far horizon. Olivia is looking in the glove compartment. A Ford Galaxie Fairlane convertible with seats the color of camel. The dashboard and inside of the car are lit, making it seem otherworldly.*)

MAGGIE: Now what.

OLIVIA: I'm looking for a map.

MAGGIE: They just told me: Keep on driving. Till you get to the airport.

OLIVIA: Keep on driving *(sits up)* where? On this road?

MAGGIE: I took it to mean the Interstate. I just pick up the information on the radio. And that thing goes in and out.

OLIVIA: Why are you bringing me with you? *(No answer.)* *(Matter-of-fact)* Does this have to do with my incident?

MAGGIE: No. Everyone has a tunnel there's no light at the other end of. No, not at all. I just don't want to do it alone. Who wants to go the airport alone? Nobody. Not unless you're rail-thin and looking for love.

   (Looks her up and down.)

OLIVIA: No?

MAGGIE: Not at all. Airport's full of the wrong mysteries. *(Pause.)* Olivia, don't you recognize me?

OLIVIA: I knew your daughter.

MAGGIE: Celia. You and Celia were joined at the hip. I know I look different. That was a long time ago.

OLIVIA: I only come here sometimes. I have a whole other life you know.

MAGGIE: Well, that makes one of us. *(She gets back in the car and starts it up.)* I thought you'd want to get a look at her anyway. Feeling like you did about her mother.

OLIVIA: That was years ago. You aren't seriously going to bring that up.

MAGGIE *(raises a hand):* Who's counting now? *(Shifts the car into gear with stick on the driving column.)* "Out we go, our perilous journey, in we come, resplendent light."

OLIVIA: Is that from the Bible?

MAGGIE: Not unless they've added something recently.

> *(Sound of a plane landing and skidding to a stop.)*

> *(Lu appears, wheeling her bag through the automatic doors. She is in Denver. She gets to the curb and waits. She readjusts the viola strapped to her back. She waits. She takes out her cell phone and texts her mother.)*

LU: "Miracle! Landed in Denver. Choppy flight. Waiting by the baggage claim. R U dating yet?"

> *(Celia, by her marble island, hears a blip and reads the text. Texts back.)*

CELIA: "Not funny. That is not at all funny. That is just rude, missy. Try not being so rude while UR away. Practice."

> *(Lu puts phone away and waits. And waits. Maggie and Olivia pull up to curb outside the baggage claim in the Ford Fairlane.)*

OLIVIA: Is that her?

MAGGIE: Gotta be. Look at the hair. And the way she's standing. Looks just like Celia. *(Shouts her name.)* Lou-ise?

> *(Louise gives a small wave hello and doesn't move. Maggie puts the car in PARK and shrugs.)*

MAGGIE *(to Louise, and loudly):* Let's go on in to baggage claim and get the rest of your luggage.

(Lu points to her very small roller bag.)

LU: This is it.

MAGGIE: That's your luggage?

LU: I'm only staying three weeks.

MAGGIE: That's three weeks?

LU: My mother's very organized.

MAGGIE: Always was. *(Pause.)*

MAGGIE: Well. *(Looks up at the sky.)* I was worried about your plane, late afternoon thunder burst, all that electricity in the air. They must have had to do one of those radar landings. *(Intently)* Did it just go *kunk* when you landed?

(Lu nods her head, Maggie nodding hers.)

Radar landing. Well, hop on in. This is Olivia.

(Lu gets in the car.)

Better get in. Better get going.

LU *(looking around the car):* I like that it's a convertible. It doesn't say Camp Kanoah.

MAGGIE: You bet it doesn't! A Ford Fairlane says, "We're good to go!" "Pull the cork outa your heart!" "Live it up!"

LU: O.K.

(She glances at Olivia, who shrugs her shoulders.)

Do you play an instrument?

OLIVIA: No. *(Puts a scarf around her hair.)* Is that your violin?

LU: Viola. I've been playing for eleven years. Did you pick up the others girls already? From camp?

> *(Maggie and Olivia just watch the road. Lights down.)*
>
> *(Lights up. Low dinner music and tinkling sounds. Celia is out on a date: a glass of wine in front of her, white tablecloth. We only hear her side of the conversation. She keeps touching the stem of her glass.)*

CELIA: I went to Harvard Law to prove I wasn't. *(She laughs. Takes a sip.)* I know. I didn't. *(Takes another sip. Waits.)* That's in Connecticut. *(Nodding.)* Hmm. Right. Just one. She's an avid musician. I know. Me? No. Not at work or anything. *(Listens.)* Before? Middlebury. That's unusual. Right. That's what they say. *(Listens.)* I don't remember. No. I was born in Colorado, but I didn't stay long. NO they don't. No kidding. Exactly. So who knows, right? Me too. I know.

> *(Lights cross fade back to car in the desert.)*
>
> *(Lu has cramps and is half lying down in the backseat, clutching the door handle, a low, long groan is coming from her.)*

OLIVIA *(looking in the rearview)*: Lu? You need some aspirin back there?

LU *(half shouting)*: I got some trouble in here. I have no idea.

OLIVIA: Maggie, why don't you give her some aspirin.

LU *(surprised):* I think I got my period on the airplane. I am late on my period. Most girls have it by like twelve. People throw their antidepressants in the river water, and now there's too much estrogen.

MAGGIE: Why in the world would they do that?

LU: I don't know, but it's happening.

> *(Pause.)*

OLIVIA: I've been on antidepressants.

LU: So?

MAGGIE *(looking in the rearview):* Lu? Do they consider you an odd girl?

OLIVIA: Hey. Maggie.

LU *(tentatively):* I guess they do.

MAGGIE: Honey, I'm sorry if I sound insulting. It's the way I am now.

LU: Let's just say, I'm used to spending a lot of time by myself.

MAGGIE: Maybe that's why you called me.

LU *(thinking about this):* I don't think I called you. I'm on my way to Camp Kanoah. Music Camp.

MAGGIE: Well, someone called me.

LU *(lifting up her viola case):* Outside Denver?

> *(Maggie lets out a long, descending whistle.)*

MAGGIE: Let's not compare worlds right now, okay, sweetie?

LU *(slumping back down)*: Okay.

> *(Maggie, Lu and Olivia keep driving on the Interstate. Olivia turns on the radio, but instead of music, there is the sound of sonar, like inside a submarine.)*
>
> *(Back in Celia's apartment, she has woken up, in blue light from the street outside. She checks the other side of the bed, sees that it is empty.)*

CELIA: Well that's good. *(Takes a drink of water by the bed, puts on her glasses, checks the time.)* Shit. *(Takes out a small pad and writes down her dream.)* "On an airplane, they are showing a movie about swimming pools. The development of the backyard pool industry. Very engaging. I am eating shrimp. Must be first class. It's very dark outside the plane. Someone in a uniform coming by and tells me "Hug your seat cushion to your chest" because we aren't over water. Sudden piercing dread. Then I wake up." *(Stops writing.)* No more dating. Horrible. *(Celia gets up and turns on the light. Puts on a robe.)*

MAGGIE *(getting flustered, speaking to Olivia)*: Hook up with the two of you. Last thing I would picture. Last thing I would picture of the Afterlife. Honestly. *(Taps the steering wheel.)* Honestly! I thought I'd either be feeding Gabriel grapes or *(flattens out her hand and passes it out the window)* over and out. Buried by a willow.

OLIVIA *(to Lu)*: She's pretty much saying anything that comes into her head right now.

LU: Is it safe for to her to drive?

OLIVIA: Let's just say we're driving through a desert with someone unpredictable.

MAGGIE: Given your scintillating approach to life, Olivia, I'm not at all insulted to know you think of me as unpredictable.

OLIVIA: That's really not a very nice thing to say.

LU *(looks around for highway signs; to Olivia, very worried)*: Where are we heading? Is this the way we're supposed to be headed?

MAGGIE *(accusingly)*: When I was little, I enjoyed family outings.

LU: When I was a little, I was afraid of being murdered. I was taught French at an early age. I drew tulips, stiff and uneven, next to poems about tulips, in French.

MAGGIE: That's because you're a city girl.

LU: Are we heading for one? A city.

> *(Silence.)*

No one knows. *(Looks out window.)* No one knows.

> *(She groans, lying back against the seat.)*

The cramps. They come in on waves.

MAGGIE *(fishing in her purse for a tin of aspirin while driving)*: 'Livia, why don't you get the iced tea? And help me find my aspirin.

> *(Olivia opens up a thermos.)*

(To Lu) And don't be so dramatical. Not a one of us hasn't had the time of month, so take these and sit up straight.

> *(Lu does so immediately.)*

> *(Celia, back in her apartment, has answered a call*

and is listening to the other end.)

CELIA: Well that's impossible. Who you got then? A girl from White Plains? My daughter lives on the Upper West Side. No, she doesn't have a retainer. No. Or bangs. That's not my daughter. You have someone else. Listen, I am certain she is still at the airport, so you get someone to get back in the minivan and go pick her up. She knows to find the help desk. She knows what to do. Just go back to Denver International and have her paged. Louise Montague-Haupenhauser. And seriously don't fuck with me or I will have Camp Kanoah and Music Camp, nestled in the Rocky Mountains, wish to God they hadn't left the daughter of a criminal defense attorney just-made-partner, at the baggage claim.

> *(Slams the phone down. Pulls out her cell and rapidly texts Louise, whose phone pings, but she can't hear it for the highway wind.)*

> *(Lights down. A short pause.)*

> *(Lights up on Lu's father, sitting in a booth in a diner in a uniform. His jacket is hanging on the hook behind him. He's drinking coffee from a white cup with a faded pattern on it, staring straight ahead.)*

ECKERT: I don't much think about her. Not anymore. It's not that I don't know I have a daughter somewhere, it's just not a thing I'd answer for. *Daughter* is a strange word to use if I'm not in her family, don't you think?

> *(He wipes his mouth with a napkin, carefully.)*

Last time I saw her she was lying in a crib, wrapped in a blanket like a little burrito. Eyes squeezed tight, two little fists at her side. That's not a thing you think about, like some horse crashing slow motion into a fence. That can't be good for you. Not here.

(Early evening on the Interstate. Music. Dashboard lights. Maggie is at the wheel staring hard at the road, driving very slowly. Lu is slumped in back, sleeping on a coat. Olivia is rocking slowly, staring up at the sky, an eerie yellow light is shining from upholstery. Maggie turns down the radio.)

MAGGIE: Are you awake?

OLIVIA: Yes.

MAGGIE: I may need you to drive. I may need to pull over.

OLIVIA: Okay.

MAGGIE: I'm coming loose. Nothing big: just: my nails are kinda separating from my nail beds. I can feel it holding the wheel.

OLIVIA: Uh-huh. *(She is looking up.)* You never see stars like this. You never do.

MAGGIE: My knees are coming loose too. The new hip replacement feels just like the old one.

OLIVIA: I'm beginning to wonder why the hell you dragged me along.

MAGGIE: Oh no you don't. This isn't my longing. *(Looks in back at Lu.)* Far as I know. I was zipping around, going about my Afterlife, till they contacted me. I guess she needs to see the father. From what I gather.

OLIVIA: Oh God, not that guy. Hate that guy. Is he dead too?

MAGGIE: Suppose so.

OLIVIA: You made her go out with him in the first place.

MAGGIE: Oh, tell me you aren't still holding on to that one. Your chances with her were between slim and none.

OLIVIA: How in the *hell* would you know that, Maggie?

(Lu sits bolt upright in the backseat.)

MAGGIE *(cheerfully)*: You up?

LU: My cramps are gone. Where are we anyway?

OLIVIA *(covering)*: We're on the Interstate and Maggie thinks it's only an hour.

MAGGIE: We're going to make a little unplanned detour. We thought you'd like to see your father.

LU: I'm supposed to be on my way to Camp Kanoah Music Camp. And I don't know my father.

MAGGIE: Just a quick visit.

(Maggie and Olivia both raise eyebrows, staring at the road.)

(Celia is dressed; it is morning. She is back on the phone with the authorities.)

CELIA: I don't see how she could have been kidnapped. Who would want to kidnap her? She's extremely aware of her surroundings. She carries mace. She lives in New York City. She's probably lost in the airport somewhere and her phone ran out of juice. Relatives? There are no relatives. Her grandmother lived outside of Denver but she passed away a while ago. Besides she didn't know her. Am I supposed to come out there?? Am I speaking directly to a detective? That Camp is taking no responsibility, but I will sue them, so that's something you might want to mention. Yes. Yes. I'll wait for your call.

(Slams phone down and takes out her cell phone and rapidly texts Louise.)

CELIA: "WHERE ARE U? VERY CONCERNED. IS THIS A GAME? IT BETTER NOT BE. NOT FUNNY. CONTACT. m. o. m."

(Back in the Ford Fairlane, it is night, and the interior is lit in an eerie way. The car seems to emitting light. They are listening to a song and all three join in on the chorus, with no expression as if they've been hearing it for many hours.)

MAGGIE *(turning down the knob):* Okay everybody. I got some more information. We are going to meet him in a lunch place, name of Nemnem's, down the road a piece.

LU: Does he know that we are coming?

MAGGIE: A-ppa-ren-tly. This is what they say. Now Lu, don't get cold feet on me — but I've bought you a new dress and I want you to wear it. I'm going to pull into a Texaco so you can change.

LU: I'm fine the way I am.

MAGGIE: Something told me that you were going to say that. Have I ever steered you wrong?

LU *(thinks about it):* But I just got here.

MAGGIE: So far.

LU: So far: no.

MAGGIE: Well things go better in a new dress. Things the nature of this. Now don't look grim. Part of the program. Just trust me. *(Presents her with a brush.)* And do the hair too, sweetie.

LU: He's already walked away from me once. What do I care what he thinks?

OLIVIA: Well, if you want to have a conversation with him, it's better if you don't look like you took that to heart. Believe me.

LU *(snapping):* Why do you suddenly know so much about it?

OLIVIA: I've had some problems with letting people ask themselves if I was worth it. *(Shoots a look at Maggie.)* I'm working on them.

LU: He was my FATHER. What does that have to do with your love life?

OLIVIA: What did I say about my love life? This has nothing to do with my love life.

MAGGIE *(pulling over the car, almost shouting):* Can we just: remember? Can we remember that there is no immediate way out of this particular situation?

> *(Pause.)*

It took YEARS to get into. Years. NO one remembers how we got into it because 1) we have no new information coming in, and 2) no one bothered to signal. Is that perfectly clear? Can anyone say, with a shred of conviction, they had no part in landing here?

> *(Silence.)*

Lu?

LU *(loudly):* Yes, ma'am.

MAGGIE *(looking at her in the rearview mirror):* No one answers the phone where you came from. Way back. Got me? You are from a scattered people. Hear me? And I'm not talking about New York. So, I want you to put on this dress …

> *(Lifts a shopping bag stuffed with fancy tissue from behind her seat.)*

MAGGIE: And sparkle up your hair a bit and we will bring you to see him, and we will wait for you in the parking lot, and will bring you back again. *(Pause.)* O.K. sweetie pie?

LU *(crossing her arms):* Okay. Okay.

> *(A pause. A small shift.)*

> *(Celia comes home from work. She turns on all the lights up bright. She walks into her apartment, throws down keys, drops her attaché case to the floor, takes her coat off, opens the freezer and takes out a thin box, opens the microwave oven and slams it inside. Turns it on. Then she takes off her shoes. Then she picks up her phone, listens to the dial tone, puts it back down. She flicks on the TV. She sits on the couch and crosses her legs at the ankles. She holds the remote in both hands as we see the light of the evening news flicker on her face.)*

> *(Inside the ladies' room of the gas station. Lu is talking to the mirror, putting on the new dress.)*

LU: They're trying to make a woman outta me. Jesus Christ! My mother's going to be furious. I have to text her. Tell her where I am. I always tell her where I am.

> *(Gets the dress on and regards herself in the mirror. Finds a small plastic box of eye shadow and rubs a smudge on her eyelids.)*

Last time you saw me I was a little baby, wrapped in a blanket. Probably in a row of other little babies: like an appetizer. *(Tries to put her hair up.)* Easy to pick up. Did you see me? *(She puts on Chapstick in the mirror.)* Maybe you just signed the paperwork.

I only have one small window, a short amount of time to affect the outcome. *(Tries a smile, holds it.)* Plain-looking when serious, but pretty when smiling.

> *(Maggie and Olivia are at a deserted gas station: a sign on one pump says FULL, on the other says SELF. It is hot, in the desert. Olivia is pacing and fanning herself, Maggie is in the driver's seat, door open, fixing a pair of reading glasses with her other glasses on. She is using a tiny screwdriver.)*

MAGGIE: Thing is, these aren't even my prescription. The one eye is fine, but the other just keeps seeing things out of the corner of it. *(Looks at the horizon.)*

OLIVIA: Depth perception. There's very little of it out here.

MAGGIE *(looks at Olivia, who is cleaning out her purse)*: Lu's taking forever in the ladies' room.

OLIVIA: It's hot.

MAGGIE *(looks around)*: I'm about to suck off that "FREE AIR" hose over there.

OLIVIA: Maggie, that would strike me as out of character.

MAGGIE: That's why I'd do it.

OLIVIA: That said, I'd walk over to the "FREE WATER" hose and aim some right down my dress.

MAGGIE: Oh do it! Do something out of character!

OLIVIA: I'm trying! My God. You've just never been in love. Is that it?

(Pause.)

MAGGIE: Got a little something buried? Got unfinished business waiting for you in a motel room?

OLIVIA: You wouldn't know about my kind of unfinished business.

MAGGIE: You think I don't know about pay phones?

OLIVIA: No one stands around begging in pay phones anymore.

MAGGIE: I am sorry to hear that.

OLIVIA: What is it, Maggie, you never had a bad idea? Is that it?

MAGGIE: Not with a married woman, point of fact. *(Starts to hear something.)* I keep getting the weirdest information.

OLIVIA: From where?

MAGGIE *(makes a small circle with the screwdriver)*: Prairie songs, Wind turbines. Forts.

OLIVIA: Oh. *(Deflated)* I thought you had some advice.

MAGGIE: What about that did not feel like advice? Put it behind you. Keep moving. Start over. Shift gears. *(Points to the ladies' room.)* What's Lu doing in there?

OLIVIA: Screwing up her courage. Probably a bit unhappy about the dress.

(Three loud knocks from Maggie at the door.)

MAGGIE: You redecorating?

LU *(shouts):* I'll be right out!

> *(A light up on Celia, by the phone but staring straight ahead; Lu begins to address the mirror and ask it questions.)*

LU: Did you ever think that I would look for you? *(No answer.)* Were you sorry that I didn't? *(No answer.)* Did you wonder how I'd turn out? *(No answer.)*

Cause I do. I wonder.

> *(Three loud knocks from Maggie at the door. Lu shouts at the door.)*

LU: OKAY! *(Back into the mirror.)* Here goes nothing. Remember not to try too hard.

> *(Lights out on Celia. Lu grabs her stuff and goes back out, she practically bumps into Maggie, who is stunned by her appearance.)*

MAGGIE: You look sharp, Lu. Dress fits you like a glove.

LU *(confronting her):* I need to ask you something.

MAGGIE: Okay.

LU: Didn't you die?

> *(Maggie waits.)*

(Whispers loudly.) So what are you doing here??

MAGGIE: What are *you* doing here? Must have had a question. Some regret. This is where we are: *regrets.* So you must have one.

LU: I don't. I don't think so. Isn't it too soon for that? I only just got my period.

(Lights down on the desert, up on Celia.)

CELIA *(picks up phone, dials):* Thank you for picking up. It's Celia Montague-Haupenhauser. I know. Look. I have an idea. I have a strong intuition that she is still at the airport, somewhere, probably in the ladies' room. Maybe she's hiding. She knows she's done something … irresponsible … and she doesn't want to get into more trouble. It's possible I misinterpreted her interest in music camp. I have a strong request that you call Denver International Airport and ask them to search for a white girl, young-looking, wheeling a roller bag, who looks like she maybe made some rash decisions, some poor choices, not sure what she is doing there or what exactly to do next. You have? And what did they tell you? That's not at all unusual? Really? Is that the word they used? I see. Right. I'll call you back.

(Hangs up.)

(Maggie and Olivia pull up to The Thruway Diner. It is dusk and the neon sign is on. Lu gets out of the car.)

OLIVIA: You look really nice. Your hair.

MAGGIE: Take your time. Have the pie. And let him do the talking.

LU: Which booth is he in? What's he wearing?

MAGGIE: He's in a uniform. I think his jacket's off, but it's a uniform. Go on, Sweetie Pie. This is your stop.

> *(Lu walks into the diner where a man is eating pie at a booth with his jacket off. He has on a big silver watch, which he keeps checking as he eats. Lu advances enough to get his attention. He stands up halfway, smoothing his tie and offers the seat across the booth.)*

LU: Hi. It's me.

ECKERT: Hello.

(Blackout.)

(Lights up on Maggie using a personal portable pocket fan, and Olivia is behind the wheel eating slowly from a small bag of chips. She wipes her fingers on a napkin after each one. Olivia is watching Lu and Eckert in their booth through the plate glass window.)

MAGGIE: I remember when you were in high school. I remember you always ate your chips like that. One by one.

OLIVIA: You never talk about Celia or where she ended up. Why is that, Maggie?

MAGGIE: My daughter and I don't talk a lot.

OLIVIA: So I guess we both lost her.

MAGGIE: That's one way to put it.

OLIVIA: Your daughter taught me how to kiss, you know.

MAGGIE: Is that my fault now? Really? Why not? Everything's the mother's fault. Go on. Why not?

(Olivia smiles.)

(Raising a hand.) Well, don't go giving demonstrations.

OLIVIA: Not to worry. You really aren't very nice you know.

MAGGIE: I spent my life on nice. Nice life. Turns out that's not the point. You'll find out.

OLIVIA *(looks over at Lu through the diner window)*: God I just HATE that.

MAGGIE *(tired)*: What?

OLIVIA: The hope; that tiny seed. See the way she's leaning in? How come it's never HIM? Why isn't he leaning in?

(Maggie looks at them, then looks away.)

I feel for her.

MAGGIE: I can see that.

OLIVIA: I can empathize.

MAGGIE: I can see that. But don't get too attached here.

OLIVIA: I'm not getting attached. I just feel for her.

MAGGIE: Listen. I'm about to move on. And you're about to go back. This is no place for you; you've got your whole life to live.

OLIVIA: They always say that. You have your whole life to live. As if you ever do live your whole life.

(Lights up on Nemnem's Diner. The Father has rearranged the salt and pepper shakers, napkin dispenser to represent parts of the story. He is animated, speaks in rapid fire, as if he has told this story many times over.)

ECKERT: It happened in the desert, over there, but in a small city. Outside. Details interrupt the offshore flow. That's what you got to keep your eye on. See, I know how to deploy. That's what I know. I know how to call my men forward. I know how to take the plans and take the means necessary for them to happen. I know how to bring my men forward. And so I do. The order comes to call them off. And so I do.

(He opens up his arms.)

We are on a Holy Site and must be wary of destroying the relics. What relics these might be: unclear. Order comes. We need to back off and hold. Well, my men hold. And then they get thoughtful. My men hold for long enough, in the desert, in the heat, and they see the flies gather at the edge of the lips of the fallen. And the lips of the fallen, who cannot be retrieved as they are directly in a sniper lane of "risk it not, my man;" they are lying in the dust of their own bad luck ... and my men can see and ruminate on the flies on the lips and eyes of the fallen. They can see. They have come to be thoughtful, in a place where thoughts have left. You have turned my marines into poets. Detail. My detail. See?

    (Lu nods, trying to follow, she takes a sip of water.)

Like a belt buckle from a plane crash, fallen right on your own front lawn. Hard to shake. Maybe you just find it there one day. Maybe you bring it inside with you, place it on the ledge against the other things above your sink. Nowhere special, but still: It interrupts. What to do with it?

    (Lu nods, trying to follow.)

Like a scream inside a shoe box. It's a practical measure. "Practice for grace for when you really need it" my father always told me. So I decided I was going to move my men forward anyway. I rose up, with my gun, and ran right through that square.

    (Lu sits across from her father in the silence. He is dipping a tea bag over and over in a cup of hot water and slowly pouring milk in.)

LU: Did you ever wonder how I'd turn out?

ECKERT *(takes a sip of tea, not sure what to say)*: Sometimes.

LU: Would you describe my mother as a person given to rash decisions?

293

ECKERT: No.

LU: When she was very young was she ever known to change her mind once she had time to think about it and then make up her mind another way?

ECKERT: No.

LU: Was she unfair and difficult to talk to?

ECKERT: Not especially. I honestly didn't really get to know your mother all too well. Just the once.

LU: Oh.

ECKERT: She knew her own mind, that much I can say.

LU: Okay.

(Pause.)

So what happened with your men? After you said, "Practice grace for when you really need it."

ECKERT: I got blown up.

LU: Blown up?

ECKERT: Yep. Blown up. And since I'm scattered it's a bit hard to give an answer to your questions.

LU: Sorry.

ECKERT: Don't be. You aren't scattered.

LU: Well, I'm not in one piece, per se.

ECKERT: Per se. Well.

LU: It means: you could say.

ECKERT: I know what it means.

LU *(takes another sip of water.)* Okay. *(Pause.)* Was she pretty?

ECKERT: Of course she was pretty. Pretty and *(he thinks)* complicated. Like you seem on your way to be.

LU *(singing):* "Oh we're on our way to Temp-or-rai-rie! And we don't know when we'll be back."

ECKERT: She had a singing voice. She sure did.

> *(They are at an impasse.)*

ECKERT: I had a recruit once, a small woman, compact, very blond, black eyes. She had no concept of the anger she carried. It was: impossible to train this woman. And that was my job. Drill sergeant, basic training.

She did a sit-up like she was getting up to get herself something. That way, she'd follow a command you gave, but acted like it was her idea. You could not intimidate this woman. I think I fell in love with her, the way I fell in love with your mother. I disobeyed an order straight from her not to love her. An order is not a thing you bargain with. It is a fact. A fact I disobeyed.

LU: Was this before or after me?

ECKERT *(he's lost in his own thought here):* Manners. Small, bird-like manners. That's what she had. Un-trainable. Kicked to shit as she was, internally, the usual: incest, boredom and a series of bad haircuts in photos, sitting next to overweight aunts. Still. She had this indelible stain. An embarrassed dignity you could not crack. She'd give you laps like it was her idea, a good way for her to blow off steam. Finally I couldn't take it anymore. I got four inches from her face and told her, she was personally, in her own way, very incrementally and specifically: an asshole. "Yes sir." She says. Can you believe that? Reminded me exactly of your mother.

LU: Was she like that?

ECKERT (*pretends to be angry*): "Do you doubt what I am saying?" I said to her. "No sir, no," she said. Right back. Smile on her face. She had a spirit. That's what it was.

LU: I think I have that. I think I have a spirit.

ECKERT: Is that a fact?

LU: Only my mother won't let me use it.

ECKERT: No? Now that's a bit unfair.

LU: All the things I do are the same. They're all the same. They're for the future.

ECKERT (*leaning in*): What things do you do?

LU (*she leans in, intensely*): I get good grades! I play the viola! I live in a nice neighborhood. I learn how to Manage My Time. My time! And this is in the NINTH GRADE. I take those practice tests. I live close to the Upper West Side. When you grow up close to the Upper West Side, everything is for the future. Your grades. Your looks. It's for the future. Everything.

ECKERT: Well. I am sorry about that. I am. (*Leaning back.*) But they should have never raised you like that.

LU: Is there something you need to say to me?

ECKERT: I was thinking that might be the question here. And I know there would be many things to say; in truth, on my conscience, I really don't. My battles took place: elsewhere.

LU: Mine didn't.

ECKERT *(looking around):* I was supposed to order you a piece of pie.

LU: I have people waiting in a car. In the parking lot. I have people waiting for me.

ECKERT: Good. Well then. Shouldn't keep people waiting.

LU: That would be painful.

> *(Pause: He reaches over and takes her hand, shakes it, then holds it.)*

ECKERT: You turned out fine. You have a spirit. I can see that.
> *(Lu gets up out of the booth and walks out of the diner.)*

> *(Maggie looks up and sees Lu leaving the diner and walking toward them.)*

MAGGIE: Start the car. Here she comes. She looks a little rearranged. Say: let's take her somewhere there's a water ride. That's it! Something like one of those water rides — where you all get in the boat.

OLIVIA: We gotta get her back, now, Maggie. Seriously. No water rides.

MAGGIE *(whispering):* What makes you such "a coper" all of a sudden?

> *(Lu walks over to the car, stands by the passenger door.)*

How'd that go?

LU: He is completely uninteresting.

MAGGIE: That can't be true.

OLIVIA *(suddenly fierce)*: She can say whatever she needs to say! That can't have been easy! How can that have been easy? Get in the car!

MAGGIE *(calmly)*: Lu? We were going to take a breather. How about we go to one of those water rides? One where they pretend you're on safari or we all go over a waterfall? Cool us off. Want to come?

> *(Lu just stands there.)*

MAGGIE: Want to come?

LU: This is like one of those TV shows where you have to keep trying not to get voted off the island.

MAGGIE *(to Olivia)*: What is she talking about?

OLIVIA: They have these TV shows where you are on an island with people you don't know and you try and survive.

LU *(holding back tears)*: Maybe that's why they're so popular.

MAGGIE: Honestly, the more I hear the news of the world, the less I miss it.

OLIVIA: Lu? Just open the door of the car and get in.

MAGGIE *(to Olivia)*: These ones coming up they frighten me, Olivia, they really do. *(Makes gestures with her thumbs as if she's texting.)* Makes my hair come out.

LU: Your hair's coming out anyway.

> *(She whips out her cell phone and rapidly texts her mother in front of them, reading it out loud as she goes.)*

"Miracle! I am in the desert with Maggie and person named Olivia, who seems to have some problems with love. We are in the afterlife. I am fine, per se. Will text you details as they become available."

(Lu gets in the car, slams the door. Olivia guns it in neutral.)

OLIVIA: Well. That does it.

(MAGGIE smiles, but to herself.)

(Blackout.)

(Morning. At the island. Celia stands and pushes the little plunger of her coffee press. She is dressed for work and holding her shoes in one hand. She is leaving a message on Louise's cell phone voice mail.)

CELIA: Listen. I am beyond language here. This is just a simple matter of courtesy. If you would call me — just so I know you are okay. That is just decency. *(Pause.)* Do NOT TEXT ME riddles. I swear to God, Louise, when you come back from camp I'm going to send you to a therapist. A therapist, Louise! Maybe a psychiatrist.

I know that things have been building up in you, but you cannot worry people like this. I am involving authorities here. I am making threats. And you are playing practical jokes with your newfound "sense of humor" which is getting you nowhere, Louise. I mean it. You call me up. And you apologize to me.

(She hangs up, throws phone down on the counter and starts to put on her shoes.)

These fucking shoes. *(She opens the huge door of the fridge.)* They make you wear them. Jimmy Choo. Power shoes. That way they know you can take inordinate pain and still ask questions in a calm voice.

(Lights out.)

(Lu and Maggie at a hair salon. The place is deserted, but well appointed. Lu is in a chair facing a three-way mirror. Maggie enters pushing a tray on wheels, on which is a bowl and a flat paintbrush. She puts a cloak around Lu with a flourish. Olivia is leafing through a Mademoiselle.)

MAGGIE: Highlights!

(She takes out small foil wrappers and paints little sections of Lu's head, then wraps them up in little packets.)

LU: Is it going to be red?

MAGGIE: Auburn, with some blond backlights.

LU: Have you done this before?

MAGGIE *(stops, looks at her in the mirror)*: Many, many times. I am not a willy-nilly try this and then try that. I have a license from the Beauty Academy of Naples Beach, 1961. Cosmetology. You can check it, if you want.

LU: Haven't things changed?

MAGGIE: Not with hair. Not with technique. Not with anything that's really in your way, I can guarantee you.

LU: I want to look womanly. Like a person carrying a purse.

MAGGIE: Carry one then. You're from prairie people. You can carry anything you want to carry.

LU: But it feels so awkward. I just carry books in a backpack. I was studying for my ... what are those called?

OLIVIA *(not looking up)*: The SATs.

MAGGIE: Backpacks just hang off you like a saddlebag. What are these people thinking? They had you plodding along like a pack mule. *(Cocks her arm.)* It's the crook. The crook of your arm. Put the strap of a purse there *(she touches the crook of Lu's arm)*, the end of a shawl, a bag of oranges, the hand of a man. That's what they forgot on you.

> *(Lu crooks her arm, with her foil packets shimmering on her head.)*

See now?

LU: I do!

MAGGIE: Backpacks! Talk about chasing the fun out of things. Now. Tuck it close *(she pulls her elbow in)*, and let it lift your bosom just the smallest amount.

> *(Lu does this.)*

Now cast your eyes down! To the ground. That's it. Turn your head two inches to the left. Now look up at me quick!

> *(Lu does this.)*

That's it. En-chanting! Hold that. Can you remember that? *(Points a finger right at her.)* Cause if you do I will not worry when I send you back.

LU: I'm going back?

MAGGIE: Of course, you're going back, sweetie. Did you think you weren't going back? Oh yes. *(Opening the foils and taking them out of Lu's hair.)* Just gave you some highlights for the journey. You're going back and Olivia's going with you.

OLIVIA: I'm what?

LU: You're coming back with me? Is she really?

(Maggie nods.)

Olivia's coming with me? Maybe she can explain this to my mother.

OLIVIA: I cannot explain a thing.

MAGGIE: She's just going to make sure you get back there okay.

(Olivia pulls Maggie over to her, close. They speak in heated whispers.)

OLIVIA: I think I still need more time.

MAGGIE: No time. Not here.

OLIVIA: God I hate that about this place! I have some things to think through.

MAGGIE: Oh, my dear Lord, more? I have never seen so much thinking in all my life. No. You are going back.

OLIVIA: How do you know?

MAGGIE: Well I do think when they told me "send her back" I took it to mean, I send you back! Don't fret. You're lucky. It means you're still connected, somewhere. Connections are everything. I have some — that's how I'm going up a level.

LU: You are?

MAGGIE: Starting to pull away from This Whole, Thing. This in between. I'm starting to feel like wind.

LU: Does that feel good?

MAGGIE: Very. Like dropping something to the ground that you don't have to fix.

OLIVIA: I want to go up a level.

MAGGIE: That'll take some work.

> (She takes Olivia by the hand and pulls her to her feet.)

Going back.

> (Pulls Lu up and puts her next to Olivia. She gives them both little pink overnight bags. She hands Lu a purse. Lu's hair is all grown-up-looking. They both put on traveling coats.)

MAGGIE: Well, you two. I'm real proud of you. I'm proud of both of you.

OLIVIA: So now we go back.

> (They all look at each other.)

How?

MAGGIE: Cruise ship. People on cruise ships get lost, thrown overboard, get off at port and never come back. It's the perfect ticket. It's how we work. We just put you on the deck of a cruise ship, you mingle, when it docks, off you go. Down the plank.

LU: How will we know when to get off?

MAGGIE: They usually try to get you pretty close to where you need to be. We have a wonderful travel department.

OLIVIA: I bet.

MAGGIE: I think it sounds adventurous. Intercontinental.

OLIVIA: Ever tried it?

MAGGIE: You've got a point. Still, it's an excellent travel department. Have no fear. Be brave. Pretend you're French.

> (She takes out two small white handkerchiefs and hands one to each.)

Wave. Wave from the deck of the cruise ship.

LU: Where is it?

MAGGIE (draws a line with her shoe, steps back a foot): Here! Right here.

> (Olivia and Lu start to wave their kerchiefs slowly.)

OLIVIA and LU: Bye!

> (Maggie steps back a yard and they start to wave their kerchiefs energetically.)

OLIVIA and LU: Bye-bye!

> (They all step back again and wave. Maggie drops to one knee and Lu runs into her arms, gets a quick, strong hug.)

MAGGIE: Don't forget now.

LU: No, I won't.

> (And Lu runs back to join Olivia. They all step back again.)

OLIVIA and LU : Bye- bye. *Au revoir!*

> (Maggie starts to wave as if they are already almost out of sight.)

OLIVIA and LU : *Au revoir!* Bye-bye.

(They all keep backing up and waving as the lights fade.)

ACT TWO

(A sign saying "Chelsea Savoy Hotel" appears upstage right. Lights up. Olivia sits on a nonflammable lime green quilted bedspread in a tiny, lightless hotel room. Her shoes are off and sit beside her on the floor. She is staring into the middle distance.)

(Lights up down stage center on a well-appointed Psychiatrist's office on the Upper West Side. A couch with a pillow headrest is draped in a tribal blanket, unknown origin. The psychiatrist, Dr. Eckert, played by the actor who plays Lu's father, is sitting on a chair just at the end of the coach. He is in a sand-colored corduroy jacket and a knitted tie. His legs are crossed. Celia is lying on the sofa.)

CELIA: So I just finally said *(controlling herself)* if you didn't want to go to camp so badly, why didn't you just tell me? Did I overestimate your love of the viola? Just tell me!

DR. ECKERT: And what did she say?

CELIA: What does she say? What does she say?

> *(She lifts her head off the couch to look at him, he motions for her to lie back down)*

She says she was in the desert in a Buick with her dead grandmother. *(Pause.)*

DR. ECKERT: And that makes you feel …

CELIA: Feel? I've got her in a lockdown. She is under curfew, studying vocabulary words and vacuuming. I dismantled her cell phone. *(Lifts her head off the couch; he makes a gesture for her to lie back down.*) And I cut her emergency Am Ex in half. You know … I may never come to know what happened. I don't think I really will ever come to know exactly what happened.

DR. ECKERT: Does she ever change her story?

CELIA: That's her story.

DR. ECKERT: Puzzling.

CELIA *(getting distraught):* And no one seems to …

DR. ECKERT: No one seems to …

CELIA: Just that …no one seems to … Are you expecting me to free associate?

DR. ECKERT: Is that what you imagine I expect of you?

CELIA: In your professional opinion, as a doctor, do you think she was hallucinating?

DR. ECKERT: I have no way of making that determination.

CELIA: And why did this happen outside Denver? Fucking Denver. *(Lifts arm.)* I wasn't even thinking about Denver when I signed her up for camp. *(Lets her arm drop.)* I was thinking more of Aspen. Music. Outdoor discussions. Outside of Aspen. Not Denver.

DR. ECKERT: No. What's in Denver.

CELIA: The West. Hate it. Dust, fences, acres and acres of "not particularly," unasked for, pushing, distances, the nonessential items, municipal swimming pools, hair salons with dartboards in them, business meetings in horseshoe-shaped booths. Frosted plastic water glasses.

DR. ECKERT: You don't have to free associate if you don't want to.

CELIA: I wasn't free associating. *(Pause.)* But I can if I need to.

DR. ECKERT: Do you always strive to get things right?

CELIA: What else would I try? I mean, what else would you have me try, mister?

> *(She raises her head off the couch; he makes a gesture for her to lie back down.)*

She's driving me crazy.

DR. ECKERT: You just called me mister.

CELIA: Is that not allowed all of a sudden? Listen, I don't know why I am lying down. *(Sits up and picks up her purse.)* I came here to try and determine if you could help me with my daughter. Help me get her into reality. There is no doubt in my mind that I am probably in dire need of therapy of some kind, but, and I mean no offense to you with this, I would probably pick object-relations, something a little more tangible.

DR. ECKERT *(holds up his palm):* Your choice.

> *(Celia sits, puts her purse down. She looks at Dr. Eckert. She lies back on the couch.)*

CELIA: What else would you have me try? Mister. *(She smiles.)*

DR. ECKERT: Just try and meet her at the level of her story.

CELIA: Uh-huh.

DR. ECKERT: She's not having it any other way.

(Lights up on Lu, back in room upstage left, in a corduroy pleated skirt. She is vacuuming mechanically with a cordless, orange stand-up vacuum.)

(Olivia, in her hotel room, sits on an orange bedspread looking at pamphlets.)

(Blip of walkie-talkie sounds. Again.)

(Lu picks up the walkie-talkie and turns it on. A light goes on in Lu's room. They both lift the handsets to their mouths. They have never used them before.)

OLIVIA *(warily):* That you? You here?

LU: Yes. Over.

OLIVIA: Where? Over.

LU: I'm back in my apartment. I'm under a curfew. You? Over.

OLIVIA *(reads the side of a ballpoint pen):* Chelsea Savoy Hotel. West 23rd. Over.

LU: What are you doing? *(Pause.)* Over.

OLIVIA: So far I've been to the Guggenheim, The Frick, the Cooper-Hewitt and the Met. I'm just skidding across the zone of masterpieces. Trying to make eye contact. I just got back from a Georgia O'Keeffe exhibit.

LU: Is she the one who paints the insides of flowers?

OLIVIA: On the plaque they say she painted pictures specific to the area, and I was wondering which area are they referring to? The West? The prairie?

(She gets up and starts to pour herself a cup of water. It is a plastic cup.)

OLIVIA: The Plaque says O'Keeffe abstracts the flower to the point where it is almost unrecognizable. To who? Who can't fucking recognize that? You really have to be a shut-in with night blindness not to recognize that. The things they let us not say! So, I guess that's what living in Colorado as a lesbian has earned me. Living in plain sight and no one sees you. Like a Georgia O'Keeffe postcard sitting just on a rack in a museum gift shop.

LU: Okay. Wow, you haven't changed. *(Pause.)* Doing a lot of thinking? Over.

OLIVIA: Thinking things over. I'm in one of those hotel rooms that makes you think things over.

LU: Want to meet me at the Reservoir? Over.

OLIVIA: You're under curfew.

LU: My mom's still got to go to work.

OLIVIA *(picks up a pamphlet):* Want to meet me at the Hayden Planetarium? They've got an exhibit on the Known Universe. I've got all these pamphlets for museums in here.

LU: Thank God Maggie gave us walkie-talkies.

OLIVIA: I know.

LU: My mom destroyed my cell phone. She dismantled it with a fork. It's a side of her I've never ever seen.

(Pause. She just keeps holding her button down.)

I'm seeing a psychiatrist.

OLIVIA: I've seen a psychiatrist. I was considered suicidal. At one time.

LU: What made them think you were suicidal?

OLIVIA: I tried to commit suicide.

LU: Oh. Hm. How?

OLIVIA: I'd rather not.

LU: You want to meet me at the Reservoir?

> *(Lights up on Celia, by the island; she has a short apron on over her work skirt and blouse and she is making poached eggs. The toast pops in the toaster, she pushes her little plunger on her coffee press and pours two small glasses of orange juice. Lu comes in from her bedroom with her practice test and sits on one of the stools.)*

CELIA: Hey. I was just about to call for you. I thought I'd make us breakfast today. Before I go to work. *(Points.)* There's your juice.

> *(She slides an egg on each piece of toast on a plate toward Lu.)*

And a poached egg. What time's your appointment today?

LU: Two-thirty.

CELIA: What are you going to do till then?

LU *(with deliberate neutrality)*: Study vocabulary.

CELIA: Want me to test you?

LU: That's okay.

CELIA: I could test you. Look. Let me test you on your SATs then. *(Picks up Lu's study book.)* Okay then.

> *(Reading quickly.)*

"His *blank* nature allowed him to see the bright side of a situation, even when very few others could. Pessimistic, humane, original, biological, optimistic."

LU *(looking hard at her mother):* Optimistic.

CELIA: Correct. "The *blank* party was boring, but impulsive Ann did her best to liven it up with her trademark *blank.*"

LU: Can I just say one thing about my father?

CELIA: Let's do words. *(Reading from list.) Abduct.*

LU: To kidnap.

CELIA: *Capricious.*

LU: Subject to whim.

CELIA: *Enervate.*

LU: To make weary. Can I just say one thing about my father?

CELIA: God. *(Blows out a breath.)* All right.

LU: He said he was a Marine.

CELIA: I heard that.

LU *(carefully):* And that he was killed.

CELIA: I heard that.

LU: He said he went ahead. They ordered them to wait and just stay. But he said he saw it made his men go soft. The waiting. So he went ahead.

CELIA: He told you that?

LU: He said he saw them turning into poets. So he went ahead.

> *(Celia just stares at her. They both hold still.)*

CELIA: Why would he tell you that, Lu?

LU *(shrugs):* I don't know.

CELIA *(exasperated):* Why does it have to be a metaphor, Lu? Why? Why can't you just tell me what happened? Why?

LU: I don't know.

CELIA: Well. I am really trying here. I am.

LU: I know Mom.

> *(Blackout.)*

> *(Galaxy Music. Hayden Planetarium. Lu and Olivia are looking up as a Universe of stars and galaxies plays across their faces. They sit very close together, looking up.)*

> *(Lights back up on Celia at the psychiatrist.)*

CELIA: Try forging on ahead. Try setting limits. Look at the outcomes. Stick to the selective truths. Don't veer. Don't show a pulse. Don't scatter. Try evening out. Try applying miles to an upgrade. Buy things on credit and get the miles. Miles can get you more miles. Try free returns. See the multiple options. See the comfort in those. Don't let things pile up: get to them as soon as you can. Skip it. Ship it. Try free returns. Have them deliver it. Have them hold it till you get them. See another person open the door to go. See another person fail to recognize you. Try another shade, or less of it. See the evening out. Mark things off once you've done them, the brain likes to see things happen. Try opening things carefully. Never tighten the screws all the way until you are sure you've assembled this properly.

DR. ECKERT: Quite a list.

CELIA *(suddenly cheerful):* Once you get started. I could go on and on like this. It just feels so good.

DR. ECKERT: A lot of instructions.

CELIA: Aren't there? *(She lifts her head up to look at him, he motions for her to lie back down.)* A *lot* of instructions. I could go on and on.

> *(Olivia and Lu are sitting on a low wall outside the planetarium. They both are holding programs and are in a kind of shock.)*

OLIVIA: Well, that was a letdown. Not even close.

LU: Not even close. The movie going out from Earth, out to the satellites, out to the Moon's orbit, just pulling out and further into space with that music, holding that one chord the whole time?

OLIVIA: Ten light years away, a hundred light years away. Like you could measure it like that. They just have no idea.

LU: I guess we've seen too many 3-D simulations.

OLIVIA: I know I have. Too many 3-D simulations. Better to just bring us into an auditorium, tell us to all close our eyes. And tell us, there is no way we can picture it.

LU: That won't work with school trips. They'll still expect a show.

(Pause.)

OLIVIA: I've got to go back to Denver soon.

LU: Back to Denver? Why?

OLIVIA: I'm running out of museums. I have a life in Denver.

LU: You do??

OLIVIA: I teach geology. At the Colorado School of Mines. In Golden.

LU: Rocks?

OLIVIA: Rocks. It's a very good way to look at the past. Striations. Ridges. Clamber around. Follow the interbedded shales. In layers you can follow. Exactly what drew me to it.

LU: It's in layers you can follow? *(She shuts her eyes.)* That sounds lonely.

OLIVIA *(defensively)*: It isn't lonely. It's a profession.

LU: But layers squash each other. Layers make you feel like it's over.

OLIVIA: I had a person. Who I loved. Living with me.

LU: What happened to him?

OLIVIA: She left me. She got married. I got sad something terrible.

LU: You sounded like Maggie just then! Just like her.

OLIVIA *(smiling)*: Wonder what Galaxy she's zooming around in.

LU: Remember? No more driving. That's what she said. Why go back then if it makes you sad?

OLIVIA: She's the one who left me. Doesn't mean I have to.

LU *(grabs her arm):* Come to dinner before you leave!

OLIVIA: Where?

LU: My house! My mother isn't much of a cook, so we'll just order delivery. Why not? Do it! Oh, come on. Just a dinner, before you leave.

OLIVIA: What would you tell her?

LU: That you're in New York for a Rock Formation Convention. No, wait. How would I know that? You're going to have to call her up and ask her out yourself!

OLIVIA *(firmly):* I will do nothing of the kind.

LU: Why not? She's already kissed you.

OLIVIA: Did Maggie tell you that? How the hell would you know that?

LU: *(leans in):* And when she goes on dates? She goes with women. She doesn't even know I know. They kiss for a long time outside our building. When they bring her home. I look down at them from my window. I used to have to go and get a stool, but now I'm tall enough.

OLIVIA: What a spy. Gotta watch you. Seriously. Lu. You're a sneak.

LU: Got to be sneaky to get the truth around here.

> *(Lu takes out a pen and writes their number on Olivia's program.)*

Call and say you looked her up after all this time. Don't say a thing about me. Leave me out of it.

OLIVIA: That'll be hard. *(Looks at her program.)*

LU: Just before you leave. What would Maggie say?

OLIVIA *(she opens up her hands and looks at both her palms):* Do it. Do something out of character! *(Looking up)* Where would I take her?

LU: Café Luxembourg! Café Fiorello!

OLIVIA: Something café! Okay I get it.

LU *(looks at her watch):* I've got to head off to my analyst.

OLIVIA: Good. You need an analyst.

LU: Just do it once. Just meet her again. And then I'll know she's met you. And I won't feel so crazy alone about … *(makes a circling gesture)*

OLIVIA: About what?

LU: About … *(makes the gesture again)*

OLIVIA: Oh. Our swirling world. Our road trip. Okay. For you, Miss Lu. I'll try. I'll try and call.

> *(Lu stops and turns)*

And Lu? Stay out of it. Okay? Do something out of character.

LU: Okay.

> *(Lu runs off. Olivia sits with the pamphlet on her lap and looks at the number, then gets up and walks the other direction.)*

(Lights up on a well-appointed Psychiatrist's office on the Upper West Side. A couch with a circular pillow headrest is draped in a tribal blanket, unknown origin. The psychiatrist, Dr. Eckert, is sitting on a chair just at the end of the couch, and is angled upstage so we see his back. His legs are crossed. Lu is lying on the couch, staring at the ceiling.)

LU: When I was little I played viola, next to someone playing a little cello, next to someone playing a little violin. It was an orchestra. *(Lifts up her head.)* A children's orchestra.

> *(Psychiatrist gestures for her to lay her head back down.)*

DR. ECKERT: Hu-huh. Your mother thinks there's something about the viola that might be upsetting you. *(Pause.)* You think she's got a point?

LU: My mother thinks it wasn't real. She thinks I'm making it up.

DR. ECKERT: She's concerned by what she sees as some new, erratic behavior.

LU: Coming back from camp without an explanation.

DR. ECKERT: That.

LU: And texting her about the dead.

DR. ECKERT: And that. *(Pause. He waits.)* And the hair …

LU *(interrupting):* And the alteration in my hair.

DR. ECKERT: Why the change in hair?

LU: I wanted to see if it would make a difference. In the kind of girl I was.

DR. ECKERT: And what kind of girl were you?

LU: A daughter.

DR. ECKERT: And what else?

LU: Just that.

DR. ECKERT: Just a daughter. So. If you were me, sitting here. What would be your explanation?

LU *(she props herself up on her elbows):* I think the closest thing that comes to it would be midlife crisis.

(He motions for her to lie back down on the couch.)

Midlife crisis. *(She counts it out on her hand.)* Nothing I do has any meaning to me, the same old grind to nowhere, dampened libido, I'm haunted by the things I didn't try, didn't risk.

DR. ECKERT: Did you read this in a book?

LU: I even want a light orange sports car.

DR. ECKERT: It's red. A little red sports car, but ...

LU: At the level of hallucination this makes sense.

DR. ECKERT: Do you think, in your opinion, you were hallucinating?

LU: No. That's not what "at the level of hallucination" even means.

DR. ECKERT: No. I would tend to agree. So up till now, this summer, things were going on an even keel. Hunky-dory. Get up, go to school, come home. Take the elevator. Perhaps some pervasive feelings of detached fury at having to rise to unreachable expectations, but, the life of a fourteen-year-old girl in New York. Not saying everything was grand, but...

LU: Right.

DR. ECKERT: Right. And so you head off to camp. Outside of Denver. Back where your mother's from. Music, foothills, old paths to the river. Mistakes. Perceived mistakes. And all these pieces of her past came up to meet you.

LU: They did come to meet me!

DR. ECKERT: Right. Aspects of self she left behind. What would make her leave them all behind? Having a child? Was she married when she had you? *(Silence.)* No. So she had to find a way to raise you. Some viable new way. She would have had to make a clean break. A stinging pain, right in her sternum telling her: Go tonight if you have to. Bring what little you have.

LU: Why don't you ask her about it? What does that have to do with me?

DR. ECKERT: Feeling angry?

LU: Feeling like you're on her side?

DR. ECKERT: I won't be very useful if I'm not on *your* side. Besides, you can't have your own adventures if you don't know about your mother's.

LU *(aghast):* Really? Is that true? How can that be true?

DR. ECKERT: So what she does is she comes East and goes to law school and becomes successful, quite successful and raises you. She gets you into top-tier schools.

LU: And she expects me to adapt. To climb.

DR. ECKERT: That's right. She wants you to adapt and want the things she wants for you. Perhaps she fears an unwanted pregnancy of not just the literal kind. But an animus driven urge could easily slip inside the well-guarded walls of the female psyche.

(Lifts her head up.)

LU: She took my cell phone permanently away from me and destroyed it with a fork. I've never seen her like this.

DR. ECKERT: You both are expressing some erratic behavior.

LU: She cut my emergency American Express card in half. With a meat cleaver. It just went *kunk!* against the butcher block. She's scaring me.

DR. ECKERT: This might be a good place and let whatever comes into your mind to just come out.

LU: (lifts her head): The automatic thing?

DR. ECKERT: Yes, that.

(He gestures for her to put her head back down; they both wait awhile.)

LU: Does your wife jog around the reservoir? In a padded headset?

DR. ECKERT: Hhmm.

LU: Cause I used to watch psychiatrists' wives jog around the reservoir from my bedroom window. All the time. Through binoculars.

DR. ECKERT: All the time. Don't you have friends your own age?

(Pause.)

LU: I'm not very popular.

DR. ECKERT: How did you know that they were married to psychiatrists?

LU: Well …

DR. ECKERT: Let me rephrase that. How did you know, in your fantasy, they were married to psychiatrists?

LU: The tracksuits. The free time. Not sure. I just imagined if they were? That would be difficult. I think that being married to anyone would be difficult. Especially psychiatrists.

DR. ECKERT: Why is that?

LU: Just that … you would expect them to be good listeners.

> *(Blackout.)*

> *(Restaurant sounds. Lights up on a table, set for two, with a white linen cloth, two glasses of wine facing each other. Celia is sitting across from Olivia at the Café Luxembourg. Olivia is uncharacteristically confident. Flirtatious but also confronting Celia.)*

CELIA: So, you're here on business.

OLIVIA: Me? No.

CELIA: You said you're here for a Rock Formation Convention.

OLIVIA: Did I? I think of that as pleasure. I'm not married.

CELIA *(holding up her hand):* Neither am I, not to worry.

OLIVIA: How'd you end up with two extra last names?

CELIA: You know me. Ever hopeful.

(Pause.)

OLIVIA: Why would I worry?

CELIA: I don't know. I'm sorry. I don't know what I meant.

OLIVIA: I didn't know you had a daughter.

CELIA: Did I mention her? Louise?

OLIVIA: She picked up the phone when I called.

CELIA: Ah.

OLIVIA: But you never mentioned her before. She sounded: self-assured.

CELIA: Well, I try to keep that separate from my dating world.

OLIVIA: Am I in your dating world?

CELIA: No. Not what I meant.

(They both take a sip of wine.)

When we last saw each other, you were working on your master's thesis.

OLIVIA: I think we kissed that night.

CELIA: Did we? That's right.

OLIVIA: We spent the night.

CELIA: We did. That's right.

OLIVIA: That's right. We spent the night. And you went back to New York. I can't remember.

CELIA: You were working on your thesis. Something about barite-silver mineralization and detachment faults. Is that right?

OLIVIA: After all those years of longing. *(Shrugs.)* We spend the night. To think. *(Pause.)*

CELIA: You were working on your master's thesis. On detachment faults. I remembered 'cause I liked the term.

> *(Olivia grabs Celia's lapels, pulls her up toward her, a little out of her chair, looks her in the eye, might even kiss her, then lets her back down slowly.)*

CELIA *(straightening her jacket):* You look good. It's good to see you.

OLIVIA: You too. You look good. You look very successful. Very at home here.

CELIA: Well I'm not at home. Are you at home, I mean wherever that is?

OLIVIA: Oh God no! I hate my life. *(She smiles broadly.)*

CELIA: You know, you're a lot different than I remember.

OLIVIA: Really. What do you remember?

CELIA: Well, you were very, earnest. You are a lot more … unpredictable. *(Leans in.)*

OLIVIA: Oh I'm still earnest. Just more selective.

CELIA: Are you seeing somebody?

OLIVIA: Not in a while. I got a nasty shock. I'm sort of unexpectedly single. So I'm pretty unpredictable. *(Takes a sip of wine.)*

CELIA: I'm sorry.

OLIVIA: Oh, it was pretty serious. Pretty serious. We were living together. She seemed to feel that her dog was really adjusting well to my dog.

CELIA: That's good. That's a factor. Right?

OLIVIA: It can be. Well. There's just no good way to say this. We were going to do a Commitment Ceremony? *(Celia nods.)* And decided to design rings. *(Celia nods.)* Only we couldn't settle on a design. All over the map. Should they look alike? Should they be silver? Should they swirl? It required a lot of lengthy meetings with the jeweler.

CELIA: Okay. And …

OLIVIA: She ended up marrying the jeweler.

CELIA: Oh that's awful.

OLIVIA: Ya.

CELIA: Oh that's really awful.

OLIVIA: She said he was just so good to talk to, about the whole thing.

CELIA: App-ar-ently. The shit.

OLIVIA: He had long hair, some sort of custom-made bike. A gentle voice. I don't know, Celia. This is West of Denver. No one wants to be a lesbian, if they can possibly, possibly find a way.

CELIA: No one wants to be a lesbian and this is the Upper West Side. I just call myself a single parent. This seems to relieve everyone so much, I never say anything after that. I don't think even Louise knows I'm a lesbian.

OLIVIA: You sure about that?

CELIA: You'd like Louise, I think. She's earnest. Little bit of a lying thing right now, but.

OLIVIA: It'll pass.

CELIA: You get a certain window when you have a daughter. A window of time to explain things, before she becomes ashamed and wants with all her might to turn into anything but you.

OLIVIA: Is that the way you felt about your mother?

CELIA: Exactly like that.

OLIVIA: No wonder we're not getting anywhere.

CELIA: Who?

OLIVIA: Jesus, just: us. All of us. *(She leans in.)* You should tell your daughter. There's no such thing as a goddamn window. We're in a galaxy here.

CELIA *(leaning in):* And that woman? However much you loved her? *(Like this is a fact)* She was an asshole. And now she's married to a fucking jeweler and has a maladjusted dog. And that's just what we know for sure.

OLIVIA: God, you remind me so much of Maggie.

CELIA: Of Maggie. Really? What made you say that?

OLIVIA: Just the first thing that came into my head. Unpredictable.

CELIA: Do you still live in Denver?

OLIVIA: I've recently recommitted. Do you ever come back?

CELIA: To Denver? I could. Sometime. Route a trip through Denver. Do a stopover.

OLIVIA: A stopover. A trip. Bring your daughter. See the sights.

> *(They smile.)*

> *(Lights down on Cafe Luxembourg.)*

> *(Lights up on Maggie, on a bench at the Central Park Zoo. There is a box with a handle on it sitting next to her. She is holding a bag of peanuts. She calls to Lu, who is on her way home from therapy.)*

MAGGIE: Hey. Hey there! See? I just knew you'd find me at the Central Park Zoo if I sat here long enough. I put it in my mind and sent it off to you just as clear as a bell. I'm getting better. *(Motions to Lu and whispers.)* It's the next level. *(Lu nods.)* How you doing? *(Lu nods.)* Want a peanut? Don't let you even feed the animals anymore.

LU *(in a bit of shock):* Oh. There's a penguin feeding. You can watch someone else feed the penguins.

MAGGIE: You can watch someone else do anything. How's things at the lockdown? How's it going with the analyst.

LU: Mom's got me vacuuming.

MAGGIE: Well, good.

LU: I've got the only analyst in New York who does all the talking.

MAGGIE: That sounds refreshing: You already know what *you're* thinking. Mix it up a bit. What's he say?

LU: He kinda rambles. Things like my mother felt she had to make a clean break when she had me. When she had a baby.

MAGGIE: I don't claim to speak for the woman.

LU: Maybe she felt she had to start out fresh, in the East.

(Pause.)

MAGGIE: Your people set out over the ridges, crossed over prairies in the most uncomfortable wagons, anything, just to *leave* the East. They'd do anything. Just a tinge of irony there; just pointing it out.

(Pause. Lu sits beside her on the bench.)

Long wagon train winding into God knows what terrain. Over God knows what dark passage. Horses got so tired and hungry, every now and then they'd yell to the women (she cups her mouth) "Throw something overboard."

Rocking chairs, side tables. To lighten up the load. Can't you see it? Heaving out the things they had hoped to start their new life with. Grandfather clocks flying out of a wagon, landing on their side. Staring at the mountain. Looking for the Northwest Passage. Looking for the Great Divide. And when they found it? Kept on going. Throw more stuff off on out of the back. Never can bring all of you. That's the sad part. There isn't an armoire or an upright piano made it over the Great Divide. Had to have them shipped in from Europe once they had some money from the mines. We come from crazy people, Lu. That's the truth. That's why we have to take care of the little that's left, because it must have been important what they kept. Must have been what they couldn't be parted with.

LU: Everything can be parted with.

MAGGIE: My grandmother had a victrola that she clung to like a last prayer. But I don't have that anymore. Sold it at a yard sale.

> (*Picks up the pink-and-white metal box, closed with a latch and places it in between her and Lu.*)

So I brought you these. They don't usually let us "manifest" but I told them there's no way I'm gonna remember every tune in there and hum it for her. Can you imagine?

> (*Lu opens the metal box and is mystified.*)

Can't expect me to hum all that. Like 'em?

> (*Lu doesn't seem to know what they are.*)

Records! All my records. Go on. Flip through them. LPs. 33s. That's the collection. Your mother knows these songs. I taught her all those dances, on the living room rug. Lindy Hop. Jitterbug. Swing.

LU: Can I have them? Really?

MAGGIE: We come from crazy people, Lu. That's the truth. That's why we have to take care of what little that's left.

LU: Won't you miss them?

MAGGIE: Not if you hold on to them. (*Lu nods.*) You won't let them slip through your hands will you?

LU: No.

MAGGIE: Don't just look at them. Take them out and play them every now and then.

LU: Okay.

MAGGIE: Okay then. *(Rises up with great purpose.)* Gotta scat. I'm late for something. *(Opens her arms.)* Who knows what? Can you believe you can still be late and you're not even here? Wonderful to see you Lu. Keep up the vacuuming. She'll forgive you soon enough.

LU: Did my mom really have to leave? To start fresh?

(Maggie has to think about this.)

MAGGIE: To be entirely honest, her chances of coming this far *(Maggie looks around at Central Park)* were slim and none. If she had stayed. So. Live it up. You're at the next level. *(She starts to leave.)* But play those records every now and then.

(Lights down.)

(Lu is playing one of the records on a turntable, on her feet, trying to dance to the music. She is just in the light coming in from the street. Celia comes in and sees her. She watches her for a while, then turns on a lamp.)

CELIA *(her tone is soft)*: Where did you get that?

LU *(startled)*: It was in your closet.

CELIA: It was not in my closet.

LU: Yes it was. It was in the back. I found it in there. *(She lifts the needle.)*

CELIA *(sits down on Lu's bed)*: I may never, ever know what is going on here. I should just get used to that. But you are lying to me, Lu. And I don't want you to do that anymore. *(Pause.)* Now listen. I want to tell you. I need to tell you, that I'm gay.

LU *(was braced for something else)*: Oh, I know that.

329

CELIA: Ya, but I never told you that. You never heard it from me. So that is different. And so, actually? That is something that you did not know. From me. *(Stern pause. It's hard to share this.)* I never wanted you to be underestimated. I never wanted people to ignore you if you sang off-key. To not correct you. Give you the benefit of their care. Or give you an extra warm nod 'cause you are different. Or I am different. And they expect less of you in this slippery way.

If I didn't confide in you how terrified I was, that's because parents shouldn't do that.

I didn't want you getting swept under the rug, or up in a flash flood. Swept under. I didn't want to see you sweeping. Plenty of people behind us in our line sweeping.

LU *(placing her hand completely over her mother's)*: We come from crazy people: We should tell the truth.

   (Celia is close to tears.)

CELIA *(puts her head in her hand)*: I don't know where you got that song box: holy roller songs, in love with a girl songs, grab your hat and walk on the sunny side of the street. I know the songs. I listened to them all afternoon lying on my white chenille bedspread. I got a thousand kisses, a thousand radar landings, and heart-breaking farewells carrying a little suitcase across the prairie songs, all in my head. But when I had you, I had to take a good look around. I took a look at all those songs. What those 33s don't see.

LU: I know Mom. It's okay.

CELIA: And I said to myself: I've got to get you into college. A good enough college.

LU: I know.

CELIA: A college good enough so that it becomes sort of like your new last name. You hear me? So that they always kinda mention it with your name.

LU: I know, Mom. You always told me.

CELIA *(looking at her):* After that, you can do the Lindy Hop on a prairie in a high wind.

LU: After that, I won't remember anything about the Lindy Hop.

CELIA: Can we work together here? *(Forcefully)* Never hope your way through a storm, Louise.

LU: I know. You always say that, Mom. "Can we work together here?"

> *(Pause. Lu looks at her mother till she smiles.)*

If I get into college? If I get into a good college. If I get into a really good college. Will you teach me how the dances go?

> *(Long pause. Celia thinks this over.)*

All of them. Every one of them.

CELIA: Louise, are we talking about an Ivy?

LU: An Ivy. If I get into an Ivy. And after we open that thick letter and put it on the table right in front of us, will you teach me how the dances go? Cause I can't do one without the other.

> *(Celia starts to smile. Lights fade.)*

End of Play

IN CONVERSATION WITH THE PLAYWRIGHT

Maya: Can you share a snapshot of what inspired **FULL/SELF?**

Claire: When my daughter was two, I would drive her to day care in the morning and stop at a particular red light that seemed to never change. At the intersection was a filling station with two rows of pumps, one with the sign FULL and the other one said SELF. I would stare at these choices and the existential quandary they presented and started to write this play about where I might look for my full self.

Maya: How would you distill this play for your ideal reader?

Claire: Ambition, parenting, Buicks, ravishing girl love, talking to dead fathers, portals to the afterlife, the indelibility of the past.

Maya: When you think about your body of work over time, what themes, images, ideas or forms emerge as emblematic?

Claire: Themes: fishing, lakes, frozen foods, a profound ambivalence toward families, desire between women, unspoken heritage. Car crashes, investigations. Feminist dilemmas.

Maya: You're amazing at snapshots, where themes and images overlap. How do you see your work fitting into a feminist framework. Do you consciously identify as a feminist playwright? A lesbian playwright?

Claire: I identify as a lesbian feminist playwright, because those two things have shaped what part of the world I behold, what part of the world excludes me, what small resonances I am included in. It's a small club whose members don't belong in clubs.

I am not sure how you can be besotted with women and not fight for their rights, but it seems to happen all the time.

Maya: Your play **Why We Have a Body** *hit such a cultural nerve when it came out — moving from its premiere in San Francisco to Off-Broadway. Rather like Chambers, you wrote an iconic lesbian feminist play of its times, also crossing over to mainstream audiences and acclaim. Why do you think* **Why We Have a Body***, in particular, was such a huge hit?*

Claire: It may have hit a nerve because it was first produced in 1993, when the cultural discussion about 'lesbian chic' culminated in *Newsweek*'s June cover titled "The Lesbians." The picture showed two attractive, open-faced women in each other's arms, staring directly at the camera, similar to a nature special like "The Cheetahs." It was a strange fascination with "lesbians" who were not sidelined by taboo but living amongst the general population, watering their lawns, starting their families and looking elegant in denim shirts.

Like a lot of American cultural curiosities, it didn't go very deep or last very long, but it did result in a broader acceptance of lesbians in the public eye without furthering much nuanced discussion about lesbian art, or history or philosophy or true sexuality.

As a result, there is this feeling that the battles are behind us, or should be.

The women in *Why We Have a Body* are spies, investigators or self-hypnotized incarnations of Joan of Arc. They are delivering monologues that are unsettling, unusual. I wrote these soliloquies, having gone through a year of conservatory acting training in London, that I myself never had the chance to deliver.

I think that the idea of women delivering pronouncements about lesbian issues that were entirely whimsical, inaccurate and bold appealed to the tone of the time. It was unexpected. I was seeking to counter the societal gaze on lesbians as a topic and grab back the microphone. At that point, I wasn't sure which was worse: being taboo or being normalized within an inch of our lives.

Maya: What an insightful rendering of the web... You've been writing fiction, as well as stage plays, in the past decade or so. What does each form allow you to explore especially well?

Claire: Working in prose offers a directness that theatre isn't constructed to provide. I started extending my monologues into stories. I was inspired by experimental […] poetry, essay, fiction and non-fiction by writers such as Maggie Nelson, Claudine Rankine, Clarice Lispector, Ali Smith. Mary Robison's "Why Did I Ever" affected me a lot. I thought that she was writing beautiful plays with her short fiction. Turns out she was writing chapters on index cards, so that they were short, very short.

I was inspired by the acceptance of the fragment as a worthy messenger of elliptical and varying truths.

I think the theatrical form is a superior one to train in and is underused […] in MFA programs today. Learning how to construct dialogue alone should be a required focus for novelists. In theatre, we learn immediately that people don't say what they mean. Subtext is the primary motor. Theatre taught me the enormous power of intercutting scenes, of a lights up/lights down randomness, the luxury of having darkness between each chapter. And then the lights find us again in another unexpected place, favoring accumulation and compression over story and plot. These seemed current to me, and very favorable to lesbian experience, which survives by intermittent elusions and sudden truths.

FEMMES:
A TRAGEDY

by
Gina Young

Partially inspired by Clare Boothe Luce's *The Women*

**Winner of the
2014 Jane Chambers Prize**

FIRST WORKSHOP PRODUCTION

Directed by Gina Young, Highways Performance Space, March 22, 2013.

MARIGOLD	Sara Ann Buccolo
RIOT	Arielle Marie McFadden
GUERRA	Kristelle Monterrosa
LIBBY	Devri Richmond
DEXY	Alessandra Pinkston
DUTCH	CT Treibel
COURTNEY	Sarah Dryden
CALLIE	Olivia Bellafontaine

Femmes also received a staged reading at the Association for Theatre in Higher Education Conference in 2014, with Holly Hughes in the role of DUTCH.

CAST OF CHARACTERS

MARIGOLD	A martyr. Curator of a performance series for femme lesbians. Late 20s.
RIOT	A diva. Asian/Pacific Islander. Early 20s.
GUERRA	An activist. Latina. Early 30s. Can double as BIBIANA.
LIBBY	An academic. 30s–40s. White.
DEXY	An anarchist. Early 20s. African American.

336

| | Can double as SARAH and GABRIELA. |

| DUTCH | Doyenne of the lesbian community. 40s–60s. Can double as IRMA VET and PILATES INSTRUCTOR. |

| COURTNEY | A babydyke. 19. |

| CALLIE | An asshole. Late 20s. Can double as DENISE DID IT and HOMOROBICS INSTRUCTOR. |

An array of other characters who appear in single scenes, including BIBIANA, SARAH, GABRIELA, IRMA VET, PILATES INSTRUCTOR, DENISE DID IT and HOMOROBICS INSTRUCTOR, to be performed by members of the ensemble, as suggested above or in alternate pairings that better serve your cast.

Unless specified, roles are open to any ethnicity.

Every character in this show is a queer femme … whatever that means.

PRODUCTION NOTE

A diverse cast is essential. Casting should include diverse body types and gender identities. (RIOT could be transgender, DEXY could be nonbinary, LIBBY could be fat, and so on.) Great care should be taken to understand the nuances of contemporary queer femme culture. As the script details, "Femmes are not just lesbians who look like straight girls." Hallmarks of the aesthetic could include but are not limited to: bright lipstick, winged eyeliner, armpit hair, multiple tattoos, cat's-eye glasses and vintage thrift store dresses. Punk influence and 1960s style should be felt throughout.

SETTING

An ambiguous American big city; most likely Los Angeles.

TIME

On the verge of same-sex marriage being legally recognized nationwide.

ACT ONE

SCENE ONE
POST-SHOW AFTERGLOW

(Backstage. The tiny dressing room of a semi-professional burlesque show at a small theater in any major American city.)

(Riot and Guerra sit at lighted mirrors. Marigold sits off in a corner, texting. All are tattooed, urban and hip: ironic fringed leather jackets, high-waisted jean skirts and big, teased hair. These are some seriously sexy hipster femme dykes.)

(Libby, Denise Did It, Dexy and Irma Vet burst in and start changing out of their costumes; removing false eyelashes, wigs and stockings. Armpit hair. General noise.)

ALL: Oh my god, you were so good. --No, YOU were so good. *(Etc.)*

RIOT: Wait, so it's done? I can be loud? Okay, so I wanna do this one where I dress like a guy...

DENISE DID IT: Wait, Riot. Did you say hi to everyone already?

RIOT: Oh hell no. Are you kidding? I have like 27 exes out there.

DENISE DID IT: Ugh, which means I do too.

RIOT: I wanna wait for at least half of them to leave. So, I wanna do this one where I dress like a guy, strip down into lingerie, and then pull out my penis, at the end, and it's a giant tube of lipstick.

LIBBY: Marigold, are you going to go out there and hang out?

MARIGOLD: No, I'm just waiting for Dylan to pick me up.

DEXY: I wanna do an act where I dress up like Bettie Page and stick myself into famous portraits of the Founding Fathers.

IRMA VET: Like a slide show? And you're like … photobomb?

DEXY: No, more like having all of you guys sitting in white powdered wigs, frozen … And I'll just stand there. Until the audience gets really uncomfortable. And then I'll show them a boob.

GUERRA: I wanna do one where I wear all pink and dance with fans. I'm getting sick of doing political shit. It feels weird to do my Immigration Gyration number in front of an audience that's like ninety percent white.

(The room gets tense and quiet.)

GUERRA: Guys! It's okay! We can talk about it.

(They all speak at the same time.)

RIOT: Well, *I* think that the reason the audience is so white is because we keep doing shows on this side of town. This neighborhood, and this strip in particular, only caters to white hipster gentrifiers. Nobody who's actually *from* this neighborhood goes to the new bars —

GUERRA: — yeah, it's like *pupusas, bodega, supermercado,* "Slurp: an urban tea experience."

LIBBY: Yeah, but how many people who are actually *from* this neighborhood are queer? I grew up really close to here and it used to be like, gay bashing central. I would not have felt safe walking around at night.

DEXY: That doesn't mean there aren't queer people here. Just because you don't see them —

RIOT: A trans woman was murdered here just a few years ago. Why haven't we done something about that yet? We could do a memorial piece about it, like maybe something site specific, where we go to the spot where it happened.[1]

DEXY: We should collaborate with trans performers then too, though. I'll get my friend Becky, who leads workshops on transfemme solidarity.

GUERRA: Totally. Yes. But what I was *TRYING* to say was, our audience just represents *us*. Like, hello, we had a predominantly white lineup tonight, so of course we had a predominantly white audience.

LIBBY: Ugh, I was so bummed that Rolling Brownouts didn't want to perform tonight! They're awesome, three women of color, plus they totally bring in the boylesque element too. Femme-identified off stage, but on stage they're sort of like drag kings, except deconstructed —

RIOT: — which is really fucking important, because as much as I love burlesque, why does it always have to be

---

[1] This is not a joke or intended to be funny in any way. Please defer to the comfort of transgender cast members when staging this beat. It might also offer a great jumping-off point for a discussion about how, in many queer spaces, lip service is paid to trans issues without any actual real movement toward making the space safer for trans people.

the femmes taking off our clothes? I wanna see some boy titties and strap-ons.

IRMA VET: I wore a strap-on last Saturday. You weren't very excited.

RIOT: Right, because I don't want to do it with you.

IRMA VET: Heterosexism!

LIBBY: We should think about that. With so many butches and transmen in the audience cheering and whipping out their dollar bills, it's like, fucked up straight power dynamic recapitulated. Maybe we *should* bring in more boylesque. Except I really admire Marigold's commitment to producing a show that's entirely about femmes.

> (*Everyone looks over to Marigold appreciatively. An awkward pause as Marigold doesn't look up from her phone.*)

LIBBY: All right, bye, ladies! I'll see you at the after party, if you come!

GUERRA: Wait, wait one second before you go, back to the point. I have an idea, which I just wanna say really quickly. Which is that if it's okay with you guys, I really want to start curating this series in a way that brings in more women of color.

DEXY: Yeah, of course we're okay with that.

> (*The whole room nods and voices agreement except Marigold, still texting, tight-lipped.*)

GUERRA: Well the reason I'm asking permission is because, I really think we should use some of the budget money to pay for some touring women-of-color performers to come through. Like bigger names. Nationally touring acts. Maybe not even strictly burlesque, but performance art and slam poetry or hip-hop even …

LIBBY: That's a really good idea, but we don't have a lot of money in the budget…

DENISE DID IT: Come on! Money where your mouth is people!

RIOT: I'm totally into it.

IRMA VET: Yeah, I think we should all be on board with this. Seriously. And, seriously, I have to go. I'll see you at the after-party.

(Irma Vet and Denise Did It exit.)

LIBBY: I'm just trying to be the Treasurer! I'm not trying to be a white girl about it!

GUERRA: Okay. Awesome. I'll start sending emails and put together a short list of who I think we should be booking, and then of course we can discuss budget and everything else. Don't worry Libby, I won't bankrupt us. All right, I'm fucking tired. Have fun if you go out. Bye, ladies!

ALL: Bye!

(Guerra goes to leave. Libby tags along behind her.)

LIBBY: You think I'm fucked up now don't you.

GUERRA (nonchalant): Are you always such a naysayer?

LIBBY: Ohmigod, now I feel terrible…

GUERRA: Yeah, I really don't have time for that though. Not my problem. Love you!

(Guerra exits.)

(Courtney enters.)

COURTNEY: Hi ... Hey ... I hope it's okay if I come back here? That was just *so awesome*. I just really wanted to tell you guys that it was soooo good.

(Thanks, etc., all around. Courtney goes to Libby and starts a hushed, fawning conversation. Marigold finally stands.)

MARIGOLD: Dylan's here. I'm gonna go.

LIBBY: Did she miss your act?

MARIGOLD: Yeah. But I mean, she's seen me dance like a million times. Bye.

ALL: Bye. *(Etc.)*

MARIGOLD: See you all back here *tomorrow*, don't forget. Planning meeting and major cleanup party. You can be late if you're hungover. But don't forget. Ciao!

(The whole room watches her leave. ... And waits to make sure she's really gone.)

LIBBY: Okay, so is she *really* still dating Dylan?

RIOT: Oh my god, I was just going to say the exact same thing.

COURTNEY: Wait, is Dylan the really hot one from Portland?

(Libby and Riot raise an eyebrow.)

COURTNEY: Sorry, I just ... I mean I think I stalk her on Instagram. She's sort of androgynous or ... wait what's their pronoun?

DEXY: She goes by she. Sort of looks like a young kd lang?

COURTNEY: I don't know who that is.

(Dexy pulls up a photo.)

COURTNEY: Yes. SO hot.

RIOT: Yeah. Well … I don't want to make a big deal out of it and I definitely don't want to tell Marigold, but I'm pretty sure Dylan tried to take me home after Gayzer Fag last week.

LIBBY: Oh no. Really?

RIOT: Yeah. I mean, not overtly? Like, she didn't outright invite me over for a wild night of scissoring or anything, but she was pretty sober — sober enough to know what she was doing — and she kept grabbing me around the waist and going, "Woah, you are *not* driving; you're really drunk." And I was like, "First of all, I drive much better when I'm drunk, and second of all, two out of the three drinks I've had tonight were bought by YOU. So …"

LIBBY: Woah, she was totally trying to take you home.

COURTNEY: I think they have an open relationship though.

DEXY: Do they?

COURTNEY: Yeah, I think so. I mean they haven't changed their Facebook statuses or anything.

RIOT: Yeah, but nobody does that, because we're not fucking sixteen.

COURTNEY: Right … No of course not. Yeah. But I think they have an open relationship anyway. They must, right?

RIOT: Still. No. I'm sorry. If they have an open relationship or are poly or whatever that's cool. But Marigold and I dance together. And we're on the Femme Committee together. We've been friends since this city had a riot grrrl chapter. She's like my best friend. I would *seriously* need her go-ahead before we could hook up with the same person.

LIBBY: *I'm* your best friend. *You* talk shit about Marigold all the time, but I actually believe her to be one of the purest, most amazing souls I have ever met.

RIOT: *Anyway*, don't think I wasn't tempted. Dylan's so hot… you can tell that she's the type that's a total top in the bedroom, will slap you around and disrespect you and treat you like shit…

COURTNEY: Woah, that's not very feminist, is it?

LIBBY: Ugh, you'll understand when you're older.

RIOT: Of course it's feminist! I'm exhausted from being this awesome all the time! I need someone to show me who's boss!

LIBBY: Riot, your sex tastes are so retrograde. You've just set us back over fifty years. *(She doesn't mean it.)* Wait, seventy years!

RIOT: Can you believe it's been over seventy years since rich white women started having jobs? Anyway Libby, we can't all be like you and get off on green tea and the love letters of Gertrude Stein.

LIBBY: Uptight girls are the kinkiest in bed, are you kidding me? All Virgos are great at sex.

RIOT: Whatever. Poor Marigold. That's why I import.

COURTNEY: *(to Libby)* What?

LIBBY: She flies them in from San Fran or Portland or wherever they proliferate…

RIOT: We go halfsies on a flight, I ship them in for the weekend, ship 'em back to *their* stomping ground, you never shit where you eat, you're never jealous!

DEXY: Oh right, you're never jealous?

RIOT: Never.

DEXY: I call bullshit.

RIOT: What?

DEXY: I call bullshit! You're telling me that if Sprocket Wrench were sleeping with a bunch of other girls in San Francisco, you wouldn't be slightly jealous? Cuz I'm pretty sure you only ever date girls you can completely control and have following you around like a puppy.

COURTNEY: Sprocket Wrench?

LIBBY: A lot of people choose their own names in this scene, honey.

RIOT: Polyamory is humanity's natural state. Plus a lot of people think that femmes are sexually passive and that butches have all the control. The world would be a better place if we acknowledged that Pillow Princesses are healers, receivers, transformers…

LIBBY: …And in your case, topping from the bottom.

COURTNEY: Sprocket Wrench?

RIOT: We're not meant to spend the rest of our life with one person —

COURTNEY: Yeah but, Sprocket Wrench…

RIOT: — and the sooner you realize that, the happier you'll be. I refuse to compete with other girls, I refuse to get caught up in any drama, I don't expect to be "everything" to the person I'm fucking, and I refuse —

LIBBY: — to ever actually have a real relationship.

RIOT SPOTLIGHT NUMBER
(Music starts. Riot performs an impromptu comedic burlesque routine to a classic musical theater song — "I Enjoy Being a Girl," perhaps, in a send-up of Asian stereotypes — pulling costumes from the dressing room racks. The other girls join in.)

DEXY: Well me, I just wish Marigold would quit rubbing it in. She's codependent. She never hangs out with her friends anymore, always has plans with Dylan and it's just like… you *do* know there's only like three eligible butches in this town, and you're obsessed with yours, and what the hell are the rest of us supposed to do?

RIOT: She really is showing off. Which is sad if you think about it.

COURTNEY: Because Dylan's flirting with other girls.

LIBBY: It's *not* just flirting.

RIOT: You seem awfully sure of that.

LIBBY: Oh, I don't know…

RIOT: What do you know.

LIBBY: I don't know if I should say.

RIOT: Now you have to.

LIBBY: God, I just don't know if I should…

DEXY: Blah blah, for the love of Josephine Baker and Jesus Christ. I'm gonna go to the after party.

LIBBY: Okay! My ex-girlfriend Jasper is now roommates with this girl I can't fucking stand. I never even see either of them anymore so it doesn't even matter, but the other night I was thinking about Jasper, and what an inexcusable psychic vampire she is, and how completely untenable our relationship was, and I fell into one of those internet K-holes that you just can't get out of…

ALL: Totally

LIBBY: …where you just, like, fall to the bottom of the earth… and next thing you know you're looking at her photos all the way back to 2005? So, you're all on that new app, Jungle Red, right? It's like Facebook meets Grindr meets Instagram… for lesbians? Well, I started looking at this other girl, her new roommate, the girl I can't stand. Her name is Callie and she suffers from a major case of bitchface…

> *(Callie appears stage left. Under the following text, she poses for a ridiculous series of sexy cell phone selfies.)*

LIBBY: Her pictures are all set to private, so I can't see them because we're not friends. But she was just in San Francisco for the weekend, hanging out with a whole bunch of people that I *AM* friends with, so I started looking through *THEIR* photos from the weekend and… I saw some photos of her and Dylan together.

> *(Silence.)*

RIOT: So? Who cares. That could be anything.

LIBBY: No, but this was like, close-up photos, you know, where the one person is holding the phone out on a group of people, you know… and you could totally see that this girl's hand was on Dylan's leg.

> *(Callie places her hand on an unseen thigh, takes one last photo, and exits.)*

RIOT: So? That still doesn't prove anything.

LIBBY: Ugh! Okay! Fine! You guys are forcing me to say this. I still know Jasper's password. From back when we were dating? She uses the same one for everything. So after I saw that picture, I used Jasper's password to go on her Jungle Red profile and look at Callie's page, because of course Jasper can see all the photos that I can't see… and…

(Libby's face says it all.)

RIOT: Dylan would *NOT* put pictures of herself in bed with another girl on the internet… would she?

(Libby pulls out her phone and works her magic. General shock.)

COURTNEY: You guys should totally say something.

LIBBY: No. And please don't tell her. Seriously. Don't say anything. It's just so crazy that we really need to process it.

(Dexy finally gets her chance to look at the pictures. She gasps.)

DEXY: I totally know that girl! She's a bartender at Spex and she's always at that thrift store on Downey.

COURTNEY: What do we do?

(Riot pushes Courtney out of the group.)

RIOT: We can't say anything. But it's going to get back to her, and she will cry.

COURTNEY: Aw, I don't want to see that. She's so cool. I like, love her.

LIBBY: I know, she's the best. She's like *THE BEST*.

DEXY: She's the sweetest. The most amazing.

RIOT: I would kill anyone who tried to hurt her.

LIBBY: I love her. She's just so pure.

DEXY: Okay, can we go? It's starting to die down out there and I don't want to lose my ride to the after-party.

RIOT: Oh my god, I know what we should do.

LIBBY: What?

RIOT: Marigold's on Jungle Red too, right? *(Dramatic pause.)* Tag her in the photo.

LIBBY: You can't do that, can you?

RIOT: I think you can…

> *(Courtney triumphantly grabs the phone.)*

COURTNEY: Of course, you can.

> *(They're impressed. Exit all. We hear them greeting friends and dates in the hallway — "Hey, sexy!" etc. — as they leave the dressing room.)*

SCENE TWO
BACKSTAGE AT THE BURLESQUE

> *(Same dressing room, the next morning. Marigold stands amid piles of costumes and props, alone.)*

MARIGOLD *(on her cell phone)*: Yes, baby… Haha I *know* you want to come… Yeah, but my show is for femmes, no butches allowed in the acts… Yes I *know* that's why you want to come… Uh-huh, you've already made that joke… You're hilarious. Okay I gotta go… Yes… yes, it was amazing… I love it when you wear that letterman's jacket…

*(Courtney tiptoes in, cute as can be but totally tragic —
spiky hair and pride rings, maybe a messenger bag
covered in pins or a T-shirt from her Midwestern
hometown. She is obviously younger than the others and
doesn't have it together yet.)*

MARIGOLD: Dylan? I gotta go. For reals. Ciao baby.

(Marigold hangs up the phone.)

COURTNEY: I can't believe planning meetings are that
long!

MARIGOLD: Some people think it's group therapy.

(A pause as she surveys the mess.)

MARIGOLD: Did you want to stay and help clean up?
Please say that's why you're here.

COURTNEY: Did everyone else just leave?

MARIGOLD: Yeah, they all promised to help clean up, but
then someone suggested they go to brunch instead.

(Marigold's almost pissed, but then she smiles.)

MARIGOLD: I don't blame them. They're high off a great
show. Courtney, there is nothing like the feeling of being
in a great show. Onstage is the only time the noise in your
head stops. Last night was amazing.

COURTNEY: I just wanted to come say that I'm such a fan.

MARIGOLD: I know, right? Riot — she's the glamazon
one — Riot is so fucking fierce. Super sexy and feminine
but she really *owns* her sexuality, a sex subject instead of a
sex object. And then there's Libby, you know Libby, right?

COURTNEY: No, I mean you! You like organize this whole thing. I know they all left or whatever, but they appreciate you so much. When you talk at the meeting it's like... everyone pays attention. I was thinking maybe I could be your intern or something.

MARIGOLD: We do not have the budget for an intern.

COURTNEY: Free intern! Free nonsexual intern!

MARIGOLD: Sold! But you know, I don't even really do anything. I mean, I never even get to perform half the time because there's so much other stuff to do. I just like being part of a community and... you know, doing something real. Something that's not TV, not housework... As your first intern duty, will you please help me clean up?

(Courtney helps. Poorly.)

COURTNEY: So, I have to be honest about something.

MARIGOLD: Okay?

COURTNEY: I'm not sure about this whole femme thing.

MARIGOLD: Okay?

COURTNEY: When Libby was talking about this, and she kept saying *"The Femme Show, The Femme Show,"* I just thought she meant feminist. Or lesbian. Or something cool. And I got really excited. So... I came.

MARIGOLD: Okay?

COURTNEY: But now that I'm here I'm like... woah... I can't possibly be femme. I don't own nearly enough eyeliner.

MARIGOLD: Fear of not being femme enough.

COURTNEY: What?

MARIGOLD: Fear of not being femme enough. It's normal. Ignore it and it'll go away.

COURTNEY: Can I ask without being offensive, why is the show femmes only?

MARIGOLD: Well… some of us felt like butches already get a lot of attention in this town. The whole drag king scene is butches, most of the hot DJs are butches, most of the party promoters are butches…

COURTNEY: Yeah, I can't get into clubs yet.

MARIGOLD: …there's like three "tomboy" clothing lines, that traveling "Butch Eye" photo show, and then on the flip side, all of the mainstream lesbian clubs, without fail, just have some straight girl on the flyer, in her underwear.

COURTNEY: Oh… I wouldn't really know …

MARIGOLD: Representations of queer femmes are really hard to find. And a femme is not just a lesbian who looks like a straight girl. Anyway, we wanted to keep the show really inclusive, so even though it's for femmes, that can mean queer femme, lesbian, trans femme, high femme, low femme, garbage pail femme… we might even branch out to queer males that identify as femme, but we're pretty committed to letting the ladies dominate the conversation…

COURTNEY: Is that why some of the girls kept calling themselves drag queens?

MARIGOLD: Well, all gender is drag. Even a girl doing female gender. All gender is a performance and a choice. We all have unlimited options.

COURTNEY: So what you're saying is… more eyeliner.

MARIGOLD: We're conceptualizing a queer femme aesthetic that exists outside of being the yin to a butch's yang. It's not about butch/femme, male/female. We do not exist only in opposition. We exist on our own. Although of course, some of us are super into butch/femme. It's a very sexy dynamic.

(Marigold smiles to herself. Courtney is seemingly taking notes on her phone.)

COURTNEY: Okay, but let's say just for the sake of argument, like I'm not saying *I'm* saying this, but like, why would you want to be a lesbian and like butches? I mean, if you're into women, don't you want... women? Like, *feminine* women? If you like masculinity, why wouldn't you just date a guy?

MARIGOLD: Dating a butch is only like dating a guy if you want it to be. Listen. Don't think I'm not conflicted about femme identity too. I used to say that girls who are good at putting on makeup are ONLY good at putting on makeup, if you know what I mean. I shaved my head when I came out, and stopped shaving my legs. And wore cargo shorts.

COURTNEY: YOU were butch?

MARIGOLD: No...

COURTNEY: Then why'd you do it?

MARIGOLD: Because I wanted to be queer! I wanted to walk into a room and have other women know me! But I missed dressing up, and short skirts, and makeup... and I didn't want to deny the things I like, just to be seen a certain way.

COURTNEY: So you decided to be more normative.

MARIGOLD: No. You're not getting it. My relationship to my gender is just as complicated or radical as any other queer's. At my most natural, I wouldn't have a gender at all. I always saw myself as neither one thing nor the other. If no one were around to see, I'd just wear curtains, white sheets, run through a field wrapped in swaths of cotton, let all my hair grow long, stroke my beard like a philosopher, read all the great literature with the pronouns taken out, neither bleeding nor ejaculating, white sheets that stay clean, the daintiest tomboy you've ever seen…

(Marigold has clearly gone somewhere else.)

COURNTEY: Haha … wearing sheets… that sounds kind of feminine though. Like the *Venus de Milo.*

MARIGOLD: I find her very butch.

(A pause.)

Okay so… cleaning! *(They get back to it.)* So, what are all these questions for, anyway? Is this for school or something?

COURTNEY: What?

MARIGOLD: You're taking notes on your phone. Are you doing a project for school?

COURTNEY: Um… yes kinda. I mean, no! No!!! I mean, I'm in Libby's class, that's what I thought you were asking. I mean, I'm taking Gender and Sexuality at State U and Libby's the TA. You know what I mean.

MARIGOLD *(smiling):* Sure I do.

COURNTEY: Did you go there?

MARIGOLD: Oh, no. I actually didn't go to college.

COURTNEY: That's cool. I mean not everybody's into it. School and getting really good grades and stuff.

MARIGOLD: Oh, I was into it. I loved high school. I got straight As.

COURTNEY: You did? Then why didn't you go to State?

MARIGOLD: Well, I couldn't afford it.

COURTNEY: Why didn't you just make your parents pay for it?

(A pause.)

MARIGOLD: Will you help me lift this? So what's your major? You're probably sick of everybody asking you that, huh?

COURTNEY: I'm undeclared. I would have been a Women's Studies major, but they don't have that anymore.

MARIGOLD: They don't?

COURTNEY: Yeah. The Women's Studies Department got turned into the Center for the Study of Gender and Sexuality.

MARIGOLD: So?

COURTNEY: Now everyone's just studying men.

MARIGOLD: What would you rather be studying?

COURTNEY: I don't know… I think maybe Art History? I'm really into Frida Kahlo and zombies.

(The dressing room is finally looking shipshape. They breathe.)

COURTNEY: Marigold, it's so exciting to be living in the city now. My life is so different! I need all new clothes! So, one more question. Is that okay? I know I should ask Libby this stuff cuz she's my teacher, but she's like, super scary, so.

MARIGOLD: I don't mind at all but we have to be out of here in five minutes.

COURTNEY: Okay well I was just wondering, I mean... do I have to choose or you'll kick me out?

MARIGOLD: Choose what?

COURTNEY: Butch or femme? I mean it seems like all of you are like, "I'm femme" and that's this huge thing to you. But I don't know why it has to be such a dichotomy. I mean why do I have to be one or the other? Why can't I just be me?

MARIGOLD: You can. Of course you can. You should be exactly whomever you want to be. Oh my god, come here.

(*She hugs her.*)

MARIGOLD: You are like the tiniest baby duckling in the entire world, and I want to put you in my apron pocket before the farmer steps on you.

COURTNEY: What?

MARIGOLD: Plenty of lesbians HATE the whole butch/femme thing.

COURTNEY: But you don't.

MARIGOLD: I hate labels when they're limiting, but I love labels when they help us find community, and help us make sense of what we're feeling. Go home. You have my email right?

COURNTEY: No. But I added you on Jungle Red. You accepted me, right?

MARIGOLD: Right.

COURTNEY: I know you did.

(Courtney starts to leave. Marigold is busy. Courtney lingers.)

COURTNEY: I used to have no idea what a lesbian even was. I mean other than church camp and stuff where pretty much all they ever told us was that it was bad. Because of Sodom and Gomorrah. You know, like it makes cities fall? And burn? I had never even seen a lesbian before Tumblr. I was like, woah, fuckyeahdykes.tumblr dot-com — oh my god. Oh my god! But... I thought all that stuff was only online. Like I mean I figured that everybody else was like... really isolated, like me. You know? Like, the only one? Anyway, you guys seem to need to label yourselves, and I kind of think maybe I'm kind of beyond that, but... I think you're really cool, regardless.

MARIGOLD: Bye sweetie.

COURTNEY: Bye.

(About to leave again...)

COURTNEY: Oh! I almost forgot! I took a bunch of pictures of you guys during the meeting. They're really good.

MARIGOLD: That's sweet.

COURTNEY: I tagged you in all of them. Did you see them yet?

MARIGOLD: Already? Oh, no... I never look at my tagged photos.

COURTNEY: You have to! Look at all your tagged photos. Right now. On Jungle Red. They're really cute. You totally have to.

(*Courtney exits slowly.*)

SCENE THREE
DISCOVERY

(*Continuous from scene two. Worldless.*)

(*Marigold, in a splotlight, looks through her tagged photos.*)

(*Marigold discovers that Dylan is cheating.*)

SCENE FOUR
THRIFT STORE

(*Racks of clothes. The thrift store on Downey. Libby and Riot are browsing the varicolored clothing.*)

LIBBY: She's. Driving. Me. Crazy! She has *thousands* of questions. I mean thousands. How is it possible to have that many questions when you were born with an iPad in your hand? It is like raising a toddler. Dear Parents, my barren spinster uterus feels your pain.

RIOT: Well, I didn't even remember who she *was*! She added me on Facebook and then liked all of my photos. Seriously, all of them. After coming to one meeting! I was like, *Girl*, you need to not do that. And then she tried to send me a message about "Operation Dylan" and I was like, that's not a thing. That is not a thing we're doing. Especially not with you.

LIBBY: Oh, my god… is she bad crazy? I can't tell if she's bad crazy. Good crazy is fine… I think she's just enthusiastic. I try to support that. Enthusiasm. Being an undergrad… getting turned on to all these amazing authors for the first time… Judith Butler and Jack

Halberstam and just being so excited not to be in my parents' house.

RIOT: Amen.

LIBBY: But when I was an undergrad, we were cynical. Nihilistic. I just don't understand this generation!

RIOT: Blame Hot Topic. Your generation had to really work at looking angry.

> *(She holds up a dress)*

RIOT: Ooh, this one is cute…

LIBBY: Undergrads. I had an extra-credit question where I asked them to define *femme*. And do you know what kind of answers I got? "You know, being a feminine female who likes to look like a woman."

RIOT: Well you can't expect everyone to know the history of femme.

LIBBY: That's the name of the course. I'm not really sure they're literate. Oh my god, do *not* look now.

> *(Callie and Sarah have entered. Rocker chicks with tattoos and big hair.)*

SARAH: Callie, I've been waiting for almost an hour.

CALLIE: Yeah, but I told you. I've been having really complicated feelings about the solstice. What's wrong with you?

SARAH: Well, I started telling you on the phone. My grandmother is sick.

CALLIE: Mmm. Your grandmother, right.

SARAH: Callie, she's really sick. Like they don't think she's going to make it. Callie, are you even listening?

CALLIE: Yes. Are you like, really sad about it?

SARAH: She practically raised me!

CALLIE: Ugh, I know. Everything is awful. I was hanging out with Donna right before this, and this guy followed us in his car for like thirty-three blocks being like, "Make out. Make out. I wanna watch you guys make out." So creepers. I'm like, just because you jerk off to girls that look like us all the time does not mean you're actually holding a remote control out in the real world. I am a fucking human being.

SARAH: So what did you do?

CALLIE: Sauntered up, leaned into his car window and emptied hot coffee into his lap.

 (Meanwhile…)

RIOT: Okay, I'm not looking. Am I being cruised by a hipster with a handlebar moustache? Should I be like, "Guess which one of us is straight and into you… Neither!"

LIBBY: No, it's that trampitty-tramp-TRAMP who's sleeping with Dylan.

RIOT: Oh, shhh… that Callie girl? I thought you were going to say something way more fun.

LIBBY: Ha! And she's totally wearing UGGs.

RIOT: Stop it. You used to wear UGG boots. Don't freak out at her.

LIBBY: No, I did not wear UGGs. They were soft boots that kind of had the same basic shape, but I would never buy something that has UGG in its name... UGG—

RIOT: — ly.

LIBBY: UGG —

RIOT: — ly. Okay, but can we not judge her based on what she's wearing?

LIBBY: Should I mean mug her? I'm totally going to mean mug her.

RIOT: Don't. Come on. Don't. You don't even know her side of the story.

LIBBY: Okay okay, but you can just tell what a trashy person she is. Ugh, I mean look at her. She has permanent bitchface.

RIOT: It's true, she does kind of have bitchface. But don't be mean to her, Libby. Don't be mean. This isn't what you're about.

> (Callie walks over, right near Riot and Libby, who immediately jump apart and become very intent on shopping. Callie passes right in front of Riot, who glares her down.)

RIOT: Nice UGG boots.

CALLIE: I have cold feet because of my asthma.

> (Callie coolly approaches Libby.)

CALLIE: Hey, aren't you Libby?

LIBBY: Yeah...

CALLIE: I saw you when you hosted FemmeFest last year. You were really funny.

LIBBY: Oh cool, thanks. You should totally come to the next one, in six months. This year's is going to be even bigger.

CALLIE: Sure, I will. I really like your outfit. That's so cute. I actually used to dance a little bit.

LIBBY: Thanks. Well, we always need performers and volunteers! Hey, don't you work at Spex?

CALLIE: Yeah totally.

LIBBY: That's why I'm like, "I know this girl."

CALLIE: Come by sometime and I'll hook you and your friends up with drinks.

LIBBY: Cool yeah, totally.

> (Callie and Sarah leave. Riot gives Libby the look of death.)

LIBBY: Don't.

> (Riot stares.)

LIBBY: What?

RIOT: So much for loyalty.

LIBBY: You said not to be mean to her!

RIOT: Yeah but I didn't mean you had to get her pregnant! You guys have matching lockets that say *"best friends*?"

LIBBY: Whatever, I think she got the message.

RIOT: The message?

LIBBY: Oh yeah. Like when she was like, "I used to dance…" and I was like, "Psh… pole dance."

RIOT: You didn't say that.

LIBBY: Oh, she got the message.

RIOT: You told her to come volunteer! *(She throws up her hands.)* I'm going to try this on.

> *(We go back to Callie and Sarah, outside, maybe about to have a cigarette.)*

SARAH: What was up with that bitchy girl, talking about your boots?

CALLIE: If I wasted my time thinking about every lesbian that looks at me funny…

SARAH: You don't even know what that was about?

CALLIE: Everybody hates me.

SARAH: No, they don't.

CALLIE: I'm everybody's evil ex. Once any femme finds out that her girlfriend once dated me, that's it. Distrust and drama and bullshit. Nobody ever wants to leave me alone with their girlfriends, nobody ever invites me to anything because they're scared their girlfriend will talk to me; it's such bullshit. You're my only femme friend.

SARAH: I thought you were just hanging out with Donna before you came here?

CALLIE: Donna hates me! She's only my friend because she's afraid to have me as an enemy. Never trust other femmes. They're so shady. You'd think that lesbians would be less catty than straight girls because of, you know, community and solidarity and whatever, but it's all just fucking high school all over again. All girls are insecure, competitive and bitchy — gay, straight or dead.

SARAH: None of my friends are like that.

(Callie's phone rings.)

CALLIE: All of your friends are boring. Shh! *(She answers her phone; instant bedroom voice.)* Hi Dylan. Are you done already? I can't wait to see you tonight. Wait, what? Oh, with Marigold? You're going to spend the night with Marigold instead? But why? Why would you wanna do that? She *needs* you? She doesn't need you, I need you. I told you I'm going through a really hard time right now. Everything is awful. I spilled my coffee this morning. I keep getting written up at work… and this guy, this guy just sexually harassed me really badly, I'm *really* shaken up. Dylan, no! Okay fine, I wasn't going to tell you this until I saw you tonight, but my grandmother is sick. Really sick. Like they don't think she's going to make it. I know. That's why I really need you tonight. I mean, she practically raised me! Okay. Okay, thank you. Thank you, baby, I'll see you then. Haha, well of course. Mmm… I always get what I want.

(Callie closes her phone, oblivious to Sarah's look of horror.)

And what everybody else wants too.

SCENE FIVE
THE BREAKDOWN / THE FEMMESIS

(Marigold's bedroom. A lovely dressing table. Vintage dressing table accoutrements. Perhaps wall posters of androgynous, "visibly" queer icons like JD Samson, Kim Ann Foxman or the like. The saddest song in the world —maybe Bat for Lashes' "Siren" or similar— plays.)

(Marigold dances with dresses.)

(She cries.)

(She collapses in a pile of pretty colors.)

(Guerra appears in the doorway.)

MARIGOLD: I don't want to get hard, Guerra.

GUERRA: Hard?

MARIGOLD: I don't want to become bitter, or see the world in a fixed way. I don't want to become suspicious or petty or distrustful of other girls. I have to fight for everything; I don't want to have to fight for love. I just want love to come easily, and without pain.

(Marigold collapses again, crying. Guerra holds her.)

GUERRA: Well, I think you can achieve most of that. In pieces and over time.

MARIGOLD: I tried calling my mother.

GUERRA: Good!

MARIGOLD: No. Not good. She was kind for about two seconds before the agenda set in. "Well you know, Honey… Dylan… she looks like a man. You, there's absolutely no reason why a boy wouldn't love you. It's not too late to change your mind!"

GUERRA: Change your mind?

MARIGOLD: My mother clings to the idea that I'll be straight again someday. She cites as proof that I had three boyfriends in high school. I'm like, "Ma! Have you seen how many boyfriends I've had in the ten years SINCE high school?" You'd think that would matter more. But the longer my hair gets, the more the flame of hope grows in her eyes. She thinks because I look like this, I can't possibly be gay. My entire life, some twisted, bastard phase.

GUERRA: Oh girl, I've been there. The idea that "You're pretty! You could get a man!" I'm like, uh, contrary to every movie and TV show ever, men are not actually that hard to get.

MARIGOLD: And do you know my mom would never even ask me about Dylan anyway? My high school boyfriends all had names, were all real to her, something that she believed in. All the women I've dated since? Might as well be the same person. Interchangeable. All representing some demon beast that got hold of her pretty, pretty daughter.

GUERRA: You're not that pretty.

MARIGOLD: Haha.

GUERRA: My dad is this total macho. He'll pretend to be sensitive and be like, "*Mija, mija* come here… why do you hate men?" And I'll be like, "I don't hate men." And he'll be like, "But always with the women… you can tell me… what happened… who hurt you." And I'll be like, "Dad! I don't hate men. I love you, I love my brothers, I love Justin Bieber, I just hate most Republicans, evangelicals, guys who read *Maxim*, guys who don't read anything... Ugh, and Carlos Cerda!"

MARIGOLD: I hate that guy!

GUERRA: Fucking asshole.

MARIGOLD: No, who is that guy.

GUERRA: This guy at work. Had the nerve. To say that I'm not oppressed as a lesbian because I don't look like one. And we're talking a Salvadorean man who calls himself a crusader for social justice. A community organizer.

MARIGOLD: What happened?

GUERRA: He said this at a staff meeting, in front of everyone, while talking about why we shouldn't let a gay organization's name be listed among our affinity groups on this goddamn banner for the worker's solidarity march. He was like, "Why do you care so much? You're not gay." And I was like, "First of all, I *am* gay. Second of all, this is the *third* time I've had to embarrassingly come out at work, thanks for remembering, and third, you don't have to 'look' gay to suffer the effects of discrimination!" I have never been so close to violence in my life.

MARIGOLD: Not to mention that you shouldn't have to "be" gay to understand that gay rights matter. People just don't understand. They don't understand us, and they don't even care to TRY. I mean, what's in it for them?

GUERRA: Most days I don't even feel that oppressed, you know? I live in a big city, I have an amazing job; I see what my sisters in Central and South America are going through and I'm like, I'm blessed. I have nothing to complain about. My life is fucking good. But then something like this will happen. Or I'll get on the bus and some guy'll make me scared for the entire hour home from work and I'm like, nope, I'm still at the shit fucking bottom of the pile, and the worst part is, I just take it as a matter of course. Like, *of course* I feel threatened on a daily basis. That's what it *is* to be a woman in this city.

MARIGOLD: What's the point. What's the point of falling in love. Ten million advertisements are wrong; you can't make yourself unforgettable with perfume. You can't! And if *this* is all you did *(she gestures at the pretty dresses around her)*, if *this* is all you're doing, there'll be nothing left to remember you by.

GUERRA: I don't think you need to be worried about that.

MARIGOLD: I don't know what to say to Dylan.

GUERRA: What do you mean? You don't say anything.

MARIGOLD: How can I not say anything?

GUERRA: Are you and Dylan officially together? Did you have the conversation about being exclusive and not seeing other people?

MARIGOLD: No.

GUERRA: Then by acting jealous you'll push her right into the arms of this other girl. Listen. I don't know this Callie girl, but I know her type. She's like every girl I used to know in Seattle. Looks like a fine-ass fox every time she goes out, and will *never acknowledge your presence* unless you're with a good-looking butch. Then all of a sudden, she'll act like she's your best friend and you guys hang out all the time. Next thing you know, she's getting your butch's number and texting her 24/7, and at first your girlfriend is innocent, like, "Your friend, she was really nice, we should all hang out, I should set her up with somebody…" Next thing you know your girlfriend is bringing her phone into the bathroom in the middle of the night when she thinks you're asleep, and you have to pretend not to notice…

MARIGOLD: Personal experience?

GUERRA: Yeah.

MARIGOLD: So fake. I don't understand why some femmes are fake like that.

GUERRA: Oh, you know, the myth that there aren't enough butches to go around.

MARIGOLD: Why would Dylan do this to me? Why?

GUERRA: Because she's insecure.

MARIGOLD: She's not insecure. Her confidence is the sexiest thing about her.

GUERRA: Okay, but you know her. Like really. She went most of her life feeling ugly. She got teased for being a tomboy, her only friends were the boys in her karate class... *(This speech isn't working on Marigold.)* You told me that she spent all of high school *not* being hot, being called a freak and a dyke and denying it, *not* dating guys like you did, pining after straight girls and knowing just from the look in their eyes that they knew, they knew it and were disgusted... and then all of a sudden, she graduates high school, moves to the big city, figures a few things out fashion-wise, realizes there's a niche that's buying what she's selling, and after a few years of transformation, suddenly she's hot property.

MARIGOLD: I wanna be hot property!

> *(Marigold collapses into the pile of clothes. Guerra is over it.)*

GUERRA: Marigold, you're an able-bodied, thin, cisgender white American citizen. To many people, you represent an unattainable beauty standard against which they will always be measured and found wanting. You've gotta give Dylan at least some credit for walking down the street looking like she does. That's brave.

MARIGOLD: Why are you making excuses for her?

GUERRA: I'm not. I'm just saying that some butches, not all of them, but some, feel the need to overcompensate by acting like the worst possible kind of guy. Come on, sweetie, look at this face. You're unlikely to suffer from loneliness for long.

> *(Guerra starts dressing up a pouting Marigold, maybe putting on funny hats and costume jewelry. Marigold starts to feel better.)*

MARIGOLD: The power dynamic in this town is so OFF. Like, there's this scarcity of butches, and this *glut* of femmes trying to find a person they can truly connect with in this already hypersmall dating pool. You'd think the whole beauty of being lesbian is that we never have to fight over men or base our worth on how perfect our marriage is…

GUERRA: …but hello, we *are* women. I mean, even though almost nothing in culture represents us, everything in culture has shaped us.

MARIGOLD: Femme competition. Femme-on-femme crime.

GUERRA: Callie knoweth not what she do.

MARIGOLD: She's my femmesis.

GUERRA: Yeah, she is

    (A silence. Then Marigold's phone buzzes.)

MARIGOLD: Hello? *(To Guerra)* It's Riot. *(To Riot)* Yeah, no, the FemmeFest lineup isn't solidified at all. *(A pause.)* Huh? No… Oh, is that why you're really calling me? No, I don't really stalk Dylan's Facebook profile, but it's nice to know that *YOU* do. No, I'm really not interested. It doesn't concern me. Things with me and Dylan are fine. Thanks though.

    (Marigold hangs up the phone and screams in pure frustration and rage. Guerra reaches out to support her.)

MARIGOLD: Riot says Callie has made her profile picture a picture of her and Dylan together. *(There's acid in her voice.)* Riot said, "Oh, I thought you knew already. I hope this doesn't ruin your night." And then you know what else she said?

GUERRA: What?

MARIGOLD: Callie wants to perform at FemmeFest!

GUERRA: NO. (Curses in Spanish.) That girl has so much nerve.

MARIGOLD: She's trying to steal my entire life!

GUERRA: No. No no no, FemmeFest is like six months from now. This girl will forget all about it by then. She's just trying to shake you. Don't let her fuck with you. You have a chance to be the bigger person here. We know you're a better person than she is. Mari. Mari…

MARIGOLD: I'm sick of being the bigger person. I'm sick of being a good person at all. FUCK. THAT. Where has it gotten me? Messing with Dylan is one thing, but messing with FemmeFest? That's my baby. This girl is going down.

SCENE SIX
THE SHOWDOWN

(The Lexington. The Wild Rose. The E-room. Or any of a million bars like them. Oh wait, except there's only one lesbian bar in every metropolis.[2] Callie is working behind the bar, polishing glasses; it's the beginning of her shift. The bar is virtually empty. She is the ultimate hipster cliché: tall, arms sleeved with cheesy tattoos [visible music notes and vintage pinup girls, ideally], long, layered dark hair, faded "ironic" rocker tee and cutoff shorts. Marigold approaches the bar, tentatively.)

CALLIE (barely looking up): Hi.

MARIGOLD: Hi.

---

[2] This was true at the time of writing. The Lexington and the E-Room have since closed, as has the Palms in Los Angeles. At the time of publication, few lesbian bars exist in the US.

CALLIE: We're not really open yet, but if you just want a beer or something uncomplicated I can hook you up, just give me one … second…

MARIGOLD: Oh… thank you…

(Callie finally looks up and really sees Marigold.)

CALLIE: Well hello, nurse! You're not a regular here or I would remember you. You're gorgeous.

MARIGOLD *(trepidatious):* Thank you.

CALLIE: And you look really familiar. Are you a stripper at Diamond Desi's?

MARIGOLD: No…

CALLIE: Too bad…I'm there all the time and I'd wanna see you dance!

MARIGOLD: I wouldn't think I'd be your type. I'd think you'd be more into butches.

CALLIE: Oh. *(Suspicious.)* Well sure, I love me a good butch top. Who doesn't? I'm mostly into butches. Or trans guys. Sometimes straight dudes if I'm really hard up. But when I see a girl as pretty as you, I can't help but sigh and think I'm doing it all wrong.

MARIGOLD: You must make a lot of tips buttering up the ladies like that.

CALLIE: No… I wish. Lesbians don't tip for shit. Some of the butch bartenders make good money, but only from certain femmes that hit on them all night. I'd like to work at a better bar, actually— *(Callie looks behind her to make sure the boss is out of earshot.)* — you didn't hear me say that, but I am looking, so if you know anywhere I should take my résumé, I'd like to work somewhere less divey, but —

MARIGOLD: None of the classy places will hire you?

CALLIE: Nah.

MARIGOLD: I'm shocked.

CALLIE *(more suspicious):* Okay, where do I know you from?

MARIGOLD: Maybe I've come up in your Facebook suggestions for "people you may know."

CALLIE: Oh yeah, haha, that shit's pretty much only ever your exes and your mortal enemies —

MARIGOLD: I'm one of the organizers of FemmeFest ... and I think you know my girlfriend, Dylan?

(Callie realizes what's going on here.)

CALLIE: I'm pretty sure Dylan's not *actually* your girlfriend.

MARIGOLD: Oh yeah? Is that what she tells you? Or just what you tell yourself?

CALLIE: I just mean, you guys aren't together.

MARIGOLD: That depends how you define *together*. And I'm pretty sure it wouldn't matter to you either way. You knew that I was dating her when you started throwing yourself at her.

CALLIE: *Throwing myself at her?* Is that what she told you?

MARIGOLD: She didn't tell me anything. We happen to have a lot of friends in common. Hilarious that you thought you'd keep it secret in this town.

CALLIE: Okay, wow. We're doing this. We're really doing this now? You come to my job to start shit with me? I thought maybe you were going to be mature and not act like it was a big deal and maybe just tell me you're not comfortable with it or whatever…

MARIGOLD: Oh, and if I said I wasn't comfortable with it, you would stop?

CALLIE: Well I won't now! I would have before, maybe, before I knew what an enormous cunt you are.

MARIGOLD: I'm a cunt?! I'M the cunt? Oh wow, it is taking every bit of my self-restraint not to tell you what *you* are right now!

CALLIE: What, too many Women's Studies courses to call me a slut? Go 'head. You know you want to.

MARIGOLD: I have way too much respect for my friends in the sex industry to call you a whore. You're… at least whores get paid to offer a service that's been in demand for all eternity! You just do this because you're… vain! To feed your… narcissistic personality disorder!

CALLIE: *(Has all the power.)* Oh wow, we're not even on a first-name basis, but now you have my *diagnosis*? You're pathetic.

MARIGOLD: You're part of the femme solidarity group! You're supposedly a feminist! You are such a fucking hypocrite!

CALLIE: Am I? Well it actually takes TWO people to hook up, so it's not very feminist of YOU to pin the blame on me like I'm some kind of homewrecker, when your girlfriend was ready and willing. No matter what she tells you, she hit on *me*, not the other way around. Would you like to apologize now, and go be mad at her instead? "Ciao."

MARIGOLD: Yeah… no. Dylan's a flirt. Dylan likes femme attention. But you… you hit on EVERYONE's girlfriend. Dylan's not even special to you. You PREFER someone else's girlfriend to any of the many, many people that are paying attention to you, right now, who are available. You're that girl. You're only interested in messes. You would never want to be with someone unless you could fuck someone else over in the process.

(Callie is visibly humbled.)

CALLIE: Didn't you ever think maybe Dylan would get bored of all your grad school bullshit? Pretentious, over-intellectual, neurotic…

MARIGOLD (shaken): I'm not *in* grad school. Did Dylan say that?

CALLIE: Maybe.

MARIGOLD: I get it. I get it. I'm uptight, you're fun. I like books; you like wearing short skirts and getting shitfaced and being like, "Let's score some blow tonight" while I'm at home trying to plan stupid events to make the world a better place that nobody comes to. I get it. But you know what? You may have a lot of hot sexy pics of yourself on the internet, but I HAVE ACTUAL GOALS. You might be the girl that everyone likes to look at and thinks is so mysterious and interesting, but you're *not* interesting. Surrounding yourself with cool things does not make you cool. Taking a million Instagram photos of yourself does not make you any more beautiful.

CALLIE (smirking): Oh, so you stalk my Instagram?

MARIGOLD: YES. How could I not? It's like you curated your whole feed for silly dupes like Dylan to jerk off to. "Oh, here's me pouting with my Patti Smith album. Here's me at a coffee shop reading Henry Miller. Oh, here's me in a sexy field reading Jack Kerouac."

CALLIE: Wow, who's more in love with me, Dylan or you?

MARIGOLD: But the difference is, those people DID things — Kerouac and Henry Miller and Bukowski and all those painters you like were fucking misogynists, first off, so congratulations on that company — but those people MADE ART and PLAYED MUSIC and STAYED UP LATE and FOUGHT IN THE STREET and DRANK WINE and RECORDED THEIR HISTORY, and yes, there was narcissism, gobs of it, and YES, there was pretension, absolutely, and navel-gazing galore, but at least they DID SOMETHING WITH IT. And none of them, and I mean NONE of them, EVER thought their life as fucking worthy of documentation as you do.

CALLIE (*finally hurt to the core*): I'm an artist too, you know.

MARIGOLD: Really? Is that so? Because last I heard, you were a bartender. Who isn't even making good tips.

(*Marigold Exits*)

SCENE SEVEN
THE BREAKUP

(*Continuous with Scene Six. Marigold steps out of the bar into a pool of light. She talks into her phone.*)

MARIGOLD (*on her phone*): Hey, baby. I was just… no, I know… no, I *know*. I'm not trying to control you. I'm not trying to control you! I just… I was just wondering if maybe I could see you tonight. You haven't been back in three days and I miss you. Have you been sleeping at your mom's, like last weekend? Is she okay? What? No! I'm not trying to be controlling, I'm trying to *care* about you. Dylan, you haven't been home in three nights. I just wanna make sure you're okay. Okay, but so your mom's okay, right? I mean, she's fine? She didn't, like get a run in her leopard-print stockings or sprain her ankle in those disgusting trashy stripper shoes she was wearing last night? Oh, you're surprised that the internet's public? Or wait, you didn't know that I *had* the internet? That it's a thing that my friends and I use on a daily fucking basis? You thought I was into Morse code these days? Baby, wait… over the phone? You're telling me this *over the phone*? So, you just started fucking her? You just started *fucking* her? Oh please, do NOT try to pretend that you haven't slept with her yet. She wouldn't be confident enough to put pictures of you two on the internet if you weren't having sex. Yes, I know. I know not everyone is monogamous. I know you identify as polyamorous. But you've been practically living with me… I kind of assumed that you had changed your mind! Okay *fine*, fine. Yes, you're right. I'm sorry. I know it's not a thing you just change your mind on. That's not what I meant. I just mean… Dylan, you've been living with me *rent-free*. I was helping you pay your fucking car insurance … And now what? You're just not coming home? Is *she* going to pay your rent? Is she taking care of you now? (*Crying.*) No… No no no…

(*Pulling herself together.*)

Yes, you told me you were polyamorous. You did. But I thought that meant that if, someday, you met someone, we would communicate about it. Talk about opening up the relationship. Set some boundaries. And you know, you've been stopping me from hanging out with anyone who's even *slightly* masculine-of-center, wouldn't polyamory mean that I could see other people too? I didn't think it meant you would just DROP me, at the drop of a hat! Oh wait, I'm sorry — *relentlessly* flirt with my friends, in front of my face, for months, and then start fucking a girl who actually tried out for *my* burlesque show last year, and wasn't good enough! — who, by the way, is dead to me, and you can tell her what a really great feminist I think she is. … So that's all you have to say? You used me! You fucking used me! Okay. Fine. You can come get your shit. It'll be in the front yard, covered in milk since you're so *vegan* now, so passionate about *veganism*, since you met her. No Dylan, I DO understand that not everyone is monogamous. I do. Not everyone thinks that way. Or feels that way. But what you're doing isn't non-monogamy. You missed one key element when you read *The Ethical Slut*: The word *ethical* was in the title.

(*Intermission.*)

ACT TWO

SCENE ONE
"THE MAIDS"

(*MUSIC: "We rockin' stilettos, ho!" or other similarly aggressive, femme-centric hip-hop. Bibiana is cleaning the women's room at the Taco Joint. She's listening to music on an iPod, the white cable visible, rapping along with something absolutely filthy. Gabriela enters. Gabi and Bibi are 19, Mexican American and femme lesbians. Their style is a little bit emo and a little bit goth, while still proudly "street" —something the rest of the women in this play most definitely are not.*)

GABRIELA: Girl. GIRL. BIBIANA!

(*Bibiana realizes she's being spoken to, and stops the music.*)

BIBIANA: *Ay, me asustaste!* Damn girl! Haha…

GABI: You need to chill with that shit, man. *El Pendejo* is going to kill you if you keep singing at the top of your lungs like that!

BIBI: I just love these badass bitch female rappers.

GABI: Who are you listening to?

(*She grabs the headphones. They both dance to the music.*)

Kiyomara is so hot, right? Have you seen that video where she's all …(*Imitates a female rapper pulling her hat low and dancing like a thug.)*

BIBI: Yes, YES… the one where she looks like a dude, in a throwback jersey and baggy jeans? She looks like a fuckin' *Vato* in that video.

GABI: Yeah, like a AG. And then in the next video she's all got the long hair and the lipstick and I'm like, no girl. We've seen you now. We know.

BIBI: Haha!

GABI: Haha yeah. Okay so I told Adán I'm gonna help you clean so we can all get out of here sooner. So, can we do this?

BIBI: Cool, thank you. You seeing that girl again tonight?

GABI: Yeah. She's cool. Kinda thuggish. She borrowed me her cousin's ID so we can get into Club Ruby.

> *(They clean, synchronized spritzing of spray bottles, wiping down the mirrors, counters and sinks.)*

BIBI: Oh my god, what was that drama earlier? That shit was crazy!

GABI: Oh, just some white girls on some bullshit.

BIBI: They were gay too, right?

GABI: Yeah, these two white bitches that come in here all the time were like, breaking up or something. And I'm just like, do that shit in your car! What is wrong with you? The stud one kept, like, trying to say that she loved the fem one and just needed a little space sometimes, and the fem one was like, "Oh and by space you mean slut? You need a little white trash slut sometimes?"

BIBI: *Eso le dijo?*

GABI: No. Not really, but that's the basics of it. And then the stud one was like…

(She imitates a hipster "Shane" type, brushing the hair out of her eyes)

GABI: "You know, I just want a simple life. I go to my job, I work, I come home to my girl. That's all I want. Callie gets that." And the fem girl was like, "I get that too. That's what *I* want, baby."

BIBI: Oh my god, you are so good at this acting thing.

GABI: And then the AG one was like, "No, you don't. You want, like, planning meetings and farmers' markets and shit. And Butch/Femme Ball and feminist book club…" And the fem was like, "So you just want a normal life. To be like complete fucking straight people, no queer community, completely hetero in every way except for the fact of who you're fucking? You want me to give it all up?"

BIBI: Daaaaamn, that shit got deep REAL quick!

GABI: And the stud was like, "I just think you'd be a lot happier if you weren't so stressed out all the time, and spent a little more time at home with me having a normal relationship." And the fem was like, "I'd much rather have a stressful life full of meaning and purpose than an empty, happy life with you." I was like, *mami*, that stud has got one foot out the DOOR now, if she didn't before. You're telling her that all that other shit you're doing is more important than your relationship!

BIBI: So, the fem was the one who ended it?

GABI: Yeah, but it was total bullshit! You could tell she didn't mean it so badly, and was saying the opposite of everything she really felt. And then the stud one kept saying all this really cute stuff, like how she really respected her, and how if she spent some time with the slutty one she would like her too, and that maybe they should just see other people for a while but then get back together…

BIBI: *Uta! No chingues!* Was the *vato* one like a model or something? I couldn't tell.

GABI: Yeah… maybe. Like a model on some corny *L Word* hipster shit.

> *(Bibi laughs.)*

GABI: *Y que*, did they check you out?

BIBI: *Ni madres.* They didn't even LOOK at me. One of them dropped her trash and was like *(she imitates)* "Oh, sorry…"

> *(Bibi looks at the imaginary trash, doesn't pick it up and then looks back, expectantly.)*

GABI *(laughs):* Fuckin' bitches.

BIBI: Yeah. No one ever clocks me as gay at this job except this one transgender who always comes in late, you know her? She's like "Girl, I know you like to lick some pussy."

> *(She flicks imaginary hair with imaginary long nails.)*

GABI: Haha! Oh my god, I would have cracked up laughing. I don't usually tell everybody, like, *you know*… but I did tell a few of the guys in the kitchen, because I didn't want them to keep asking me out.

BIBI: Yeah right, did that stop them?

GABI: No. At first, they were like, "Damn, can I watch?" and "I'll turn you out" And I was like…

> *(She imitates being so bored, yawn.)*

But now they just kind of look at me. DeShant doesn't even talk to me anymore. He's real Christian.

BIBI: Yeah… I don't know if I should tell them. You didn't tell them about me?

GABI: No, no. But you're new so of course they wanna holler. Anyway, that shit was a MESS. I was like, you are in a public place. You are embarrassing yourselves right now. Nobody cares about your problems!

BIBI: Haha, right? And they are THE WORST tippers. They act like I haven't waited on them like fifty times by now. *Pinches codas.*

GABI: Lesbians are always the worst tippers. It's some bullshit.

BIBI: So, then what happened? Did they make up?

GABI: The stud finally said she would stop seeing the other girl.

BIBI: Ooh, isn't that just what the fem wanted?!

GABI: *Pues si, pero* she kept saying, "No, no… It's already too late. I could never trust you again." And the stud is like, "We were never officially exclusive! I'm telling you we can be exclusive now! Come on, I've been so good to you!" And the fem is like, "You could have at least hooked up with someone I could respect. But this girl?" And the stud kept saying, "Why are you getting so upset, why can't you be chill about this, like I am…"

BIBI: It's easy to be chill when you're not the one getting hurt!

GABI: And finally, the stud was like, "Okay, I think we're done here. If you can't just talk about this calmly, without getting emotional, I'm out." And she straight up banged out the door. The fem one sat there crying. Like not even trying to hide it, tears just rolling down her face. I think the stud was her ride actually; I think she had to go wait at the bus stop to get home. I almost felt bad for her.

BIBI: *Pobresita*, if she's crying in public, you know it's bad. That's like me with my ex.

GABI: But some people just think they're on TV. Like all the time. They think they're so important and I'm like, yeah, you got shit, I got shit, she got shit, it's not even worth shit.

(*Bibi goes in the stall. It's a bad scene.*)

BIBI: Oh no. Oh shit. Shit! Gabi, get me the plunger! Quick! *Que pinche asco!*

GABI: Shit. Shit! I have a date tonight!

<u>SCENE TWO</u>
PILATES

(*Stage left: Pilates class at the gym. Libby and Courtney in capri yoga pants and tank tops. Clean-cut Pilates Instructor with silly headset mic.*)

(*Stage right: Homorobics. Guerra in sparkly, neon, ridiculous workout attire, soon joined by Riot. Queer punk Homorobics Instructor with boom box.*)

HOMOROBICS
INSTRUCTOR: Okay, homos! Let's celebrate size acceptance and self-love while still building strength and lifelong fitness!

(*They do some silly aerobics moves.*)

PILATES INSTRUCTOR: Okay. *Chicas.* Let's really pull the belly button into the spine here, yah? Toning toward that flat tummy and sculpted bum we're looking for. Bikini season is coming, yah?

(They do some tiny crunches.)

RIOT *(to Guerra):* I feel bad for her. I really do. But what the hell was she thinking, attacking Callie at her job right in front of her boss?

GUERRA: She just marched in there and called her a slut? I hate that antifeminist shit.

RIOT: I mean, if the girl didn't have it in for Marigold at first, she sure does now. And of course, Dylan's going to choose the girl that was fun and slutty through this whole ordeal, not the one who was angry and punitive and caused massive drama that almost got Callie fired. Did you hear that Marigold threw a drink on her?

GUERRA: That's so unlike her. I'm almost impressed. Who told you that?

RIOT: Oh wait, I thought you did.

GUERRA: No, it must have been Libby.

LIBBY: You didn't happen to see anything online about … anything?

COURTNEY: You mean like … Operation Dylan?

LIBBY: Militaristic slang is an offense to all those enslaved by the military industrial complex.

COURTNEY: Aah! Sorry.

LIBBY: But yeah … I may or may not have accidentally told the Marigold story to Dolly DP, completely forgetting that she does that stupid relationship blog that's full of typos and generally completely offensive. And what does she do? She goes and writes an article about polyamory and communication and setting healthy boundaries, which I've been begging her to do FOREVER — but she goes and does it NOW, using a picture of Dylan and Callie together to illustrate the "healthy communication" section.

(Pilates Instructor adjusts Courtney in an overly sexual fashion.)

PILATES INSTRUCTOR: Now what we're gonna do is really tuck *this* under, and really pull *this* way into the hip sockets.

COURTNEY *(to Libby):* I hate it when they touch me. Nobody reads that blog though, right? She has like three followers.

LIBBY: Yeah, nobody reads it, but Dolly DP sent the link to Better Homes and Lesbians, hoping they would reprint it or link to it or something …

COURTNEY: They're not gonna post it.

LIBBY: No, but they liked the photo of Dylan and Callie so much that they're putting it on the *cover* of the print edition …

COURTNEY *(gasps):* … of the issue where they're interviewing Marigold about FemmeFest? Oh no!

RIOT: It's really stressing me out. I mean, I'm friends with both of them, and Dylan, and now it's like I have to avoid ALL of them so it doesn't look like I'm taking sides.

HOMOROBICS
INSTRUCTOR: Okay! Guys!
Listen up! Try to really
express yourself. With the
music!

GUERRA: Wait, that's right,
didn't you do roller derby
with Callie?

RIOT: Well, she didn't stick
with roller derby for long,
actually. No, I kind of got to
know her more recently...

GUERRA: After you knew
she was hooking up with
Dylan?!

RIOT: I cannot keep track of
everyone's drama.

GUERRA: I think you're
doing pretty well.

HOMOROBICS
INSTRUCTOR: Guys, can
you try to pay attention,
please?

PILATES INSTRUCTOR:
And four ... three ... two ...
one.

RIOT: Anyway, this is why
Sprocket Wrench and I have
a don't ask, don't tell policy.
I'd like to see someone try to
start that kind of drama with
me.

GUERRA: You know, Marigold still isn't returning my texts? I've been so supportive, and now all of a sudden, she won't tell me anything.

RIOT: So, let her be self-absorbed. We'll find out everything at the FemmeFest planning meeting anyway.

GUERRA: I'm not gonna hang out with her for a while. I'm sick of being her caretaker.

PILATES INSTRUCTOR: Last twenty!

COURTNEY: You should warn her about the cover photo. Then at least it won't be a total surprise.

LIBBY: Hmm...

COURTNEY: Can't you just apologize?

LIBBY: Then she'd know it's my fault! And I've been SO loyal to her, completely telling off Callie that time I saw her at the thrift store.

COURTNEY: Well, then I guess you just have to wait and see how she takes it. It'll be bad.

LIBBY: Oh, whatever, this sort of thing happens to girls in the scene all the time.

COURTNEY: What do they usually do?

LIBBY *(shrugging):* Move. Usually clear across the country, or to Berlin.

PILATES INSTRUCTOR: Nice work, *chicas*… Think of that hot guy you're going to impress on the beach next weekend!

(Libby and Courtney roll their eyes and all start to exit.)

COURTNEY: Oh yeah, that's exactly what I'm thinking about.

LIBBY: Who does she think she's kidding?

SCENE THREE
THE BREAKTHROUGH

(Marigold's bedroom. Marigold is on her laptop with Guerra looking over her shoulder.)

MARIGOLD: Okay… I'm going to go ahead and post it. Count down to hate mail in five … four … three … two …

(She clicks send. They cheer. The joy is short-lived.)

MARIGOLD: Yup.

GUERRA: Surprise?

MARIGOLD: Everyone is offended.

GUERRA: What did they say?

MARIGOLD: "Wow, looks like FemmeFest will continue to be classist this year by yet again charging money at the door."

GUERRA: I don't know how they think we can pay for this event without charging money. Oh, plus the girl who wrote that lives on her dad's credit card, so I'm not sure why she's concerned.

MARIGOLD: "A show that's supposed to represent the entire femme community… with not a single femme over forty in it."

GUERRA: Crap… that one's kind of valid.

MARIGOLD: But we never said that this show was supposed to represent ALL femmes, my god, that's a huge responsibility! That's kind of impossible! Wait, here's another one. "As usual, a totally white lineup."

GUERRA: Wait, what? Okay now I'm personally offended. The lineup is at least half women of color, including me, that I personally curated. Fuck that shit. Give me the computer. (*Guerra snatches the computer from Marigold and starts typing a post.*)

GUERRA: Thanks for telling me how white I am… I wasn't aware… I'm sure that myself and all the other femmes of color in the show feel much less invisible now that you've completely invalidated our participation. Send.

MARIGOLD: Lesbians are the worst. THE WORST. I don't want to do it anymore.

GUERRA: Do what?

MARIGOLD: FemmeFest. The monthly *Femme Show*. Any of it. Trying to make art in this community isn't worth the abuse.

GUERRA: Come on, this is what art-making is.

MARIGOLD: Dealing with constant negativity and criticism?

GUERRA: We do it to others. We hate the art school queers cuz they're all so elitist; they hate the bar dykes because they're not comfortable around the working class; the bar dykes hate the power lesbians because they wear blazers instead of sports jerseys; and the power lesbians judge us because they would date us if we could just be more normal.

MARIGOLD: I just don't want to do it this year. I'm ashamed to even show my face.

GUERRA: Why would you be ashamed? Dylan's the one who looks like a dick.

MARIGOLD: True. But I'm the one everyone thinks is crazy.

GUERRA: You know, the blame isn't all yours. I'd put some blame on the friend circle.

MARIGOLD: I owe so much to my best femme friends. Frenemies. Femmemies.

GUERRA: Stop. We'll do what lesbians from time immemorial have done. We'll get out of town.

MARIGOLD: Really?

GUERRA: Really. We'll go to San Francisco for the weekend, and stay in a cute bed and breakfast, and party our faces off. I'm looking up tickets right now.

MARIGOLD: No, no we can't go to San Francisco.

GUERRA: Why not?

MARIGOLD: Because *they* went to San Francisco. Dylan and Callie. They have friends there. Everyone will be talking about it.

GUERRA: Fine. (*Shrugs*) We'll go to Oakland!

SCENE FOUR
"DIVORCE HOTEL"

(*A pulsing electro beat. A rowdy burlesque club in San Francisco. Marigold and Guerra enter with fun-looking drinks and lean on the bar, watching the performance.*)

(DUTCH SPOTLIGHT NUMBER. *The music changes and Dutch performs a retro, Gertrude Stein–inspired old-fashioned burlesque routine.*)

MARIGOLD: This is bizarre and heavenly.

GUERRA: This is just what you needed.

MARIGOLD (*toasting*): To San Francisco.

GUERRA: To Oak-town my hometown!

MARIGOLD: I cannot believe this show.

GUERRA: I know! Dutch is an icon. She's like the mayor. She's been promoting events like this for over twenty years. She can do whatever she wants.

MARIGOLD: This is fate.

GUERRA: Really? She's too femme for you. But she does have short hair …

393

MARIGOLD: No, perv, we have to invite Dutch to perform at FemmeFest!

GUERRA: Oh. Still working. Of course. I thought we were partying tonight! Are you feeling it yet?

> *(Here, they have most likely popped a molly. No need to lean too heavily on it.)*

MARIGOLD *(drinking)*: Not really. But it's perfect! She's a genius, and we really *don't* have many performers over forty, which we have to do something about...

GUERRA *(grinning)*: I knew you weren't serious about quitting. This FemmeFest is going to fuck people's minds, and you're going to perform this year too, dammit.

MARIGOLD: Maybe... I don't know...

> *(Dutch approaches them at the bar.)*

GUERRA: Can we buy you a drink?

DUTCH: You're joking, right? I drink for free.

> *(She snaps her fingers and a drink appears.)*

GUERRA: We've been standing here flipping over how great you are.

DUTCH: Oh, so you liked my moves?

GUERRA: Loved.

DUTCH: What about your friend over here? She doesn't look so sure.

GUERRA: She's going through a horrendous high-profile breakup. Listen, we're part of the collective organizing FemmeFest. We just randomly ended up here tonight and... you have to come perform. We'll pay for your flight and everything.

DUTCH: No, I'm not interested. That's perfectly charming, but no. When's the show again?

MARIGOLD: In two months. It's a huge event. It gets tons of press.

DUTCH: No, I'm not interested. There's no way I could possibly make it. I'll think about it.

> (Dutch pauses and takes a drink.)

DUTCH: So, Miss High-Profile Breakup. It can't be that high-profile or I'd know about it.

MARIGOLD: Well, we don't live here.

DUTCH: Good thinking. To your breakup! *(Dutch makes to toast.)*

GUERRA: To your breakup!

MARIGOLD: I don't think a breakup is worth celebrating.

DUTCH: Oh listen, what are you, twenty-five? You've got so many good relationships coming your way. You can wallow if you want, but I wouldn't recommend it. All my best love affairs happened much older than you are.

MARIGOLD: You're not that much older than us.

DUTCH: Would you believe I turned fifty last week? *(Or substitute forty or sixty or whatever is most appropriate for the actor playing Dutch)*

(They toast again.)

GUERRA: No way! Congratulations!

MARIGOLD: You look so young!

DUTCH: No, I look my age and I'm proud to look it. I know it may shock you to think that lesbians over thirty live exciting lives, but surprise! We do. It's fantastic. To be completely free of the *fear* of aging, because I actually *am* aging. And my generation has it the best. Completely immune to the stigma of the unmarried woman. We can do whatever the fuck we want. Now it's all changing. It'll be different for you. You're going to be pressured to marry each other, and be expected to have children. I feel bad for you…

MARIGOLD: Gay marriage is going to change everything. It's gonna happen, this is gonna be the year.

GUERRA: Yeah but when we're normal, how will we be special?

MARIGOLD: I'm sure we'll figure something out.

DUTCH: So what happened?

MARIGOLD: Oh, you know. Age-old. She left me for another woman, boring story.

DUTCH: For your best friend? For your ex-girlfriend?

MARIGOLD: No…

DUTCH: Honey, you'll be fine. You wouldn't believe the things I've seen at this point. I've seen lovers left for other women, other men, for drugs, for art, for ladder climbing and better opportunities, for money, of course, not to mention just out of boredom or insecurity or ADD. I've dated stone butches straight out of the '50s who won't let you touch them at all, to virtual teenagers who ID as genderqueer and want to try absolutely *everything* in bed, simultaneously. My current plaything is a bike punk named Sprocket Wrench…

(Guerra and Marigold elbow each other at this.)

DUTCH: …who hasn't read a single lick of queer theory or history, and doesn't put any limits on who she can love, or how. I've seen it all, and it is all amazing.

MARIGOLD: It took me a really long time to figure out who I was and what I wanted. And then for a moment I had it… someone who allowed me to be soft not because they thought I *couldn't* be strong, but because they *wanted* to be the strong one.

DUTCH: And what? You're afraid that simpatico is going somewhere? Butch/femme has been around forever.

MARIGOLD: Well, not forever.

DUTCH: But a lot longer than we have. And it'll be around when we're gone. Of course, not everyone's into it, thank god, but butch/femme has existed publicly for at least a century, right? There were more lesbian bars in New York in the 1920s than there are now. In the 1940s and 1950s you saw butch women wearing men's clothes full-time, and often being arrested or hate-crimed for it. Imagine being femme back then! How do you avoid a husband? Be a spinster schoolteacher? Be a nun? Butch/femme bar culture was a full-on thing for decades, and back then you had to play by the rules, not like now. …

GUERRA: Oh, there's still pressure. If you're perceived as one thing, god forbid you do something different one day.

DUTCH: By the '70s it got a lot more… well… "Makeup and heels are the source of our oppression so femme's gotta go…" but thankfully the '80s brought it back, with big hair, and in the '90s people *finally* started publishing books about it, and properly documenting our history. The '90s were *completely* crazy in New York… have I even gotten to when you guys were born yet?

GUERRA: Haha.

MARIGOLD: I just feel like she has all the power because she's butch, so I'm reduced to this stupid girl that has to compete for her. Isn't *she* supposed to be wrapped around *my* finger?

DUTCH: Well, I don't envy you. You're about to find out really fast who your friends are. Some femmes will suddenly act like they never met you, you know, so they can bide their time and then date what's her name— what's her name? — and then act like they didn't need to check in with you about it, cuz you were never all that close.

MARIGOLD: Her name's Dylan.

DUTCH: Oh, sure, sure. I know who Dylan is. Cuuuute.

MARIGOLD: Oh my god. *(To Guerra)* This is what I mean! Everyone knows everyone. A straight girl can go to somewhere exotic, like San Francisco, and sleep with a guy, and nobody has to know. But if you're a lesbian? There is no such thing as casual sex. No matter who you sleep with, inevitably someone's' going to be mad at you.

DUTCH: To angry lesbians.

GEURRA: To angry lesbians! *(Beat. To Dutch.)* I still can't believe you're fifty. You look amazing.

DUTCH: Stop it. I told you. Do you consider it a compliment when someone says you don't "look" like a lesbian?

GUERRA: No, I *want* to look like a lesbian. I wish they'd say I did!

DUTCH: Exactly. And I want to look like a hot fifty-year-old lesbian who's having the best sex of my life. Are you into fisting yet?

(Marigold and Guerra look at each other and shake their heads no.)

DUTCH: You will be.

(Dutch Exits)

GUERRA: Wow. So, did you catch that little Sprocket Wrench story? Should we pass that along to our dear friend Riot?

MARIGOLD: Riot is such a meddler. I told her I wasn't going to look at Jungle Red the entire time we were here, and she keeps sending me picture texts of things from Jungle Red! If she's such a good friend, why does hanging out with her hurt so much? Woah, okay I think I'm finally starting to feel it a little bit...

(Marigold pulls out her phone to show Guerra.)

Look at this crap she sent me... *(freezes.)*

GUERRA: What?

MARIGOLD: Dylan texted me.

GUERRA: Ha, she wants you back! Tell her she's a real son of a dick...

MARIGOLD: She says she wants to talk... should I call her?

GUERRA: I don't know, Mari... she's put you through a lot... don't do it. Let's just have fun tonight...

(Marigold's eyes well up with tears.)

GUERRA: Okay, no. You know what? You want her back. You still love her. Don't listen to me. Do it.

(Marigold dials the phone frantically.)

MARIGOLD: Dylan! Hey, hi. I wasn't expecting to hear from you, either… Yes, I am in a good mood. And you still sound like the handsome lady in the letterman jacket that I remember… No, I'm not home but I could be back by tonight if you wanted to come over… Oh… no I guess you can tell me over the phone… You are? You barely know each other. You're really going to make that kind of a commitment? …And be polyamorous still? Oh. No?? Yeah, well thanks for letting me know. It's definitely better than hearing it on Facebook. Oh, sorry, yeah, I can't hear you… *(She's lying.)* I'm in a club, it's really loud. I should get back to my date. She gets *so* mad when I talk to other butches. Ciao. *(She hangs up the phone, stunned.)*

GUERRA: Did they get… engaged?

MARIGOLD: Yup.

GUERRA: What are you going to do?

MARIGOLD: Dance. And then go back home and make this year's FemmeFest the best ever. And tomorrow? I'll buy you brunch and you can tell me all about what's new with that asshole at your job.

> *(Marigold turns her back on the audience and walks slowly toward the dance floor.)*

SCENE FIVE
SHOWTIME

(The stage is set for the big show. A banner proclaims: FemmeFest. A show within a show, FemmeFest should almost stand on its own as an actual variety show using the actual talents of the cast. [It's also an opportunity to touch on issues affecting your local queer community not already be covered in this play.] Dutch is the emcee and banters authentically between each act. Ad libbing

with the actual audience is encouraged. Part of the dressing room set is also visible, stage right.)

DUTCH: Hello, hello, and welcome to the fifth annual FemmeFest! My name is Dutch and I'll be your host tonight. The organizers flew me here all the way from San Francisco — coach on Southwest, thank you ladies. Well, we've got quite a lineup for you tonight. To start things off, what lesbian event would be complete without a little spoken word, am I right? So please, welcome to the stage... Dexy!

> (**DEXY SPOTLIGHT NUMBER.** *Dexy performs a political spoken-word piece. The actor playing Dexy is encouraged to write their own text. Alternately, they are welcome to use the following text written by Alessandra Pinkston, who played Dexy in the first workshop production.)*

DEXY: They say it's not normal
Right in front of me
As if I don't exist
They guess my brown skin makes me one of them
They yell that it's a sin
Preaching that "the different" will
Burn in hell
They guess my high heels make me one of them
They say it's a "White" thing
That no person of color
Can truly be "that way"
And they look to me
Waiting for my agreement
They guess my pink lipstick makes me one of them
And then my girlfriend walks in
And she kisses me
On the lips
And they stare...
I am Black
I am a Woman
And I love women
I love the smoothness of their skin

401

I love the way that we touch
I love our fearless ways
But my community
Doesn't
Love
Me
I am an outcast
I am a disease
I love who I am
I love where I am from
But I hate
How
My people don't love me

> *(Lights up on the dressing room. Riot and Callie have entered during Dexy's performance. They look bizarrely like twins.)*

CALLIE: I'm so nervous!

RIOT: Don't be. You're marvelous. You look like Joan Crawford.

CALLIE: They're going to throw vegetables.

RIOT: Well they might. But you're vegan.

CALLIE: Ugh, you're the worst! You were supposed to smooth everything over.

RIOT: Hey! Don't think you were an easy sell to the committee. Half of them think you're a homewrecker.

CALLIE: *(hopeful)* And the other half don't?

RIOT: Oh, no. That's the nice ones. The others…

CALLIE: What did they call me?

RIOT: You should be asking what they *didn't* call you. I told them, I don't like the word *slut*. I don't care how much sex someone has, good for you, knock yourself out. And I don't like the word *bitch*, because duh, the rest of the world thinks ALL of us are bitches—too much coming out the mouths, not enough coming *in* the vaginas. And they agreed with me on both points. But then they said that we DO still need SOME kind of a word that we can call someone completely self-serving and mean, who has done us soooo wrong.

CALLIE: You got me downgraded from a slut to an asshole?

RIOT: And for that, you should thank me.

> *(Back to the show.)*

DUTCH: This next performer is the reason I'm standing in front of you tonight. She accosted me on a dance floor in Oakland and told me all about how FemmeFest is the largest event of its kind in the entire world, and how it was created specifically to give queer femmes a platform and a voice. I suspect her voice would be unstoppable anyway though. Please give a round of applause for our very own warrior princess, Guerra!

> (**GUERRA SPOTLIGHT NUMBER**. *Guerra performs a highly emotional, politicized flamenco dance about women's roles in Latinx culture. It brings the house down.*)

> *(Meanwhile, back in the dressing room …)*

CALLIE: You're ruining my hair! Stop it! Oh my god, this is terrible. I can't go out there.

RIOT: Come on, square up, breathe. Listen, I lost a lot of friends over you. This is Marigold's event, she's the main organizer, everybody loves her here. But I told them, we can't allow personal feelings and petty infighting to get in the way of putting on a good show, because if we cut out every girl who ever stole someone's girlfriend or hurt someone's feelings or offended someone, there'd be no one left. I used all my pull for you, you're a babe and a doll and a great dancer. You can't make them like you, but you can make them respect you. Now get out there!

DUTCH: So, here's a little joke we used to tell back in lesbian Girl Scouts: How do you tell a femme from a straight girl? By her nails! Haha… Okay but seriously, of course we all know that's not true. Some femmes are just pillow princesses. So, let's welcome our very own pillow princess, Callie!

> (**CALLIE SPOTLIGHT NUMBER**. *Callie performs a super sexy and vampy, Bettie Page–inspired burlesque routine. The discomfort of the audience is palpable and Callie overcompensates by trying even harder. She's a good dancer, but it's all a bit… too much.*)

DUTCH: Well fuck me. That was… something else. Give it up for Callie! Okay so our next performer is someone who is near and dear to my heart, and should be to yours too. She's the founder and producer of *The Femme Show*, the monthly event that grew to give virgin birth to the monstrosity that is FemmeFest. This means that without her, none of you would be getting laid tonight. So here she is, with a performance piece inspired by the Mia Mingus keynote address at the Femmes of Color Symposium 2011. Please put your labia together for … Marigold!

> (**MARIGOLD SPOTLIGHT NUMBER**: "Running From Ugly"
>
> *Marigold enters, as a Barbie-looking white girl in a blonde wig and princess gown. Everywhere she turns, signs:*
> *"Disabled"*
> *"Fat"*
> *"Poor"*
> *"Transgender"*
> *She recoils in horror from these signs.*
> *She tries to run from them.*

The sign-holders try to pass the signs off to her, to get her to own them.
She throws them away from her and freaks out.
She wins the pageant.
She is presented with a diamond crown.
She is presented with a bouquet of flowers.
She is presented with a sign that says: "Nothing."
She holds it, smiling and waving and crying.

SCENE SIX
…REVENGE?

(Backstage at the burlesque, an echo of Scene One. Callie sits awkwardly at one of the dressing room mirrors, alone. She looks very small, for a change. Marigold bursts in immediately following her number.)

MARIGOLD: Hey, Libby? Do we have a plan for a curtain call or are you all… already gone.

(Nobody is there except Callie. They stare at each other for a second. Marigold is cool as can be.)

CALLIE: I think I may have scared them all away.

MARIGOLD: Callie. Congratulations on your first FemmeFest performance. You were really something out there.

CALLIE: Oh, so you totally still hate me too.

MARIGOLD: I'm sorry?

CALLIE: Marigold, the stuff with Dylan happened like two years ago, can we just be okay?

MARIGOLD: It was six months ago, actually. Only six months ago, but I'm fine. FemmeFest is open to all femmes, *(under her breath)* not just the ones I respect. *(She tries.)* You looked really beautiful out there, under the lights.

405

CALLIE: You're so fake.

MARIGOLD: Excuse me?

CALLIE: This is your whole problem. Why don't you ever say what you mean? You might've had a shot at keeping Dylan.

MARIGOLD: Keeping Dylan? Haha... you did me a huge favor by taking her off my hands. I dodged a bullet there. Have fun marrying that.

CALLIE: You're still doing it.

MARIGOLD: It's much better to be single than to date someone who makes you feel sick to your stomach all the time. I'm way happier now.

CALLIE: But you still hate my guts.

MARIGOLD: Hate you? Oh no, I *loved* your little number out there. You really put a lot of thought into our theme of Body Positivity and Intersectionality. I'm glad you chose to do something so profound and deep instead of a thoughtless little striptease that basically looked like you hanging out your shingle and letting all the butches know you're sooo great in bed. Do you even care about this event and what it stands for?

> *(Libby enters.)*

CALLIE: Of course, I do! *(She falters.)* I'm not as smart as you and Libby, okay?

LIBBY: Marigold, do you think that a femme and a butch passing as a straight couple is a transgressive form of accessing hetero privilege?

> *(Libby realizes what she's just walked in on.)*

LIBBY: Oh — sorry…

(Libby exits.)

MARIGOLD: You're damn right you're not. And how does Dylan feel about you putting it all out there like that? She was never okay with it when she was dating ME.

CALLIE: Oh, you haven't figured it out from Facebook stalking yet?

MARIGOLD: I blocked you. And Dylan. And pretty much anyone who talks to you. So, no.

CALLIE: Dylan and I broke up. She… was cheating on me with Dutch.

MARIGOLD: WHAT?

CALLIE: Yeah, Dylan's been dating Dutch. She dropped me a couple months ago, after taking a little trip to San Francisco on my credit card. It was pretty fucked up actually, but I don't expect you to care.

MARIGOLD: What?!

CALLIE: She bought me a ring, with my money, that I'll be paying off forever if I don't find the receipt…

(Dutch and Guerra enter, chatting.)

DUTCH: …so then I said, "Listen. You don't believe this now, but your boobs will sag. Your feet will corn. High heels will hurt. You'll gain weight at a rate you currently can't even conceive and plucking your chin hairs will be like a full-time job. And it WILL be a challenge to your femme identity. So, you have to face it head-on and say, 'I *am* desirable.'"

(Guerra elbows Dutch.)

DUTCH: What? Oh. We were just leaving!

(They exit.)

(Marigold taps her foot, seething.)

CALLIE: Wait, wait a minute. You and Dutch are friends. Was this some kind of stupid revenge? Would you really...

(Riot and Dexy enter.)

RIOT: I mean just because I present myself in a sexual way does not mean my sexuality is available to anyone who wants it —

(Riot smirks at the scene she has stumbled upon.)

RIOT: Oh... we're gonna go. Sisterhood is powerful!

(Riot and Dexy exit.)

MARIGOLD: No, Callie. The only person that calculating is you. And, hilarious, do you expect me to feel sorry for you, after everything you did to me?

(A pause. Callie looks down.)

CALLIE: I never stole Dylan from you.

MARIGOLD: Excuse me?

CALLIE: I never "stole" Dylan from you. You gave her up. She told me from the get-go that she was getting pretty serious with you —

MARIGOLD: Living with me, yeah, I guess we were getting there.

CALLIE: — she basically told me that if she got word from you that you wanted to be with her, for real, she would have to drop me at the drop of a hat.

MARIGOLD: She didn't …

CALLIE: All you would have had to do was ask Dylan to be with you. Ask her to be monogamous. Tell her that you loved her.

MARIGOLD: No, that's not how it went down at all. …

CALLIE: Did you even try? Did you even tell Dylan how you felt, or did you just come and attack me first?

MARIGOLD: None of this matters, anymore.

CALLIE: I wanted to be friends with you!

MARIGOLD: Cease and desist, for god's sake.

CALLIE: I've been trying to tell you this all along —

MARIGOLD: Fuck you.

CALLIE: You were scared and I was brave. That's the only reason Dylan left you.

> (Out of words, Callie strides across the space out of the blue, grabs Marigold and plants a kiss on her face. At the exact same moment, Riot, Dexy, Guerra, Dutch and Libby come barreling through the door.)

RIOT: Wait, I'm sorry, what the fuck is going on here?

GUERRA: Oh my god, seriously?

DUTCH: She's choking her! Oh wait… no.

CALLIE (to Marigold): I date butches. I also date trans guys. And cis guys. And femmes.

MARIGOLD: You are insane!

LIBBY: You just let her kiss you, so I'm pretty sure *you're* insane.

RIOT: I'm not sure what I just saw.

LIBBY: Femme on femme. It's been a while.

MARIGOLD: I could start dating femmes tomorrow, and if you're my friends, you better accept it!

GUERRA: Wait, you two are *dating* now? Mari, we were just coming in here to *save* you!

MARIGOLD: Well thank you. Thank you all for your concern, but I actually don't need saving. And my relationship didn't need your "saving" either.

RIOT: Why are you looking at me?

MARIGOLD: I have a hot piece of gossip for you guys. The real reason Dylan and I broke up wasn't Callie. It was you.

   (Everyone protests vehemently.)

MARIGOLD *(advancing on Riot and Libby)*: I didn't ask for your help catching Dylan doing what I already knew in my gut she was doing. *(Advancing on Dutch.)* And I didn't ask anyone to get revenge on my behalf either. ...

DUTCH: Pardon?

CALLIE: I told her. About how you stole Dylan from me.

DUTCH: Darlings. Seriously. You do know that it's not actually possible to "steal" a person from someone else.

GUERRA *(to Dutch)*: Wait, what? You saw how sad Marigold was in San Francisco. You consoled her. And the whole time you were just counting the minutes until you could jump online and hit on Dylan?

DUTCH: It was two weeks later! I don't know what the statute of limitations is in your town.

RIOT: Dylan is not even that hot, can you all get over her already?

DUTCH: Anyway, I just assumed that Callie and Dylan were non-monogamous, since Callie slept with Sprocket Wrench.

RIOT *(to Callie):* Wait, what? You said you DIDN'T sleep with Sprocket Wrench. You little fucking liar! Oh my god!

DEXY: Ooh, are you jealous? You are so busted right now.

RIOT: Jealous? Not a bit. Not a bit. By all means. Have at it, ladies. It's a fucking free-for-all!

MARIGOLD: Callie. Seriously? Why don't you at least TRY to write a book, or make an album if you're such a MUSICIAN, or contribute SOMETHING to the conversation, do SOMETHING with your life other than just being PRETTY, and doing your fucking makeup, and your fucking hair, and hitting on other people's fucking girlfriends!

DEXY: Stop, okay? Stop attacking her. I don't like what she did either but I'm not going to stand by and let you gang up on her.

CALLIE: Thank you.

(They all gang up on Dutch instead.)

GUERRA: So, how's it working out with Dylan then?

DUTCH: Dreamy.

LIBBY: That's not what I heard.

DUTCH: If you must know, Dylan ended it with me, out of the blue. She fed me some mid-twenties line about being in a weird space and not being able to deny her true feelings anymore. She's still having feelings for someone else that she can't act on because it's so complicated.

LIBBY: *Still* have feelings? Someone from her past, perhaps?

DUTCH: To think, she thinks SHE can break up with ME. Ah well. I've hit her where it hurts. You know that little squat she's been cultivating for months, decorating like crazy trying to make it into a loft for herself?

CALLIE: No, we're not exactly buddies anymore …

DUTCH: Well, I had it condemned. I suspect she doesn't know it yet, but the police seized everything inside of it today and posted it "No Trespassing." If she goes back there, she'll be arrested.

DEXY: Fucked up.

LIBBY: I kind of want to high-five you.

DEXY: I'm so not into this. You guys are making me sick.

> *(Dexy makes to exit the dressing room, then comes back just as quickly.)*

DEXY: Um. Don't all jump at once, but… Dylan's here.

ALL: What?

DEXY: Yeah. Waiting outside the stage door with a sad puppy dog expression. I think she practices it in the mirror.

DUTCH: Ooh, she dared show her face here?

RIOT *(to Callie):* Do you think she's here for you?

CALLIE *(to Marigold):* I think she's here for Marigold.

(Nobody moves.)

GUERRA: Marigold. Don't.

RIOT: Guerra! Remember how sick you are of being Marigold's caretaker?

DEXY: Riot, remember that time you stayed out of everyone's business?

(Everyone starts yelling at each other. Marigold steps through the tangle.)

MARIGOLD: This is why I hate femmes. All we do is tear each other apart. All we do is find fault with each other — who's fucked up because they said that one thing that one time. Who's offensive because they're not as radical as you are. Instead of seeing the good in each other, the potential to grow and someday NOT be offensive or fucked up... we judge each other, and we write each other off. Forever!

DEXY: You think that's just femmes?

MARIGOLD: FINE. This is why I hate WOMEN. We're SO PATHETIC. This is exactly what we do. We get so caught up in the drama of who's dating who and the pining after people we can't have and the interpersonal relationships and the planning the baby showers and the resentment over what happens at the weddings and frosting the cupcakes and the KNITTING, the fucking KNITTING, and we forget to do anything, ANYTHING WORTHWHILE. We could be saving the world, but instead, we're reading tabloids.

DUTCH: Oh, come on. You think it's only women that focus on trivial shit instead of what really matters?

MARIGOLD: FINE! THIS IS WHY I HATE ALL OF HUMANITY! OUR PRIORITIES ARE COMPLETELY AND UTTERLY WRONG!

(Courtney bursts in, now totally femmed-out. She actually looks... a lot like Callie.)

COURTNEY: Oh my god, so much yelling. Can you not?

(The whole room reacts to Courtney's sexy new look.)

ALL: Wow! Oh my god, I didn't recognize you! *(Etc.)*

COURTNEY: Yes, that's great, you're all shocked, thanks.

GUERRA: *Quelle de femme, que linda!*

COURTNEY: I'm actually a non-identified pandrogynous genderqueer who happens to be femme-presenting at the moment, but it's nice to know that this is all I had to do to get your attention.

RIOT: Did you steal my eyeliner?

COURTNEY: I'm actually writing my final paper for Libby's class on how butch/femme is really outdated, heterosexist and fucked up. You guys have been awesome source material. Thank you for an amazing ride.

DEXY: Hey, not all of us believe in the binary just because we like femme drag!

COURTNEY: My generation identifies as "queer" rather than as "lesbian," and our gender expression is way more fluid than butch or femme!

DUTCH: Oh, I love that each new generation thinks they invented that. We've all been doing that since the beginning of time, honey, it's only the language that keeps changing.

414

MARIGOLD: And language is so inadequate to begin with!

CALLIE: I have no idea what you guys are talking about.

COURTNEY: Although, confession … I am starting to develop a newfound appreciation of my own nonessentialist femme self … as seen through the eyes of a butch admirer. Believe it or not, it's the butch gaze — or, masculine-presenting of any female-bodied gender gaze, actually — that has allowed my femme self to flower. Not you guys, who made me feel like high school all over again. *Dylan* made me quite a confession tonight. I must say I was shocked and enormously flattered. So if you will excuse me, congratulations on a great show, but I won't be staying for cleanup, because she's taking me to christen her new squat tonight.

(Courtney exits. They all gape.)

DUTCH: Like a lamb being led to the slaughter.

GUERRA: Marigold, are you going to go out there? And say something to Dylan?

MARIGOLD: No. I've had two years to sharpen my claws, and I know exactly what I'm going to do. I'm moving on from *The Femme Show,* I'm moving on from producing, and I'm moving on from burlesque. Tonight was perfect. This last year has been perfect, and you all have been wonderful. Wonderful. And exactly as I would want you to be. I'm going to write a book about this. All of it. All of us. You won't see me around much anymore, so be sure to follow me, because I'm going to post the entire thing online. On Jungle Red!

(Blackout.)

End of Play

IN CONVERSATION WITH THE PLAYWRIGHT

Jen-Scott: What inspired this play?

Gina: The 1939 film *The Women*. I was familiar with Clare Boothe Luce's fantastic play, but it was the film version that gave me chills. It could have been made yesterday. Joan Crawford and Norma Shearer *et al* being icy and catty and fighting over a man... as a lesbian I think of myself as completely outside of that world, but in a lot of queer spaces, masculine- or androgynous-presenting women are valued more than femmes. I was like, "Woah, these really intense heterosexist dynamics are also present in the queer spaces that supposedly exist to fight them." What should have felt foreign to me felt unsettlingly familiar. So much has changed for women since the 1930s, and yet so little... I started updating *The Women* to be relevant to a contemporary lesbian/queer audience, and then it grew and changed and went in directions that *The Women* never would have. It became a play about queer art-making, the queer burlesque/variety show scene, public breakups and the omnipresent role social media now plays.

[...] One thing I always want to do is make queer femmes visible. We get erased a lot, which wouldn't happen if people knew what to look for. We have our own signifiers, our own fashion; nothing thrills me more than when a butch stranger immediately reads me as queer. [...] Our sexuality is sometimes deemed less valid or more unstable; we're presumed straight or outright told that we "look straight," which... uh maybe that's someone's goal, but it's not mine. I also want to look at some of the ways that masculinity is still privileged, even in queer feminist communities. Sometimes we find femmes doing all the emotional labor, or butches behaving in really overtly sexist ways, scarcity mentality in the dating pool leading to needless competition, things like that.

Jen-Scott: How would you distill this play in ten words or less to your ideal reader?

Gina: A reimagining of *The Women* set in the femme lesbian subculture. Man, ten words is not enough!

Jen-Scott: What is most key to this play in performance?

Gina: The most significant part of this play in performance is the show-within-a-show… It was very important to me to have a moment in the show that allows any production to reflect where the local queer scene is at. You can add text or use the burlesque numbers to address whatever's going on in the political landscape or your local gay bar right now. […] [T]he FemmeFest scene can give voice to any voices you wish I had. I keep the play elastic because I know how quickly things change in the queer community.

I love that this is my most-produced play so far. It's always gone up because a group of queer femmes somewhere, from Massachusetts to Minneapolis to Orange County […], has gotten their hands on the script and been like, FINALLY.

Jen-Scott: Do you identify as a feminist playwright? A lesbian or trans playwright?

Gina: Yes and yes. I mean, like anyone else there's a part of my brain that bristles and says, "I'm just a playwright, not a *lesbian* playwright"—you know, the age old, "I'm an ARTIST, not a 'woman artist!'" But then again… my work exists in a specific context: no work exists in a vacuum. All of my plays deal with lesbian/queer/transgender and feminist themes; that's who I am and that's also the audience who has been unfailingly supportive of my work. I shouldn't […] hide that to reach a mainstream audience.

Jen-Scott: How do you define feminism today? And how does your work fit within a feminist framework?

Gina: My definition of feminism is enormously broad. Any woman who believes that she *deserves*— believes she has worth as a person, deserves to learn, to create, to have rights— she's a feminist. Or any person of any gender who believes that women […] have value— you're a feminist. Not everyone relates to (the label). Some people think they don't count because they haven't marched in a protest with the "feminist movement," but that's not true. Or maybe you prefer the word womanist, or riot grrrl, or you're just a […] a badass bitch. I care about the substance of what the movement is fighting for, which should simply be women's rights to unlimited possibilities.

My work is feminist to the core. I've […] only written female protagonists. Until there's anything approaching gender parity in theater, I see no reason not to.

Jen-Scott: What advice do you have for women considering writing their first play or becoming professional playwrights?

Gina: […] Figure out how the story wants to be told — maybe it's a TV pilot, or a novel, or an inaugural blog post. If it's a play, and you're sure it's a play and it can't be anything else but a play, then you just have to do it. Don't think about it and don't be critical of yourself. The driving message of my most recent play *sSISTERSs* […] is to stop analyzing and *DO*. "Stop talking about it... Just plant." I guess the practical advice I would give is, produce your own work. Waiting around submitting to everything and racking up the rejection letters is important to do, but it can be soul crushing. There's something really satisfying and necessary about putting your writing out into the world, even if it's only a reading at a small theater with 20 of your friends. You never know what that will inspire.

TALES OF THE REVOLUTION:
An Afterword on the Life and Legacy of Jane Chambers
Sara Warner, Cornell University

Jane Chambers was in rehearsals for *Kudzu* at Playwrights Horizons in 1982 when she became ill with what would be diagnosed as a brain tumor. The cancer proved to be as malignant as the invasive vine for which the play is named. Chambers lost the ability to write and couldn't complete revisions for *Kudzu*, which had been optioned for a Broadway run. The producer backed out, and Chambers never made it to the Great White Way. She would have been the first lesbian to stage a play about lesbians – happy, well-adjusted lesbians – on Broadway. Audiences would have to wait decades for alternatives to those "god-damned sick and dirty" women whose love for other women resulted in their condemnation (*The God of Vengeance*), suicide (*The Children's Hour*), or homicidal urges (*The Killing of Sister George*).[1] Nuanced and complex lesbian characters began to appear on Broadway (often as minor players, typically in musicals) in the late 1990s (e.g., *Falsettos, Rent, The Color Purple*), but it wasn't until 2006 that a lesbian-themed work by a lesbian creator, Lisa Kron's *Well*, achieved what Chambers was poised to do in the 1980s.

The degree to which lesbians have been pathologized, criminalized, and marginalized in American drama cannot be overstated. The history of lesbians in mainstream theater is sparse and inconsistent, at best. It took Paula Vogel, the first out lesbian dramatist to garner the Pulitzer Prize, until 2016 to make her Broadway debut, which she did with *Indecent*, a play that addresses, among other topics, the history of lesbian censorship in the theater. *Indecent* premiered during the regional run of *Fun Home*, Kron's groundbreaking adaptation of Alison Bechdel's graphic novel. These Tony Award-winning shows are remarkable for their audacious and unapologetic

---

[1] Lillian Hellman, *The Children's Hour*, New York: Dramatists Play Service, 1953, 67.

exploration of lesbian desire. While stylistically distinct, *Fun Home* and *Kudzu* share similar elements. They are both set in rural America, involve patriarchal figures with destructive secrets, and feature middle-age lesbians. These paradigm-shifting productions don't plead for acceptance or inclusion. They take lesbian sexuality as a given and assume that audiences will have no trouble seeing the world from their perspective.

One of the most important dramatists of the 20th century, Chambers' reputation rests largely on "the lesbian plays" she wrote during the 1970s, though these constitute only a fraction of her astonishing creative output. In her brief life – she died one month shy of her forty-sixth birthday – Chambers wrote at least thirty-five plays, seventeen novels (two of which were published), thirty-two screenplays and television scripts, thirteen short stories, one poetry collection, and dozens of articles. The lesbian plays feature characters and plots inspired by the antics and amorous escapades of Chambers' friends and lovers. *A Late Snow* (1970), the first in this series, is set in rural Maine, where she lived with the figure on whom Pat, a charismatic butch with a drinking problem, is based. Five women, all current or former love interests of the protagonist Ellie, a college professor, find themselves trapped in a remote cabin during a blizzard. Ellie is worried that her tribe will out themselves to Margo, a famous author she has invited to campus. Margo reveals that she too is a lesbian, one who chooses, like Tally in *The Eye of the Gull* (1971), to remain in the closet to protect her reputation. The plot proved prophetic when *A Late Snow* debuted in 1974 at The Clark Center (later Playwrights Horizons). Chambers lost her job at CBS and was blacklisted from the television industry, despite having garnered a Writers Guild Award for her work on "Search for Tomorrow."

Apprehensive about the commercial viability of *A Late Snow*, no producer would risk an Off-Broadway run. The next six years were lean ones for Chambers, and the only writing jobs she could secure were with porn presses, where she penned pulp novels and articles for straight and gay men's magazines under different pseudonyms. Chambers' luck changed radically in 1980 when John Glines invited her to stage *A Late Snow* as part of the First Gay American Arts Festival in New York. The play was still under option, so Chambers proposed *Last Summer at Bluefish Cove* (1974). A resounding success, the festival run at the West Side Mainstage Theatre was extended, followed by a transfer to the Actors Playhouse in Greenwich Village. Starring a young Jean Smart as Lil, a rakish dyke who finds the love of her life just months before she dies of cancer, *Bluefish Cove* resonated with audiences and critics alike. Chambers dedicated the play to a friend who had recently died, not knowing that she would soon succumb to the same fate. Nicknamed *The Girls in the Sand* – a reference to Mart Crowley's trailblazing 1968 gay drama *The Boys in the Band* – *Bluefish Cove* received a Villager Downtown Theatre Award, and a California production garnered the Los Angeles Drama Critics Circle Award (1983). Venezuelan film director Fina Torres adapted the play in 2014 as *Liz in September*, though her plot centers on Lil's lover, Eva, interjecting both a husband and a deceased son into the lesbian enclave.

Chambers headlined the second Gay American Theatre Festival with *My Blue Heaven*, her most idealized portrait of a lesbian relationship, and one of the earliest examples of a same-sex wedding in American drama. Glines paid a posthumous tribute to Chambers by staging a one act about her life titled *In Her Own Words* at Town Hall on a double bill with *The Quintessential Image*. The latter (Chambers wanted to title it *The Quintessential Dyke*) takes place at a television studio where host Margaret Foy interviews her idol, the elusive photographer Lacey Lanier, who reveals that her success stems from a series of failed attempts to capture Bettina Adams, the object of her unconsummated obsession. The play's experimental form and use of multi-media to comment on the misogyny and homophobia of representational regimes excited feminist theorists who bristled at Chambers' use of realism, which they denounced as a pernicious genre incapable of reflecting the truth of lesbian lives.

If the lesbian plays seem formulaic, this is because Chambers was working in the early 1970s as a television and screenwriter in Hollywood, during which time she was mastering the art of melodrama and churning out scenarios for a soap opera at a furious pace. None of her film or television projects made it into production, though several were optioned, including *Here Comes the Iceman*, one of the first situation comedies to feature an African American family, and *Batt'lin Bertha: The Senator from Waterloo*, an homage to Shirley Chisholm. Chambers' screen- and teleplays reflect a deep and abiding commitment to racial justice, a position catalyzed by her upbringing in the Jim Crow South and her family's slave holding legacy. *Rosie Love-Apple*, about a middle-class Puerto Rican family who moves to Spanish Harlem, is one of several pilots based on Chambers' transformative experience with the Job Corps for Women, a cornerstone of President Johnson's War on Poverty.

Chambers' screenplays and lesbian-themed dramas stand in marked contrast to the art she produced during the 1950s and 60s, when she studied with Erwin Piscator, performed with the Actor's Mobile Theatre, and created work with the Poet's Theatre. These plays are experimental in form and many are daring in political content. Take for example, *Tales of the Revolution and Other American Fables* (1969), a bracing exploration of the sexism, homophobia, and racism of contemporary society. Set in a mixed-bar in Greenwich Village on Halloween night at closing time, this play opens with a stage full of mannequins, some of which come to life to engage in sexual banter and crude jokes. While not a lesbian-themed play, the patrons do include characters named Dyke and Faggot. If *Tales of the Revolution* is "ever produced," Chambers told her thesis advisor at Goddard College, "I'll be cell-mates with Angela [Davis]!"[2] The play earned her a fellowship to the O'Neill Playwriting Center in 1972, where it received a staged reading, its only production to-date.

---

[2] Jane Chambers, *Letters to Paul*, Goddard College Thesis 1971, 41.

That same year, Chambers was elected Chairperson of the New Jersey Women's Political Caucus (agitating alongside Bella Abzug and Gloria Steinem) and co-founded Women's Interart Theatre with Margot Lewitin, who directed four of Chambers' early, experimental plays. The first was *Random Violence*, a ninety-minute performance piece staged in the round about Eve McIntyre, "a disenfranchised woman in our electronic-sexist society, guilt-ridden about the violence which surrounds us but rendered powerless to change or stop it."[3] The following year, Lewitin staged two of Chambers' one act plays, *Mine* and *The Wife*, which examine the socio-economic conditions that keep women oppressed, a theme shared by *The Common Garden Variety*, produced at Interart and The Mark Taper Forum. Like the protagonist of this play, Sari, Chambers was raised by her grandmother after her parents' divorce, an event catalyzed by her father's alcoholism and mental illness. Both he and his brother sexually abused Chambers, and incest is one of the topics she explored in her essays.

In 1982, Chambers made her last public appearance when she received the Fund for Human Dignity Award, a fitting tribute for a lesbian feminist dramatist, who, denied the right to study playwriting at Rollins College and the Pasadena Playhouse, dropped out of school in 1956 and taught herself the craft of dramaturgy. Driven by a desire for fame and recognition, and determined to affect social change, Chambers demanded – and received – success on her own terms, without compromising her ambition, integrity, or political commitments. Filmmaker Alison McMahan is producing a documentary about Chambers, and her legacy lives on in the Women and Theatre Program's annual Jane Chambers Playwriting Award, founded in 1983. A second prize in her name, given by the Gay Theatre Alliance, ended when the organization disbanded.

---

3 Jane Chambers, *Random Violence*, unpublished manuscript, 1970, 1.

APPENDIX A

WINNERS OF THE PRIZE SINCE 1984

Grandma Shot the Cat by Karen Boettcher (1984)
Third Child by Charlotte Anker & Irene Rosenberg (1985)
Rosvitha's Review by Patricia Montley (1986)
Conversations of My Mother by Micki Goldthorpe (1987)
Conversation by Gloria Parkinson (1988)
...After April by Arlene Fanale (1989)
Burnt House by Jenna Zark (1990)
The Butcher's Daughter by Wendy Kesselman (1991)
David's Red-Haired Death by Sherry Kramer (1992)
F-64 by Christine de Lancie (1993)
The Waiting Room by Lisa Loomer (1994)
Shamanism in New Jersey by Rosemarie Caruso (1995)
The Fifth Season (retitled *Dakota Sky*) by Kathleen Cahill
    book/lyrics, Deborah Wicks LaPuma, music (1996)
Topographical Eden by Brighde Mullins (1997)
China Doll by Elizabeth Wong (1998)
The Essential Gourmet by Mindi Dickstein (1999)
Rossenstrasse by Terry Lawrence (2000)
Rise by Bernadette Flagler (2001)
Signs of Life by Deborah Brevoort (2002)
Day of Reckoning by Melody Cooper (2003)
Special Award: **Solo Performance** — Deb Margolin (2004)
The Zero Hour by Madeleine George (2004)
Carried by the Current by Nicola Pearson (2005)
Legacy Year: **Last Summer at Bluefish Cove** Staging (2006)
Trojan Barbie by Christine Evans (2007)
Unspeakable Acts by Mary F. Casey (2008)
The Siegels Montauk by Meryl Cohn (2009)
A Live Dress by MJ Kaufman (2010)
Mud Offerings (solo) by Natalie Marlena Goodnow (2011)
Still by Jen Silverman (2012)
FULL/SELF by Claire Chafee (2013)
Femmes: A Tragedy by Gina Young (2014)
Roe by Lisa Loomer (2015)
No Candy by Emma Stanton (2016)
Never, Not Once by Carey Crim (2017)
Queens by Martyna Marjok (2018)

APPENDIX B: FINALIST PLAYS HONORED 2007 to 2018

2018
Winner: *Queens* by Martyna Majok
Runner-Up: *Allond(r)a* by Gina Femia
Honorable Mentions: *Bull in a China Shop* by Bryna Turner, *Fuel* by Caridad Svitch, *Milk and Gall* by Mathilda Dratwa, *The Niceties* by Eleanor Burgess, *Wendy and the Neckbeards* by Kari Bentley-Quinn

2017
Winner: *Never, Not Once* by Carey Crim
Runner-Up: *The Great Divide* by Alix Sobler
Honorable Mentions: *Policarpa* by Diana Burbano, *Paradise* by Laura Marie Censabella, *A Small Oak Tree Runs Red* by Lekethia Dalcoe, *The O'Malley Gambit* by Kate Monaghan

2016
Winner: *No Candy* by Emma Stanton
Runners-Up: *La Llorona* by Cecelia Raker, *The Madres* by Stephanie A. Walker
Honorable Mentions: *Danny* by Jennifer Barclay, *Second Skin* by Kristen Idaszak, *The Bumps* by Rachel Kauder Nalebuff, *Wanda, Daisy and the Great Rapture* by Alexis Schaetzle

2015
Winner: *Roe* by Lisa Loomer
Runner-Up: *Manahatta* by Mary K. Nagle
Honorable Mentions: *What I Thought I Knew* by Alice Eve Cohen, *The Egg Layers* by L. Feldman, *The Taming* by Lauren Gunderson, *Other Than Honorable* by Jamie Pachino, *The 9 Fridas* by Kaite O'Reilly

2014
Winner: *Femmes* by Gina Young
Runner-Up: *Seamless* by Dorinne Kondo
Honorable Mentions: *Baby Strike!* by Liza Case, *Goddess of Mercy* by Jenny Davis, *Exile is My Home* by Domnica Radulescu

2013
Winner: *FULL/SELF* by Claire Chafee
Runners-Up: *Silent Sky* by Lauren Gunderson, *The Town with Very Nice People* by Domnica Radulescu
Honorable Mentions: *The Draper's Eye* by Fengar Gael, *Takarazuka!!!* by Susan Soon He Stanton, *A Man, His Wife, and His Hat* by Lauren Yee

2012
<u>Winner</u>: *Still* by Jen Silverman
<u>Runner-Up</u>: *The Final Say* by Meryl Cohen
<u>Honorable Mentions</u>: *Exile* by Nasaren Ahmadi, *Buzz* by Susan Ferrera, *Kali Dances* by Patricia Montley, *Tar Beach* by Tammy Ryan

2011
<u>Winner</u>: *Mud Offerings* by Natalie Marlena Goodnow
<u>Honorable Mentions</u>: *Exquisite Corpse* by Mia Chung, *Can't Complain* by Christine Evans, *Maryam's Pregnancy* by Mia McCullough, *Love Alone* by Deborah Salem Smith

2010
<u>Winner</u>: *A Live Dress* by MJ Kaufman
<u>Runner-Up</u>: *Queens for a Year* by T.D. Mitchell
<u>Honorable Mentions</u>: *Doctoring* by Nasaran Ahmadi, *Poke Her* by Lisa O'Hara

2009
<u>Winner</u>: *The Siegels of Montauk* by Meryl Cohn
<u>Runners-Up</u>: *The Wisdom of Serpents* by Diane Baia, *Charm* by Kathleen Cahill, *Topiaries* by Elizabeth Rosengeren-Cotone

2008
<u>Winner</u>: *Unspeakable Acts* by Mary F. Casey
<u>Runners-Up</u>: *Retrospect For Life* by Dominique Morrisseau, *Pony* by Sally (now Sylvan) Oswald
<u>Honorable Mentions</u>: *Quark* by Gloria Bond Clunie, *What Remains Is The (Stillness) Of Objects* by Laylage Courie, *What Once We Felt* by Ann Marie Healy, and *Big Baby* by Sibyl O'Malley

2007
<u>Winner</u>: *Trojan Barbie* by Christine Evans
<u>Runner-Up</u>: *AISLE 7* by Kendall Lynch
<u>*Honorable Mentions*</u>: *VICTORIA MARTIN: Math Team Queen* by Kathryn Walat, *The Woman Who Was Captured by Ghosts* by Julie Pearson-Little Thunder, *Passing Through* by Vynnie Meli

See our curatorial notes, posted annually on WTP's website since 2007: www.womenandtheatreprogram.com/contact.html.

APPENDIX C: STUDENT WINNERS

Winners of the Student Prize have included: **Rebecca Basham** for *Lot's Daughters* (2000); **Anne Davis Basting** for *The Last Dinosaur* (1994); **Andie Berry** for *Son of Soil* (2018); **Olivia Briggs** for *Agnes' Baby* (2012); **Merri Biechler** for *The Bathtub Play* (2005) and *Confessions Of A Reluctant Caregiver* (2007); **Rachel Calnek-Sugin** for *Flush* (2017); **Liza Case** for *The Unspoken Ones* (2010); **Karen Cronacher** for *Scavengers* (1993); **Dorothy Fortenberry** for *Good Egg* (2008); **Inda Craig Galván** for *Black Super Hero Magic Mama* (2016); **Barbara B. Goldman** for *Perfect Women* (1997); **Katherine Gwynn** for *Merely Players* (2015); **Nicola Harwood** for *Mouth* (1998); **Corrina Hodgson** for *Privilege* (2004); **Pamela Hopkins**, **Katherine Lopez** and **Linda Manning** for *Writings on the Wall* (1991); **Tania L. Katan** for *Stages* (1996); **Erin Rachel Kaplan** for *Collateral Bodies* (2009); **Jennie Kiffmeyer** for *Boy A, Boy B: After a Murder* (1999); **Martyna Majok** for *the friendship of her thighs* (2011); **Rebecca Nicholson** for *Hello, I'm Eve* (2013); **Masha Oblolensky** for *Not Enough Air* (2006); **Cecilia Rodriguez Petit** for *Ain't That A Shame — The Art of Talking Trauma* (1995); **Bianca Sams** for *Rust on the Bone* (2014); and **Naomi Wallace** for *In the Fields of Aceldama* (1992).

THE JANE CHAMBERS PRIZE recognizes plays and scripts for performance written by women which present a feminist perspective and significant roles for female performers. This annual award is given in memory of lesbian playwright Jane Chambers who, through her plays and activism, became a major feminist voice in American theater. The Contest sees feminism to refract across diverse themes and experiences; we welcome experimentations in form. Sponsored by the Women & Theatre Program (WTP) with the Association for Theater in Higher Education (ATHE), the Prize includes $1000 & a staged reading of the winning play. Submission guidelines and our archive of recent winners can be viewed at <www.athe.org/wtp/>. WTP relies upon donations to fund this Award, as well as a Student Prize. WTP is a 501(c)(3) non-profit organization that fosters feminist inquiry among scholars and artists.